EFFECTIVE FOOTBALL COACHING

COACHING

Game-Winning Techniques for Preventing Mistakes and Errors

Donald E. Fuoss
and
Rowland "Red" Smith

ALLYN AND BACON, INC.
Boston   London   Sydney   Toronto

To our grandson, Christopher Brett, the son of our cheer-leader, to whom I dedicated the first football book that I authored, in 1958.

D. E. F.

To H. C. M., without whose encouragement and assistance my contribution as the co-author of this book would not have become a reality.

R. P. S.

Library of Congress Cataloging in Publication Data

Fuoss, Donald E
  Effective football coaching.

  1. Football coaching.   I. Smith, Rowland P.,
joint author.   II. Title.
GV956.6.F86   796.332'07'7   80–17509
ISBN 0–205–07125–2

Series Editor: Hiram G. Howard

Printed in the United States of America

CONTENTS

FOREWORDS

Developing the theme and format that "a team should not defeat itself through its own mistakes and errors," the authors have focused on "breaks" that can turn around a football game quickly but that can be minimized by effective coaching. Don Fuoss and Red Smith indicate how the latter is accomplished by sharing their expertise, drawing from their broad experience in having coached and been associated with successful football programs at major universities, small colleges, and both large and small high schools.

This book does not deal with the traditional X's and O's but with the organizational and coaching "musts" that make for winning football.

I am pleased to endorse this book, as it is a welcome addition to the student or experienced football coach's library.

John Robinson
Head Football Coach
University of Southern California

Drawing from their broad background experiences and longevity in the football coaching profession, Red Smith and Don Fuoss have identified and analyzed numerous organizational and technical problem areas, which, if not corrected, can and do lose football games.

The authors then prescribe remedies to alleviate these critical mistakes and errors, minimizing the chances of a team defeating itself.

The suggestions presented in this book are sound and applicable, and, if properly applied, should result in more effective coaching and winning football.

Darryl Rogers
Head Football Coach
Arizona State University

PREFACE

This extremely practical book is intended to help football coaches recognize, analyze, and solve major coaching errors. The problem areas that we examine come from all aspects of the game, including organizational and technical concerns as well as matters pertaining to strategy and tactics. The book is organized into five distinct sections, beginning with an examination of the role errors play in the game of football as it is played at all levels (Chapter 1); this includes a discussion of how to win games by capitalizing on your opponent's errors as well as how not to lose games by committing self-defeating errors. Next, we show coaches how to avoid critical errors by developing, managing, and evaluating team personnel, which includes coaching the staff as well as the players (Chapters 2, 3, 4, and 5). The third section offers detailed and specific suggestions for running effective practice sessions (Chapter 6), while the fourth section (Chapters 7, 8, 9, 10, and 11) shows how to develop winning game strategies and conduct meaningful post-game analyses. The final chapter tells coaches how to plan for the future by effectively analyzing and interpreting the season's statistics.

WORK TOWARD THE "COULD BE" OR "SHOULD BE" SITUATION

The suggestions we offer throughout the text are neither unrealistic nor unattainable. As indicated in the Acknowledgments, many of the suggestions were garnered from comments from successful football coaches throughout the country who responded to our query, "Would you please share with us some common football mistakes and errors as you perceive them, and offer your suggestions for avoiding them?" Every coaching situation is different, and each coach must recognize his "as is" situation. However, unless he can realistically conceptualize and work toward a better "could be" or "should be" situation for improving a football program, it will become stagnated. If he does not give direction, guidance, and leadership to improving the "as is" situation, it will not improve and neither will his coaching record. The suggestions, forms, charts, checklists, and illustrations we offer are applicable to every football coaching situation and will contribute to more effective coaching and a winning program. Utilize those that you can.

Regardless of one's coaching situation, it is well to bear in mind that for a program to achieve excellence the number of coaching tasks to be accomplished remains constant. A smaller staff does not mean fewer tasks but, to the contrary, the fewer staff members the more organizational leadership a head coach must give to his program. He must have a well-organized plan, and he must then solicit the services of others in order to carry out his plan and accomplish the necessary tasks.

Our material is *not* presented in the context of an "ideal" situation but rather to point out what is essential. Our illustrative staff figures represent only a sample to work from. However, the numbers and the assigned tasks have been drawn from real life coaching situations of successful football programs and are not hypothetical. Also, while personal contacts with the players are very important in a successful program, many tasks are accomplished when the players are not available for counseling and off-the-field coaching. The theme throughout this book is to have a definite plan and then to organize that plan to the ultimate. The assistants need to be coached before they can coach the players. On many staffs the planning is either nebulous or nonexistent, and the coaching is ineffective.

DEFINITIONS: "MISTAKE" AND "ERROR"

The terms "mistake" and "error" need to be identified since we include them in the title and use them frequently throughout the book. While "error," "mistake," "blunder," "slip," "lapse" by dictionary definition are all synonymous terms that mean "a departure from what is true, right and proper," each is further defined as follows (Webster's New Collegiate Dictionary):

error—an act involving an unintentional deviation from truth or accuracy; an act that through ignorance, deficiency, or accident departs from or fails to achieve what should be done.

mistake—a misunderstanding of the meaning or implication of something; a wrong action or statement proceeding from faulty judgment, inadequate knowledge, or inattention.

blunder—a gross error or mistake resulting usually from stupidity, ignorance, or carelessness.

slip—an unintentional and trivial mistake or fault.

lapse—a slight error typically due to forgetfulness or inattention.

While there appear to us to be distinct differences among the above terms, for brevity's sake we, too, will use the terms synonymously since generally all mean "a departure from what is true, right and proper." However, one should be aware of the differences in terms and cognizant of the fact that blunders, slips, and lapses by coaches and players can lead to mistakes and errors, all of which can and do lose football games. The purpose of this book is to examine a number of such coaching mistakes and errors and to suggest ways to avoid them.

AXIOM: "FOOTBALL IS A GAME OF MISTAKES..."

A time-tried and game-tested axiom is "Football is a game of mistakes, and the team that makes fewer mistakes generally wins the game." Some mistakes are critical tactical errors, obvious even to a football fan with only a basic knowledge of the game. Other mistakes, dealing with judgment decisions, are not quite so evident, but they can be just as disastrous as critical tactical errors. Additional mistakes in the areas of sound coaching philosophy, practice organization, game planning, sideline/bench control, and similar aspects of overall football organization, may not be evident to a typical fan for the most part, but are still common and reflect on a head coach and his staff. These critical mistakes and errors will be discussed in detail in Chapters 2 through 7 and 11.

"BREAKS OF THE GAME"

A philosophic outlook toward mistakes might be that they are merely "breaks of the game," which is a typical fan's point of view. On the other hand, if a coach is to be successful he must do all that he can to avoid such breaks occurring against his team, and his team must be prepared to take full advantage of the breaks that go against the opposition.

It might be well for a coach to recognize the fact that anything you practice to accomplish or to prevent should not be minimized as a break but recognized as a failure to accomplish specific coaching goals. This is to say that the completion of a long pass or bomb, a runback of a punt or kick-off, a blocked punt or a critical fumble are not breaks if you have practiced to accomplish these objectives to your team's advantage. If your team is the victim of such breaks, however, the problem could be poor coaching. It certainly must be labeled ineffective coaching.

DO NOT DEFEAT YOURSELF OR YOUR TEAM

A logical point of view is that before you can win at anything, first you must not lose; or in order to have a chance to win you must eliminate those mistakes or errors that will cause your defeat. You have a good chance to win in any competition if you do not defeat or beat yourself! Often it is not so much what you do that brings you victory; rather it is your opponent's mistakes that contribute to his defeating himself, which in turn results in your team being victorious. Suggestions and methods for not beating yourself are presented throughout this book.

The giveaways or turnovers, the loss of possession mistakes, such as the intercepted pass, the loss of the fumbled ball, the blocked punt, the failure to make the first down especially in the three-down zone, are mistakes that are obvious. The immediate results are evident.

Other mistakes, such as roughing the punter or passer, which permits the opposition to retain possession of the football, the offensive penalty that nullifies a first down, or the defensive penalty that permits the offensive team to sustain its drive, the defensive back who blows a coverage call, the safety who handles a high punt inside his own 10-yard line, the defensive contain men who fail to contain on a punt rush and who permit the punter to run with the football from punt formation, are all judgment mistakes or errors that reflect on a coaching staff. How to avoid them will be discussed in Chapters 8 through 10.

GAME ORGANIZATION

What about the lack of bench discipline or sideline control that draws a critical 15-yard penalty or even nullifies a score or long gainer or automatically awards the opposition a touchdown? Or the mishandling of substitutes that draws a penalty because too many players are on the field? Or you have too few players in the game? Or your captain making a wrong choice or option, an obvious error to almost everyone except himself? All of these errors and mistakes are a direct reflection on a head coach and his staff, and when they occur the fans' comments range from "poor" to "no" coaching. Also, on occasion these errors can and do lose football games.

Chapters 7 and 11 deal with game organization and analyzing game mistakes and errors, and include suggestions for answering such queries as the following: Do you have a plan for everything and everyone? What occurs at half-time in your locker room? Are your players getting the help they need whether your team is ahead or behind? What kind of information are you receiving from your coaches in the coaching booth? Is it helpful or confusing? Who is on the field telephone to the sideline coach or player? Is he transmitting accurately to those for whom the information is intended, or is he reinterpreting what is being relayed through him?

During the course of a game are your opposition's previous game statistics, upon which you have based your offensive and defensive game plan, holding up? Is your opponent doing what you expected him to do when you formulated game plans? Or are you still coaching last week's statistics, despite the fact your opposition has changed offensively or defensively? Are your game plans flexible enough to adjust to what your opposition is doing now, not what he did a week or two ago? Perhaps you do not even have a game plan, but instead "play it by ear" as the game progresses. Methods and suggestions for securing answers to the above queries will be discussed in Chapters 6 and 7, including how to develop and analyze a game plan.

PRACTICE ORGANIZATION

Of the total amount of time available to a coach during a football season, the vast majority is spent in getting ready to play the games. Are your practice plans well organized? Do you give adequate consideration to all of the basic fundamentals of the game? Do you analyze each player's job and tasks in a game, and then check to see that he spends a proportionate amount of time on each phase in practice? Is your practice schedule organized so that the fundamentals, skills, and techniques are taught in the individual period, practiced in the group or combination period, and then woven into overall offensive and defensive team effort to be tested under simulated game conditions during the team period? Or do you scrimmage frequently and conduct numerous "meat" sessions and drills, and suffer the consequences of frequently injured players? Practice organization, including mistakes and errors to be avoided, will be discussed in Chapter 6.

ASSESSING AND ALIGNING PERSONNEL: PLAYERS AND COACHES

The assessment and alignment of assistants (Chapter 3) and players (Chapters 4 and 5) are very important. The complete evaluation of personnel and how it affects a winning program are covered in detail. A head coach must coach his assistants before they can effectively coach the players. Frequently erroneous assumptions are made by head coaches about their assistants simply because they do not know the strengths and weaknesses of their staff members, and they slot their assistants improperly for teaching-coaching effectively.

A pitfall of coaching is to become so captivated with the placement of the X's and O's on the chalk board that the skills and abilities of the players are overlooked. Many coaches envision a high scoring offense and a tenacious defense but fail to consider completely the characteristics and attributes of their own player personnel that make such systems operable or inoperable. To adopt some other coach's offense or defense without taking into consideration your available personnel, including what your players can do offensively or defensively, is a common mistake. Personnel is the prime factor that determines whether a coach can utilize a particular offense or defense successfully, and the failure to take this into consideration when adopting any offense or defense is a serious mistake.

KEYS TO SUCCESS

Football success all commences with a head coach. Can you organize, discipline, and control your activities, work, and time? Does your job as a head football coach run you, or do you handle your job? Do you evaluate and slot your personnel properly? Do you have a philosophy of football, offense, defense, and kicking game, or do you have only a fragmented, unrelated collection of plays and alignments? Do you know what to expect from your system and from your assistants and players? Do you analyze why your team wins and loses? Do you analyze and correct the errors and mistakes that you, your staff, and your players make? Do you have a plan for everything and for everyone? Suggestions on how to answer these questions, and how to be a more effective coach, will be discussed in Chapter 2.

WORK TO AVOID MISTAKES AND ERRORS

A well-coached team will avoid or minimize committing critical errors and mistakes, while a poorly coached team will make them frequently.

Conversely, a well-coached team will jump immediately on opponents who make critical errors and mistakes and will capitalize on an opposition's faulty play. While all things are relative, the better material a coach has the fewer errors and mistakes his team should commit if his coaching is competent and effective. Also, the better athletes a coach has, the more capable his team is of capitalizing on the opposition's faulty play.

A coaching staff and team must first work to avoid making errors and mistakes so they do not beat themselves. Then they have a chance of winning. The failure to avoid mistakes makes the odds of winning prohibitively more difficult, unless your personnel is vastly superior to that of your opposition. Our book deals in detail with how to avoid mistakes and errors; the odds of winning are greatly enhanced for a coach and team who utilize the suggestions we offer here.

ACKNOWLEDGMENTS

Grateful appreciation is herewith expressed to all persons who shared in the preparation of this book. We make no claim of originality for much of the material contained here. The interpretations and applications, however, are our responsibility.

We are grateful to the numerous football coaches throughout the country, particularly those coaching at the high school level of competition, who responded to our questionnaire and the request to share their materials with us. We do regret and apologize for being unable to give individual credit to those contributors, despite the fact it was our intent originally to do so. In time the materials became intermingled and not infrequently they became separated from the contributors' names as we moved ideas, guides, suggestions, and comments around to different chapters in preparing the manuscript. Since we would inadvertently omit the names of some contributors, we will not include individual credit by name to any of these coaches but merely state Thank you! While those words are inadequate, they are expressed with grateful appreciation.

In various sections of our book we have included, with the permission of the coaches, materials from Frank Broyles, John Ralston, and others, to whom we have given direct credit. We are appreciative of their professional courtesies in permitting us to utilize their materials, as we are for the personal comments in the Forewords by Coach John Robinson and Coach Darryl Rogers.

We would be remiss not to express our appreciation to the players, parents, administrators, and coaching and teaching colleagues with whom we have been associated at all levels of competition over the collective time span of more than sixty years in the profession, at more than a dozen different institutions and coaching positions throughout the United States. Those individuals have contributed much to our "education," particularly to our philosophy of coaching and of football, and thus to this book.

As the former head football coach of the 1977 Jesuit High School (Sacramento) football squad, and despite the fact I have changed coaching positions since then, I (R. P. S.) would like to express my personal appreciation to the Jesuit faculty, staff, students, players, and particularly Harriet C. Marx. Despite my numerous football coaching positions, I have a particular fondness for Jesuit and its football adherents.

Finally, I (D. E. F.) express loving appreciation to my wife, Frances Fuoss, our daughter and son-in-law, Donna and Jim Montich, and to the memory of my mother, Mrs. Teresa Fuoss (who passed away shortly after we concluded writing this book), for their assistance, encouragement, understanding, and unfailing support.

D. E. F.
R. P. S.

1 FOOTBALL IS A GAME OF MISTAKES AND ERRORS

Due to the human element, it is impossible to play *errorless* football. In fact, it is not illogical to state that football is actually a game of mistakes, and the team that makes the fewest mistakes generally wins the contest. This is especially true in an evenly matched, closely contested game where an error can be pinpointed as having a direct bearing on the final outcome of the game. That is precisely what occurred in a National Football Conference championship game between the Los Angeles Rams and the Minnesota Vikings.

The Rams received the kick-off and drove to the Vikings' 1-foot line, where they lined up for a field goal attempt when they were stopped. Minnesota blocked the Rams' attempted placement and returned the football for a 99-yard touchdown, the equivalent of a 10-point play. The Rams lost their opportunity for three points when their attempted field goal was blocked, and the Vikings scored seven points! Also in the first quarter the Vikes blocked a punt when the Rams' punter mishandled the snap from his center, and Minnesota regained possession of the football at the Rams' 9-yard line. The Vikes kicked a field goal and led 10–0 at the half.

At the beginning of the second half the Vikes made the score 17–0 on a 62-yard run when the ball carrier went outside the Rams' defense perimeter. The Rams came back and scored, 6–17. In the third quarter they set up their second score when their defenders sacked the Minnesota quarterback, the Rams recovered the fumbled football, and scored from the Vikes' 8-yard line on a pass, 13–17.

Late in the game when the Rams had to keep a drive alive in a fourth down and long yardage situation, the Vikes intercepted a Los Angeles pass, which shut off the Rams' last scoring opportunity. With thirty-three seconds left to play, Minnesota ran a power play over tackle for its final touchdown, 24–13.

The four turnovers or giveaways by the Rams in the first half, with both the blocked field goal attempt and the blocked punt in the first quarter resulting directly in scores for the Vikings, were too great for Los Angeles to overcome. It is significant to note that during the course of the year Minnesota blocked a total of thirteen field goals and punts plus two more in the NFC championship game, on their way to the Super Bowl.

Many times the momentum of a game shifts to the team that is able to capitalize on its opposition's errors, and the team that sustains momentum is difficult to defeat. After the blocked field goal attempt, which resulted in the first score of the game for the Vikings, the Rams were unable to recapture the momentum that they had at the beginning of the game.

In the American Football Conference championship game, the Oakland Raiders on their way to the Super Bowl capitalized on Pittsburgh Steeler mistakes to win, 24–7. The Raiders dominated play; and with the score 24–7 in the third quarter, they forced the Steelers to try to play catch-up football in the last half.

Frequently when a team is guilty of mistakes and the other team capitalizes on its faulty play, the team committing the infractions is forced to abandon its previously conceived game plan in order to play catch-up football to try to get back into the game. Not infrequently more mistakes occur, especially if a team loses its poise and becomes disorganized and dispirited.

It is significant to note the Raiders' game plan was to run the football against the Steelers' defense, which they did well, although Oakland had been known as a passing team. Conversely Pittsburgh, known for its possession type of running game offense, was forced to revert to its passing game to try to catch up in scoring. They were not successful.

RULE #1: TO WIN, DO NOT LOSE BY "BEATING" YOURSELF

Before you can win at anything, first you must not lose; or, in order to have a chance to win, you must eliminate or minimize any mistakes that might cause you to lose. In other words, you have a good chance to win if you do not defeat yourself. At times it is not so much what you do that brings you victory; it is your opposition's mistakes that contribute to its defeat and your victory. Of course you must plan and practice on capitalizing on the opportunities made available to you by your opposition's blunders.

The typical fan views mistakes as inevitable breaks of the game. While the dropped pass, fumbled ball, mishandled punt, and missed block or tackle may be labeled as "breaks," they may also be the result of poor coaching. Should these occur despite the fact you have practiced to prevent their occurrence, then they might be the result of breakdowns in player techniques, fundamentals, or skills. This rationale is not applicable, however, if players have not been coached properly. Anything you practice to accomplish or to prevent from occurring, such as turnovers, should not be minimized as breaks of the game, even if they go against your team. A turnover means your team has failed to accomplish its immediate objective, but its ultimate goal is to win the game and you have prepared your team to do this. If you are to be a consistent winner, you must do all that you can to avoid mistakes, and you must be prepared to take full advantage of the situation whenever your opposition makes a critical error.

Let us look now at various types of mistakes and errors, with game illustrations limited to this chapter. Throughout the remainder of the book we will offer suggestions and comments on how to avoid mistakes in building a winning program. First we will illustrate the most obvious mistakes, then follow up with those not so obvious. The latter deal mostly with the organization of your football program.

Giveaways or Turnovers

The giveaways or turnovers, the loss of possession mistakes, such as the intercepted pass, the fumbled ball, the blocked punt, the failure to make the critical first down, are mistakes that are fairly obvious even to the typical fan. The immediate results are fairly evident, too, especially if the errors occur in the area of the field you are defending, as your opposition may have only a short distance to go to score.

Game Illustrations A 96-yard return of an intercepted pass by Tulane in their game with Army paved the way for a Green Wave victory, 23–10. Indiana capitalized on two pass interceptions for a touchdown and a field goal to defeat Purdue, 20–14, to give the Hoosiers their first win in the Boilermakers' home stadium in fourteen years.

The University of Pacific's eleven turnovers on five interceptions, four fumbles, and their failure to score twice when inside Fresno State's 10-yard line, permitted Fresno State to win big, 35–7, by capitalizing on UOP's mistakes.

LSU's alert defense set up five touchdowns with timely interceptions and fumble recoveries in routing Ole Miss, 45–0. Oklahoma converted four second-half turnovers into touchdowns in defeating Kansas, 28–10, after trailing the Jayhawks at the end of the first half. Virginia Tech intercepted five passes and recovered two West Virginia fumbles in defeating the Mountaineers, 24–7.

Indiana came up with its first shutout since 1969 in defeating Northwestern, 7–0, with the aid of two end zone interceptions. In Oklahoma's Fiesta Bowl victory, 41–7, over Wyoming, the Sooners intercepted five of the Cowboys' passes and recovered a fumble. These six turnovers kept the Cowboys in the hole most of the game, as they were unable to generate any offense.

Colorado converted two Kansas State fumbles into fourth-period touchdowns to defeat the Wildcats, 35–28. Penn State converted three first-half fumbles into a pair of touchdowns and a field goal, and then let their defense take over in a hard fought 15–12 victory over Stanford.

In Florida's 28–23 victory over LSU, each team had two touchdowns set up by opponents' fumbles. The Georgia Bulldogs kicked a 33-yard field goal with :05 seconds left to play in the game to break a 10–10 tie with Georgia Tech. The latter had exploded for ten points in the fourth quarter to tie the game, and it took a fumble recovery by Georgia at the Tech 34-yard line to set the game winning field goal by the Bulldogs in motion.

Why passes are intercepted will be analyzed in Chapter 8. Suggestions on how to avoid offensive, defensive, and kicking game mistakes will be discussed in Chapters 8 through 10.

Kicking Game Mistakes

There are many mistakes that occur in the overall kicking game. At times the errors happen because of poor player execution when there are breakdowns in their kicking game; other times mistakes are the result of outstanding execution by opposition players who benefit from the blocked punt or placement attempt or who excel in kick coverages and returns. Many mistakes occur as the result of coaches failing to give sufficient practice time to the overall kicking game.

Game Illustrations   Colorado State recovered three of Air Force's mishandled punts and converted them into seventeen points in defeating the Falcons, 27–3. In defeating Temple, 26–25, Penn State used a 66-yard punt return to set up the winning touchdown, and later took an intentional safety and the ensuing free kick to get out of dangerous field position to preserve their hard fought victory over the Owls.

In Nebraska's 27–24 Bluebonnet Bowl victory over Texas Tech,

Nebraska blocked a Red Raiders' punt to set up the Cornhuskers' go-ahead touchdown.

The kicking game also played a very prominent part in the Oklahoma-Miami game, which the Sooners won, 20–17. Oklahoma's defense set up two touchdown runs to enable the Sooners to win. Miami marched seventy-four yards to go ahead 7–0 on its first possession. Oklahoma scored on a 34-yard field goal. The Sooners later blocked a Miami punt, recovered on the Miami 11-yard line, and scored three plays later. Two plays later the Sooners recovered a Miami fumble on the latter's 27-yard line and scored five plays later. Oklahoma later added three points on a 21-yard field goal to close out a 20-point second quarter. Despite the fact Miami fought back with a 53-yard field goal and a 72-yard touchdown strike in the fourth quarter, and outgained the Sooners by more than one hundred yards total offense, Miami came off on the short end of the score, 17–20.

With less than three minutes left to play in the fourth quarter, Maryland blocked a Wake Forest punt, kicked a 27-yard field goal, and came from behind to win, 17–15, and keep alive its winning streak and its undefeated season on its way to the Cotton Bowl.

A fumble recovery set up UCLA's only touchdown to take the lead from Ohio State, 10–7. However, the key play in UCLA's scoring drive was a 29-yard running play from punt formation near midfield in a fourth down and inches to go situation. The Buckeyes later kicked a field goal and the final score was 10–10.

In the Texas-Oklahoma contest, Texas led 6–0 with less than two minutes left to play in the game. The Longhorns fumbled, and Oklahoma recovered deep in Texas territory. The Sooners drove for their score, and on the attempted extra point the center's errant pass sailed over the holder's head denying Oklahoma the opportunity to win the game.

Florida's failure to utilize the punt in the third quarter in a fourth and 1-foot situation on their own 29-yard line, behind 27–20, undoubtedly cost the Gators their game with Georgia. The Bulldogs stopped the Gators' fourth-down running attempt, took over and scored, and went on to defeat Florida, 41–27. The momentum shifted from Florida to Georgia after the latter's fine defensive play in the third quarter, and the Gators never regained it.

Suggestions for avoiding kicking game mistakes will be offered in Chapter 10. The game examples above do not illustrate all of the kicking game errors, such as the defensive safety man mishandling the punt inside his own 10-yard line, the defensive contain men on the punt rush failing to contain properly and permitting the punter to run with the football, roughing the punter or place kicker, the offensive player on kick coverage interfering with the receiver's opportunity to catch the football, short punts, mostly as the result of the punter's slicing or shanking the ball, keeping the kicking team in poor field position, and others.

Penalties: Mistakes and Errors

Penalties frequently play a more important part in the outcome of games than you imagine, especially when the penalty nullifies a scoring play, takes a team out of field goal range, or stops an offensive drive. Conversely, penalties can keep a team's drive alive, give a team a second opportunity to score, and generally change the momentum, intensity, strategy, and tactics of the game. Penalties are "hidden yardage," because usually you are not aware of the total yards gained and the direct bearing penalties have on the outcome of the game until you analyze the statistics afterward (Chapter 11).

Game Illustrations   In the Oakland Raiders-New England Patriots play-off game to determine the American Football Conference champion, with fifty-two seconds remaining to play in the game and Patriots leading by four points, in a third and nineteen situation, the Raiders passed unsuccessfully; but New England was penalized for roughing the passer. The penalty gave Oakland a first down at the 13-yard line, and four plays later the Raiders' quarterback rolled out and dived into the end zone to win the game, 24–21.

In the counterpart game in the National Football Conference, a running into the kicker penalty was called against a Dallas player in the fourth quarter as the Rams place kicker's attempt was successful for an apparent 10–10 tie. The field goal score was declined by the Rams, and they accepted the penalty assessed to the Cowboys' 3-yard line. Three plays later the Rams scored to go ahead 14–10. Later the Rams took an intentional safety as the game ended, Rams 14–Cowboys 12. It is significant to point out that Dallas had blocked two of the Rams' punts earlier, which had permitted the Cowboys to score their ten points. In the follow-up game for the National Football Conference championship, as mentioned above, the blocked field goal attempt and the blocked punt permitted the Vikings to garner a ten-point first-half lead over the Rams, from which Los Angeles never recovered.

In Southern Methodist's upset win over Arkansas, 35–31, the Razorbacks stopped themselves three times and on three other occasions aided SMU in sustaining their drives, accumulating ten penalties. Also, one SMU score was set up by a 92-yard kick-off return. In Oregon State's 10–9 upset win over California, the latter's three field goals could not offset its one hundred and seventy-two yards in penalties, its three pass interceptions, or its tendency to fumble in critical situations. While California's turnovers or giveaways did not aid its cause, the numerous penalties California sustained destroyed the consistency of its offensive attack.

Back-to-back 15-yard penalties by Miami for roughing the kicker and grabbing the face mask permitted Nebraska to kick a key 32-yard field goal with 6:25 left to play in the game. With 3:21 left in the game, Nebraska scored on a 23-yard pass to defeat Miami, 17–9.

In Missouri's 22–21 upset win over Ohio State, the Tigers' second opportunity on their two-point play was successful. With :10 seconds remaining in the game on a third-and-goal situation, Missouri scored with the pass, went for the two-point conversion but failed. The Buckeyes were penalized for defensive holding, and the Tigers given the second opportunity succeeded on the two-point conversion, an upset win for Missouri.

In the Stanford-San Jose game, won by the former, 28–23, a late San Jose score was nullified by a penalty for too many players being on the field. San Jose scored first after recovering a fumble and driving twenty-six yards for its score. Stanford followed by recovering a fumble and going twenty-six yards for its score. Stanford had a drive stopped by a pass interception; and a San Jose drive was stopped on the Stanford 1-yard line by the half-time gun. Later the Stanford quarterback mishandled his center's exchange on his own 1-yard line and lost two points on a safety to San Jose.

In Purdue's upset win over Notre Dame, 31–20, two key penalties late in the game thwarted the Fighting Irish's chances of pulling off a come-from-behind victory. The first Irish penalty was the result of a pass completion to an ineligible receiver, and the second penalty was assessed as the result of the Irish having an ineligible receiver downfield on a pass. Purdue led throughout the game, jumping off to a 21–0 first-quarter surge as the result of three pass interceptions, one of which was returned for a touchdown. The Boilermakers also recovered a Notre Dame fumble which set up another touchdown. Purdue's final score was set up by a pass interception.

You must work to eliminate penalties, especially the 15-yard penalty. A first-and-twenty-five situation, for example, is almost an impossibility for most teams to overcome. Your offense is greatly restricted in such a situation, particularly if poor field position is also the result of the penalty. Remember Rule #1, To win, do not lose by beating yourself!

Organizational Mistakes and Errors

Organizational errors are not as easily detected by those outside the coaching staff and players, as are the obvious breakdowns in the execution of skills, fundamentals, and techniques of the offensive, defensive, and kicking games. Therefore, it is difficult to give specific game illustrations. However, a coach knows when he has been "out-coached" and is unprepared, especially when he has superior player personnel but loses to a coach and team whose personnel does not measure up to his. Generally this occurs as the result of the other coach being better organized and probably a better teacher-coach. It all falls on you, the head football coach, to organize the key control areas or elements. In Chapter 2 we commence with the head coach organizing himself and his time. In Chapters 3 through 5 we examine how to assess, align, and evaluate the performance of your assistance coaches and available player personnel.

A coach's practice organization (Chapter 6) and game plan (Chapter 7) must be geared to eliminate critical errors that can and do lose football games. Are your practice plans well organized? Do you give adequate consideration to *all* of the basic fundamentals of the game? Do you analyze each player's job in a game and then see that he spends a proportionate amount of time on each phase in practice? Is your practice schedule organized so that the fundamentals, skills, and techniques are taught in the individual period; practiced in the group or combination period; and then woven into overall offensive and defensive team effort to be tested under game simulating conditions during the team period? Suggestions and illustrations are included in Chapter 6.

Game Plan Mistakes   How do you devise game plans? Are offensive and defensive game plans necessary? During the course of the game are your opponent's previous tendencies holding up? Is your opposition doing what you expected of them when your game plans were formulated? Are your game plans flexible enough to adjust to what your opponent is now doing during your game, not to what he did a week or two ago against a different team? Mistakes to avoid in devising game plans, as well as when to abandon the game plan if it is ineffective and invalid, are discussed in Chapter 7.

Scouting Booth Information Mistakes   On the sideline you can get the "feel" and tempo of the game, but you need "eyes" in the coaching booth above ground level in order to obtain specific information relevant to defensive alignments and stunts, pass coverages, breakdowns in personnel, where and how you are being attacked offensively, and ways to capitalize on your opposition's mistakes in order to win the game. Generally this information is conveyed to the sideline coaches and players by a communications system, such as field phones. Do you know specifically what information is being sent down from the coaching booth? Is the person on the phone conveying the information directly as he receives it, or is he interpreting what is being told to him? Who is talking to your quarterbacks and defensive signal callers? Are they helping or confusing your players? Failing to organize this aspect of the overall program can lead to many errors and mistakes. As the head coach, what are you doing to avoid this confusion? Suggestions will be offered in Chapter 7.

Sideline and Bench Mistakes and Confusion   Do you have a plan for handling substitutes? Mishandling substitutes can draw a 15-yard penalty if too many are on the field. Do you always have eleven players on the field. There have been occasions when several players came out of the game, but one fewer player replaced them. Do you always have your eleven *best* players in the game? There have been instances when, through mishandling substitutes, a head coach has discovered one or two of his best players still on the bench, although he assumed they were in the game. What about the lack of bench discipline or sideline control, which draws a critical 15-yard penalty, or even nullifies a score or a long gainer? This has occurred in several nationally televised games in the past, including a bowl game where a score was nullified when an assistant coach ran on to the playing field during the scoring play. Sideline discipline and bench control will be discussed in Chapter 7.

Captain's Options Mistakes   Do you "coach" your captain so that he does not make wrong choices in the exercise of his options? There have been instances, once in a memorable nationally televised professional game, when a captain's wrong choice gave the opposition both possession of the football in receiving the kick-off and the advantage of a strong wind. That wind was the key factor and the captain, upon winning the toss, meant to exercise his choice of defending a goal so the wind would be at his team's back. Upon being asked his choice by the official, the captain replied, "Kick," and the opposing captain quickly replied, "We'll defend this goal," giving the opposition both possession of the football and the wind at its back. A captain's options and utilizing your time-outs will be discussed in Chapter 7.

Half-time Mistakes   Do you have a half-time plan to aid your players whether they are ahead or behind or tied? There is much speculation by the typical fan and sportscaster as to what a coaching staff does at half-time, ranging from preaching and praying to raving and psyching up the players. The type of information and aid that should be given to your players will be suggested in Chapter 7, too.

After the Game Analysis   It is often easy to analyze why you have lost a game. However, do you ever analyze why your team *won* a game? Do you know how many times you had possession of the football, and scored? Do you analyze how you scored, or how you gave up possession of the football? Were you defeated by a team with superior personnel, or did you beat yourself? Can you prepare your team better for your next game? Post-game analysis will be discussed in Chapter 11.

After the Season Mistakes   There are coaches who do not feel it is necessary to coach year-round. Their off-season may be from the termination of their last game of the regular season to the beginning of pre-season practice the following year. Although you might work intermittently at

getting ready for the upcoming season during this period, you can enhance your chances of winning by off-season planning. Suggestions of
how to make the best use of that time will be offered in Chapter 12.

RULE #2: TO WIN, AVOID OR MINIMIZE CRITICAL ERRORS AND MISTAKES, AND CAPITALIZE ON THOSE OF YOUR OPPOSITION

A well-coached football team will avoid or minimize committing critical
errors most of the time, while a poorly coached team will make critical errors frequently. Conversely a well-coached team will immediately
jump on opponents who make critical errors and capitalize on those mistakes. All things are relative, however, and the better material an effective coach has the fewer errors his team should make. Also, the better
athletes a coach has the more capable they are of capitalizing on their
opposition's errors.

A coaching staff and team must first work to avoid making errors
so as not to beat themselves. Then they have a chance of winning. The
failure to do so makes the odds against winning prohibitive.

2 THE KEYS TO SUCCESS

The measuring stick of excellence in football is the scoreboard. Where success means a winning record, successful coaches are obviously good organizers. Not as readily recognizable is the fact that winning coaches are good planners. Planning precedes organizing, and plans must be continually monitored or regulated. While most coaches recognize the necessity of planning and organizing, many fail to follow up with control measures. To control means to check or regulate, referring to all facets of the plan, and it is up to the head coach to determine where the control will take place, what it must do, how elaborate it must be, and how effective it will be. Control involves constantly checking progress against plans so that you can regulate and adjust, if necessary. Maintaining controls will help you anticipate problems in most cases and will enable your coaching staff to make adjustments so that the outcome is success. Control monitors performance and corrects it when necessary so that planned and actual performance coincide. Control is merely closing the planning loop.

ORGANIZING THE KEY CONTROL AREAS OR ELEMENTS

In coaching as in the business world, to be successful you must be able to plan, organize, and regulate the key control areas or elements at your disposal. These activities will largely determine the success of the operation you are directing. Through experience and possibly trial-and-error or trial-and-success, winning coaches have learned which areas or elements in building a successful program are the most important, need the major part of their time and attention, and need to be well planned, highly organized, and carefully observed and controlled. The time element alone prohibits you from devoting an equal amount of attention to all aspects of the program, nor is it necessary for you to do so. Then, too, there are some areas, elements, and facets of the football program over which you may have little or no control, depending on the type of coaching situation you have and to whom you are accountable. However, three very important areas over which you must exercise optimum planning, organizing, and control are your job, work, and time, your assistant coaches, and your squad members. How well you coordinate these areas or elements will largely decide the success of your football program. Each of these areas will be discussed separately.

Coaching Is Winning: Organize to Win

In building a successful football program, you must obviously make decisions on the formulation of a plan. The plan then must be organized. Staff need direction as to their tasks and responsibilities. Leadership is necessary to implement or activate your plan. The resulting performance must be controlled or regulated in order to complete the process and close the loop of planning.

The importance of sound organization can never be underestimated. If there is a secret to coaching success, it lies in perfect organization. Dictionary definitions of organization include:

> The act or process of grouping and arranging into one whole a set of parts dependent on one another.
> To cause to unite and work together in orderly fashion.
> A body made up of parts mutually dependent on one another.
> (Webster's Seventh Collegiate Dictionary)

The theme of this book is to identify the "parts that are mutually dependent on one another," which should be "united to work in orderly fashion" into "one whole" in order to have a high degree of efficiency organization to bring success in the football program.

While you must realistically recognize the "as is" situation, which is usually problem oriented, you must strive and work toward the "should be" or "could be" situation, which is usually opportunity or achievement oriented. Otherwise you have little chance of changing the status quo, and it is unlikely you can build a successful winning program. You should seek every opportunity to improve your football program if you expect to be a consistent winner.

KEY CONTROL AREA: YOUR JOB, WORK, AND TIME

Probably few coaches would ever acknowledge the facts that they do not plan well and are poorly organized. Most coaches feel they are pretty well organized, especially if they put in long hours at their job of coaching. Unfortunately, long hours on the job do not guarantee a well-planned and highly organized winning program. A poorly organized coach may put in even longer hours on the job and still lose, unless he has superior personnel, mainly because he does not have a well-conceived plan or because he misuses time. It is unlikely that such a coach will be able to tie all the elements together into an organized, workable plan in order to achieve winning results, until he organizes himself better and controls his time.

What and How Organizational Mistakes

A critical organizational mistake is simply not being knowledgeable or not being able to identify the necessary *what* and *how* components that should be included in a successful football program. Many coaches devote their time to "majoring in minors," unable to distinguish between the important components and the unimportant ones. The emphasis should be placed on majoring in majors, the essential components, not the minor ones.

A second critical organizational mistake is not knowing *how* to organize all of the necessary components into a workable plan to achieve the end results. The purpose of organizing is to win, because coaching is winning. You should focus your attention on the *results* to be achieved, rather than on the things to be done. The inexperienced and unsuccessful coach is likely to focus his attention on the means rather than on the end.

Why? Where Does It Fit in your Plan?   There should be a well-thought-out reason for everything you do as a coach in connection with the football program. You should constantly ask yourself and your staff, "Why are we doing this? Where does this fit into our plan? What do we expect to get out of this? Why do we believe this?" For unless you have a reason for everything you do, including what and how you teach and coach, you really do not have a firmly fixed plan to follow. Conversely, if you don't have a reason for doing something, it should be eliminated. Time is always a coaching factor. In seeking answers to the above questions, the element of time must receive serious consideration. Otherwise, your football program will lack purpose and direction, and it will not be well organized to achieve maximum results.

Develop Sound Personal, Coaching, and
Football Philosophies

A person's philosophy is the way he views things, events, and relationships, and the values he places on them. It is his point of view or attitude toward people, places, and things. The manner in which you as a coach organize your job and work, which includes all aspects of the football program, will depend on your personal philosophy, the philosophy you have toward coaching, and your philosophy of football. These attitudes in turn will depend on your experience to date both as a player and a coach, including any previous experience as an assistant coach, and on the knowledge you have gained by playing the game, by coaching the sport, and by studying and analyzing the game of football as you broaden your "football" education. This composite will aid you in formulating, broadening, and delineating your philosophy, which will dictate everything which you do as a head football coach. You need to understand that as a head coach one of your essential risks is to influence others to cooperate toward achieving desired results. Also, you must develop people, assistants and players, and to make them successful, since only successful people achieve important results.

If a head coach is going to provide the necessary leadership to his coaching staff and players, it is imperative that he develop sound philosophies in the three areas mentioned above. All three are interrelated and determine the way a coach will conduct his football program.

Personal Philosophy   The starting points for all achievement are desire and definiteness of purpose. Therefore, to become a successful winning football coach, you must have a strong desire *to be and to do*. It cannot be a hope or a wish or a vague groping to be successful, but it must be a zealous desire to be a success. It must be a definite realistic goal. One must give to get, so you must determine what you are willing to give up in order to get success. It is not sufficient to say, "I want to be a winning coach." You must establish a goal of *when* and *how*. You must create a definite plan of carrying out your desire to be a successful coach. Then you must put your plan into action. It is a mistake for a coach not to set realistic goals for himself, his assistants, and his team, and goal setting is meaningless unless time limits are determined for reaching those goals. When you establish a goal, you must consider the time and place in which you are trying to achieve it.

In developing a personal philosophy, it is important for a coach to reckon with his self-image. Therefore, you should understand yourself, your strengths, weaknesses, motives, desires, and drives, and learn to live with them. You will be far better able to handle success and failure, trials and tribulations, frustrations and anxieties, as you strive to meet your personal and professional goals and aspirations.

Coaching Philosophy   Your *coaching* philosophy will be how you look at the problems connected with football and the importance you place upon them. You will be motivated to act on these problems in accordance with your attitude or point of view toward them. Some of these problems will receive your major interest, attention, thought, time, and effort, while others will receive little because of the low priority you place on them. Therefore it might be stated that a coach's philosophy is really his attitude toward the problems of coaching.

A head football coaching position is a leadership role position. As a leader and decision maker, you must become involved in many facets of the job that are only indirectly related to coaching on the field, but all of which have an important bearing on the success of your football program. A checklist of general and collateral duties, the "nuts and bolts" problems, as compared to specific coaching duties, is located in Chapter 3.

Football Philosophy   You must develop a sound philosophy of football as well as a philosophy of coaching. Football is a game that constantly changes. Probably no other sport in the entire field of athletics undergoes as many continued modifications and variations as does the game of football. You must keep abreast of the changes in the game, and you should continue to broaden your football knowledge. However, this does not imply that a coach should change merely because of the popular trends or fashions of the times. Yet some coaches do just this, feeling a new offense or defense will solve a problem, when in fact they have a very limited knowledge of what they are adopting and trying to implement and utilize. They do it merely because other coaches have enjoyed success with a particular offense or defense. For example, a coach in his first coaching assignment decides he will use the wishbone offense, despite the fact that in all of his previous experience as a collegiate and/or professional football player he has never played the wishbone, and he lacks sufficient knowledge of the strategy.

In the final analysis, players win football games, not plays or systems. The experienced football coach knows this. The inexperienced coach learns it. Initially the coach who lacks coaching experience collects plays and systems. Should he win he is convinced he has done so because of *his* coaching and *his* plays or system. In time he learns a coach wins because of the execution of the plays and the skills of players and not because of favorite scoring plays or his outcoaching the opposition.

In developing your football philosophy, you must determine whether you favor *possession* ball control or *position* on the field football. Are you offense or defense oriented? How are you going to utilize the kicking game? Are you run or pass oriented? Obviously all three phases of the game of football are important, but the importance you attach to each is part of your philosophy of football. Your practice plans, game plans, and coaching strategy and tactics are influenced by the importance you attach to the offensive, defensive, and kicking games, all of which will be discussed in separate chapters.

The Management of Time

Although most people think of time as having only a single dimension and a single value of hours, time has in fact three interrelated dimensions—hours, energy, and money. Therefore, if you waste one, you waste others; and if you use one wisely, you enhance the value of the others. Since you cannot delay the clock, you must learn to utilize it. To disregard time, or to fail to use it properly and wisely, is a grave error. A coach must discipline himself in the vital area of time management. How well a coach can control and manage his time and the demands made on him and his time, especially during football season, is a strong indication of whether he or his job is in control.

Time factors relevant to the job and work alone that must be considered, planned for, and organized are:

The amount of daily, weekly, and total time available for *off-the-field planning* and organizing for football in pre-season, during the season, and after the football season. This means a year-round plan.

The amount of time available for actual *on-the-field coaching*.

The amount of time to be devoted to *general* and *collateral coaching duties* that are actually related to football or one's coaching position.

The amount of time to be devoted to *classroom preparation and teaching assignments*, if you have multiple teaching-coaching duties and responsibilities.

The *reasonable time demands* a head coach can impose upon his staff.

The amount of time available for on-the-field coaching (football practice time) generally is fairly well set and blocked out. How effectively a coaching staff can teach during the amount of practice time available is another matter. The amount of time in which you can actually teach, counsel, or coach your players off the field, and under what conditions, is limited, too.

All of these time demands, which relate only to coaching, cannot receive equal attention, nor should each be allotted an equally proportionate amount of time. Priorities must be made, and time assigned accordingly, two tasks that will be discussed in later chapters. ·Also, no line of work can be a 24-hour a day job, 365 days per year. Coaches, like others, need unscheduled personal time away from their work.

KEY CONTROL AREA: YOUR ASSISTANT COACHES

A head coach should utilize optimally the talents and competencies of his coaching staff. This is not always the case. You must know clearly what results you expect your assistant coaches to produce and achieve, and they in turn must know clearly what their head coach expects of them as assistants.

Staff Selection

It is readily recognized that in many high schools and small colleges, as compared to those colleges playing major football schedules, head football coaches usually have little choice in the selection of their assistants. The individual hired as the head football coach will probably inherit the present coaching staff members. Or because of the lack of funded faculty positions or teaching slots, an individual is hired first to fill a teaching vacancy in a discipline and department, and he is then given the duties and responsibilities that accompany being a football coach. Despite the fact this may be the "as is" situation, a head coach has to recognize it as a starting point and still make every effort to build a successful program. Therefore, despite the fact the head coach's position may not be structured so that he is permitted to select his own assistant coaches, he is not relieved from his other duties of organizing, orientating aligning, and assigning and evaluating his coaching staff. In situations where the head coach does have the authority to make total or partial decisions on staff selections, oftentimes he may not have established criteria to aid him in the selection process. Several are suggested below.

Do I Really Want to Coach?   This is the first question you must ask yourself, whether you are an assistant or head coach. After each coach answers this question to his own satisfaction, then the head coach should ask each of his assistants, whether they are just being hired or are already members of his staff, "Why do you want to coach?" There may be a strong likelihood that you or they really do not *want* to coach, but that you or they *like* to coach. There is a vast difference between *wanting to* and *liking to coach*, and your work, as a head or an assistant coach, reflects your attitude.

Essential Qualities of a Good Coach   In selecting, organizing, aligning, and evaluating the coaching staff, how does a head coach know whether or not he has *good* coaches? A head coach may ask himself, "Do *I* have the essential qualities of a *good* coach?" It is the consensus that a good coach must possess certain basic qualities and skills. You may use the following as a guide to evaluate your own attributes and those of assistants when you are selecting and then later evaluating them. How do you measure up to the qualities and skills that all *good* coaches should possess?

Do I have a thorough and comprehensive technical knowledge of all aspects of football (and/or my coaching specialty)—offense, defense, strategy, techniques, skills, fundamentals, rules? Do I study the game *all ways and always.*

Do I understand the characteristics and needs of the level (junior high, high school, college, professional) of the participants whom I am coaching—mentally, emotionally, physically? Or are they merely X's, O's, bodies, "studs," "jocks"? (Assessing, aligning, and evaluating player personnel will be discussed in later chapters.)

Am I skillful in the art of teaching? How well do my players comprehend and execute successfully what I teach them? A coach may possess vast technical knowledge of football and the specialty he coaches, but does he teach effectively?

Do I have the extra ingredients—energy, enthusiasm, stability, dedication, honesty, integrity, courage, loyalty, sense of humor, and the other desirable personality and character traits, which rub off on the participants and others, which are "caught" rather than "taught," and which produce the pride and morale that are necessary ingredients to be winners? *

While it is unlikely that many individuals have all of these desirable attributes, sterling qualities, and skills, obviously some individuals have more of them than others. Also, one can work on acquiring more of the essential qualities and skills of a *good* coach! Many are intangibles, but coaching is "people work," where the application of human skills is extremely important. Staff evaluation is discussed in detail in the next chapter.

Speaking on the subject of selecting a staff, Lloyd Eaton, formerly Wyoming's highly successful head football coach, listed the following criteria:

---

* Donald E. Fuoss, *Blueprinting Your Coaching Career* (New York: Pilot Industries, Inc., 1973), p. 11. This realistic blueprint was written especially for the individual seriously interested in furthering his career in coaching.

Appraise them critically, professionally.

Bring them into the fold.

Know the people you are going to hire. They in turn must get to know you, and know about Saturday, Sunday, and night work.

Get to know the wife. She has ruined many a good coach.

There is a difference in temperament, background, age, opinions, and this is good. However, I want a man to think soundly, and to present his ideas soundly. I want men with "horse sense." It is good to have new ideas, but ones which will work.

There is no place for the "yes" man. I want thinkers.

There is no place for the "second-guessers."

You must have a genuine love for working with boys. You have got to be a "father confessor" away from home.

You must have a genuine love for football, and what it can do for the people in this country.

You must be well-versed in the phase of the game you are going to handle. Can you do the job which has been assigned to you?

You must be a good teacher. You must be the master teacher at your school.*

"How do *I* measure up?" is a question each coach, head or assistant, would do well to ask himself. A head coach might do well to ask each of his assistants, "How do *you* measure up?" A head coach may not be able to measure up to the criteria he is imposing on his assistants. Only the individual coach can determine whether he can live with these standards, or whether he wants to. The initial question, however, which must be answered truthfully, is, "Do I *really want* to coach?"

The Role of the Assistant Coach

The typical fan is likely to think of the assistants as helpers whose knowledge of football is inferior to that of the head coach. This is not a valid premise, especially where the head coach is involved in many administrative details surrounding the football program and where he must rely on his assistants to do much of the actual field coaching. The assistant coach is the specialist, and in most instances, even at the high school level, the assistant coach probably has major responsibilities in planning, organizing, and implementing certain aspects of the offensive or defensive game plan, with the head coach's approval. If each coach's expertise is properly utilized, every assistant will have some input in determining the game plan.

* Fuoss, p. 12.

Staff Dynamics　Each assistant should form a part of the total teaching unit, which must function in a team approach to meet the needs of the football squad. This means the coaches must be compatible and cooperative, working together in a closely knit, harmonious relationship in order to coach effectively and to produce the desired results. When this harmony is absent, the chances of building a successful program are greatly inhibited. Since the work of assistant coaches is vital, care must be utilized in selecting each coach in order to ensure harmonious staff dynamics and effective coaching. It does not make any difference whether a head coach selects his assistants or they are inherited, he must try to orient each assistant to that individual's expected contribution to the success of the football program. Also, the head coach must stress the importance of the individual coach being a member of the collective coaching staff team.

Staff Organization and Orientation

After the staff selection has been completed, organizing, orienting, assigning, and aligning the coaching staff members must be done. Organizational policies, procedures, rules, regulations, and codes, some of which may be unwritten, must be made known to each member in order to build an effective organization. The process by which a new member learns the value system, norms, and behavior patterns of a group is known as organizational socialization.

Setting Goals and Affixing Time Expectations　To attain certain accomplishments, both personal and professional, goals must be formulated. If goals are mutually arrived at by the staff as a team, those goals are much more likely to be realized. It would be well for you as the head coach to identify the roles and expectations of *all* of the assistant coaches when you are working together in goal setting. Set goals for all phases of the game, offense, defense, kicking game; for the squad members individually and as a team; and for the overall football program. Every goal should be ranked in terms of priority, so that each is classified as a short, intermediate, or long-term goal expectation. The order or priority is most important and deserves more than a cursory examination. You may want to win *now*, but you must also build a strong foundation in order to accomplish future goals. Therefore, fix time limitations or expectations to each of the goals, too.

Loyalty to a Person or Issue?　Few speeches are likely to be given to assistant coaches on the subject of loyalty, although some coaches are almost paranoid on the importance of loyalty. Nevertheless, the unwritten code is, "Be loyal or be gone!" While *loyalty* appears to be an all-inclusive, somewhat nebulous term encompassing the head and assistant coaches, the team, and the school, be aware of the fact that loyalty does not have the same meaning for everyone. Each individual must interpret for himself the meaning and application of loyalty, and it is imperative that anyone in a subordinate position understand how his superior interprets the term. Candidly your head coach may state "I expect your support *100 percent* whether I am *right* or *wrong*." A dilemma arises for the subordinate whose value system on an issue or the resolution of a problem may be contrary to that of his superior and who believes his head coach is wrong. Does the assistant concur with the head coach's action or beliefs merely because he is his superior who demands unconditional loyalty, or does he risk the chance of being identified as disloyal merely by supporting a different point of view on a particular issue? As an example, the issue or problem could arise over opinions on the treatment of injured players, questionable recruiting tactics, clandestine scouting procedures, and other controversial areas. These are not in the same category as differences of opinion pertaining to offensive and defensive systems, strategy, practice, and game plans, unless a subordinate "bad mouths" or "second guesses" his head coach or another assistant who is responsible for these specialized areas of coaching. It is almost universally accepted in the coaching ranks that such indiscretions constitute disloyalty. The lack of loyalty, trust, and respect for each other is highly detrimental to the effective performance of a coaching staff and program, and it affects adversely the morale, attitudes, and behaviors of the coaches, players, and others. When disloyalty prevails, corrective measures must be taken; a head coach's failure to do so only creates additional problems.

Loyalty Is a Two-way Process   One need not be in complete accord with you or other assistant coaches; honest differences of opinion are acceptable and expected. The individual who speaks out honestly for what he believes is best for the team and the good of the program is likely to be respected, although at times his opinion may be unpopular. However, once a final decision becomes staff policy, differences of opinion are left in the coaches' room. It is well to remember that loyalty is a two-way process in that it runs in both directions, up and down. You cannot demand or expect loyalty, if you do not practice loyalty in your relationships with those from whom you expect to receive it.

Develop We and Us Concepts

A championship team, like a successful business, is the result of a group effort. It seldom matters how good an individual effort is; what counts is how well every individual works with everyone else to achieve the common team goal. Therefore, the coaching staff and players must be indoctrinated with the WE and US concepts. *We* win and *we* lose; it is *us* and *our* team. It is not *I* win, *you* lose. The *we* and *us* concepts start with the head coach and his assistants. Some assistants play the *I* and *you* or *they* game, which is dangerous; it implies *I* as everything.

It is impossible to build a winning program without unanimity on the coaching staff, at least as far as outsiders can see. A coach should remove any doubt about unanimity and his integrity to the coaching staff. The unwritten law, likely to be swiftly imposed, is, "If you aren't loyal to me and the program, why should I be loyal to you?"

Curbing the "Climber"   All efforts must be directed toward team results rather than toward an individual coach's selfish personal benefit and gain. It is especially true if a coach climbs over others to get what he wants, and if he has little loyalty to anyone other than himself. Such an individual will be a threat and disruptive to the unity of the coaching staff, and his selfish conduct and attitude must be curbed. A head coach must also be cognizant of "cliques" among his coaches, which can also create loyalty problems. Personal friendships among two or more of the clique members make them supportive of each other's opinions, concepts, and points of view on football business and other matters, so that their loyalty in reality is to each other and not to the total staff. While one does not refute ideas and concepts in a staff meeting just to be argumentative, cliques on a coaching staff can stifle the free flow process in the exchange of information.

Curbing Personal and Professional Jealousies   Disloyalty may arise between assistant coaches because of personal or professional jealousy. At times the coaches' wives are the catalysts. When you detect this situation as a head coach, you cannot remain aloof but you are compelled to take action cautioning the assistants, "While you may not like each other, I will not permit your personal feelings to affect your work adversely and to have a detrimental effect on the players and the program. Should this occur, you will be removed from the coaching staff." Regardless of the coaching set-up, even if the assistants are locked in by faculty rank and assignment, should the rivalries and jealousies continue, you are forced to remove the guilty party even if it means you are unable to replace the subordinate on your coaching staff. Be aware of the fact you may not receive the backing of your administrators, but it is impossible to produce a winning program where such instability and disloyalty prevails.

Motivate Your Assistant Coaches: Recognize Their Needs

While head coaches are keenly aware that they should try to motivate their players to attain greater individual and team effort and performance, many head coaches are not aware that their assistant coaches need motivation, too, for the same reasons. Your goals, whatever you formulate for yourself and the program, will probably be accomplished to the extent that you successfully motivate your assistants, players, and others. Therefore, it behooves you to try to motivate your assistants as well as your players. Motivation is a matter of recognizing and attempting to satisfy each individual's needs.*

Know Your Assistant Coaches as Individuals   It is important to know staff members as individuals rather than merely as football coaches with specialized knowledge and skills in coaching. Many head coaches readily recognize the necessity of knowing their players as individuals, but they fail to recognize their own assistant coaches as individuals. It behooves you to find out all that you can about your assistants. If a head football coach can recognize each assistant's individual needs, aligning his staff and making coaching assignments will be much easier, and the overall performance results will be more productive. You can learn a great deal in your day to day interpersonal relationship with each assistant, and as you observe how they interrelate to other staff members and the players.

Individual Goal Setting   In order to determine what "turns on" each assistant you should try to find out each coach's goals and aspirations. These may be vague. As a head coach, your career goal may be easily identified, but an assistant coach's may not be clearly formulated. In response to the question, "What do you want to do with your life? What is your career plan?" most assistant coaches are likely to reply, "To be a head coach!" However, they may have neither a definite plan of action nor a timetable for attaining this goal. By getting each assistant coach to verbalize and even to submit his goals to writing, you aid him in individual goal setting and in meeting his personal needs.

Coaching Staff and Team Goal Setting   If a head coach secures relevant and pertinent information, he not only aids each of his assistant coaches in verbalizing their goals, but he aids himself, too. He has secured input and factual information for making decisions on aligning his staff and making coaching assignments. Knowing coaching strengths and weaknesses will be helpful in setting coaching staff and team goals.

Avoid Secret Meetings   You should encourage open discussion on all subjects pertaining to football in staff meetings. Do not make major de-

---

* *See* A. H. Maslow, "A Theory of Human Motivation," *Psychological Review, vol. 50,* 1943, pp. 370–396; and A. H. Maslow, *Motivation and Personality* (New York: Harper & Row, 1954). While these are original or primary sources of Maslow's "Order of Priority of Human Needs," virtually every book on the subjects of psychology, human relations, management, motivation, discusses Maslow's theory.

cisions relevant to the program without the benefit of staff discussion and input. You must guard against the secret meeting concept, where a coach attempts to sell his ideas individually outside of the staff meetings. Not only does the lack of communication create problems, but secret meetings breed distrust among the staff members.

Do Not Create "Yes" Men   If you have avoided *selecting* the "yes" man for your staff, then you should work equally hard to avoid *creating* "yes" men as assistant coaches. This depends on your leadership style as a head coach. If you are autocratic or dictatorial, then it is likely your assistants will give you "yes" responses. A "no" response may be interpreted as uncooperative, unknowledgeable, argumentative, disloyal, or simply negative, all of which would be threatening to the assistant whose viewpoint is different from yours. Obviously if your leadership style is supportive or democratic, then assistants are likely to be more responsive and open in their comments and will not feel threatened in expressing a viewpoint contrary to yours.

Leadership Style   The very crux of supportive or participatory theory is based on strong leadership, in direct contrast to autocratic theory, which is based on power, obedience, and compliance. Regardless of one's style, assistant coaches expect certain characteristics of their head coach in his leadership role, such as: emotional stability, the ability to think clearly and to make rational decisions under pressure, to criticize constructively not destructively, to use praise intelligently, to show consideration, to be a pacesetter and to set a good example, and to develop the potential of individuals. When a cohesive coaching staff is highly motivated, their joint efforts are highly productive, and the result is generally a winning program. Successful head coaches find time to put into practice the interpersonal relationships discussed in this chapter, which is one important reason why they are winning coaches. Staff alignment, assignments, and evaluation will be discussed in Chapter 3.

KEY CONTROL AREA: YOUR PLAYERS

A third element that must be organized for optimum utilization is the players or student-athletes available for coaching. What are their talents and skills? How are they utilized? How are the players slotted? Answers to these and other questions will be presented in later chapters.

While it is an acknowledged fact that no team is stronger than its personnel, or the material the coaches have to work with, it is possible to have good material yet lose games due to a poorly conceived and/or poorly organized plan or ineffective teaching. Conversely, a coach may have mediocre personnel and yet win because he is a good planner, organizes well, and is an effective teacher. Or when he does lose, he is not outcoached and his team is not likely to lose badly; his players are well coached and he has been able to get optimum performance from his available material.

Great Coaches are Good Organizers and Good Teachers

Good or successful coaches are also good teachers. Bud Wilkinson, one of the game's winningest coaches, has been quoted as saying, "Coaching is teaching, and the kind of coach you are depends on the kind of teacher you are." Other winning coaches have made similar statements. Good organization includes effective teaching, which is frequently overlooked by the inexperienced coach as well as by the unsuccessful coach. Effective teaching has occurred when the players learn to coordinate eye, mind, and body, and when they perform as well as they are capable of performing. This generally takes place if you have taught the players the game through a system that adheres to sound principles of instruction. Good organization is also keeping everyone pointed toward the achievement of the desired results or goals. This is your responsibility as the organizer of success, the head football coach.

ADDITIONAL CONTROL AREAS OF COACHING

Only three major elements have been presented here, but additional elements you must organize, which have a direct bearing on the success of your program, are budget, equipment, travel, feeding the squad members, lodging, and other business management aspects of football. Eligibility, grade checks, discipline, and other similar time-consuming, frequently bothersome ancillaries of coaching must also be handled by you and your football staff. For the most part we will give these areas only cursory treatment. It is sufficient to state, however, that to ignore these details or the problems that might arise in these areas, with the hope they will take care of themselves, would be a most serious coaching mistake. The organizational process involves *all* aspects of the football program, preseason, during the season, post-season, and year-round, as will be stressed throughout our book, and especially in the concluding chapter, which deals specifically with off-season planning.

3 STAFF ALIGNMENT, ASSIGNMENTS, AND EVALUATION

A head football coach who is a consistent winner is one who *optimizes* the efforts of his available personnel, players and coaches. He places each player and coach where each can make the *maximum* contribution to the success of the football program. Aligning, assigning, organizing, orienting, and coordinating the coaching staff cannot be merely a cursory effort nor done on a hit-or-miss basis, if you wish to build a successful program. As head coach *you must have a plan* and *you must organize your plan* to the utmost. A fairly common practice, and a coaching mistake to be discussed in a later chapter, is to fail to have a plan for everything or to fail to organize that plan completely.

STAFF ALIGNMENT

In aligning your staff, you should evaluate each assistant's ability, competencies, proficiencies, and experience carefully *before* coaching assignments are announced to staff members. If you do not have anyone on your staff with experience or background to handle a particular position or teach a specific skill, you may make the assignment according to a coach's special interest or aptitude. By concentrated study an assistant with little previous knowledge in an area or phase could become a "student" of the game and do an outstanding teaching job.

Realignment and Reassignment of Staff Members

Reassigning staff members especially from offense to defense or vice versa, or reassigning major coaching responsibilities such as those duties performed by offensive and defensive coordinators, as an illustration, must be done on occasion in order to strengthen the overall staff and program. Or changing staff assignments may be necessary when you lose a coach or when you have two coaches with expertise in one area but need coaching assistance and strength at another position. The manner in which you make changes is very important. Privately informing an assistant coach, "I am making this change because I think you can make a *greater contribution* to the success of our overall football program in this new coaching assignment," is less caustic and is more readily accepted than informing an assistant, ". . . because you haven't been doing your job!" While a situation may dictate change, the manner in which you handle it can do much to alleviate the blow to the ego of a demoted assistant coach. If a head coach merely announces an anticipated change in a staff meeting without any prior consultation with the assistant(s) individually and privately, staff morale is likely to be shaken for awhile. If a head coach commits the grave error of making the change on the field in an emotional outburst or in order to shake up his staff, this is tantamount to a severe public reprimand and censure. If the assistant does not walk off the field and quit his job on the spot, it is very likely he will do so shortly since his effectiveness as a coach has been destroyed. It is very likely coaching staff morale will be severely strained and the other assistants will feel they, too, may be subjected to such abrupt and demeaning treatment by the head football coach's insensitivity.

Field, Collateral, and Other Coaching Duties

A suggested outline of duties and responsibilities for a six-man coaching staff,* including the head football coach, is listed below. Further, *every coach* has assignments in the following categories, *in addition to* teaching and coaching specific individual and team techniques and strategy: field coaching, and general, specific, and collateral duties. These major areas will be discussed generally first, with the specifics detailed under the coaches' titles and assignments.

---

* By necessity this may include the junior varsity and varsity assistant coaches, as well as the head football coach, depending on one's coaching set-up. If a total of six coaches is not available, the proposed plan must be modified and tailor-fitted to one's individual coaching situation, with the duties and responsibilities divided among the total number of coaches.

Field Coaching   The head football coach must break down his total on-the-field plan and ensure that all areas of individual, group, and team work are covered and receive adequate attention. Planning and organizing the practice schedule, game plan, and the game duties and responsibilities of the coaches will be discussed in later chapters.

General Duties   Assuming the coordinator role of the total program, the head football coach will make a further breakdown of all general assignments. As an illustration, the offensive and defensive coordinators, working with their position coaches, devise a proposed game plan offensively and defensively based on a statistical breakdown of scouting data and from studying films of opponents' other games. The films are used for verifying scouting reports, studying player personnel, and for staff and squad to view the overall execution and performance of the opposition. From this information, and getting statistical breakdowns offensively and defensively from the scout, game plans are devised. Since the head football coach is responsible for the overall game plan, he modifies or approves the game plan, and throughout the week he coordinates and monitors it, through field coaching assignments. The game plan will be discussed in greater detail in a later chapter. Additional general duties will be discussed later in this chapter and throughout the remainder of the book.

Specific Duties   Individual assignments to coaches *by position* would include responsibility for handling such matters as personnel evaluation, practice plans and organization, notebooks, summer letters, and so on, with some individual coaches having additional specific duties for handling such areas as the out-of-season conditioning and strength programs, film breakdown, evaluation of officials, and the like.

Collateral Duties   Individual assignments to coaches *by position* would include responsibility for handling such matters as morale and motivation, counseling, equipment, and so on, with some individual coaches having additional specific duties for handling such areas as hi-lite and training films, scout squads, offensive and defensive game plans, visiting team arrangements, and the like.

Control: Check and Regulate

Since coaching is a race against time, it is recommended that the head football coach distribute to the assistants a written list of *all* of their coaching duties and responsibilities. Because you as the head coach are actually responsible for the entire program and you must coordinate and monitor all the activities of all the staff, you should delegate judiciously as many of your duties (outlined below) as possible among your staff. You cannot assume every assistant will know how to carry out his assignment, nor that he will actually perform the task merely because it has been assigned to him. There is a close relationship between a head football coach's managerial functions of planning and control. *Planning* establishes the goals to be achieved and the means to be used to achieve them; and *control* monitors performance and corrects it when necessary so that planned and actual performance coincide. While a head coach may be successful in knowing that everything is written down and has been distributed to the assistant coaches, if he fails to follow up in monitoring and imposing controls, planned and actual performance will differ significantly.

STAFF ASSIGNMENTS

The assignments proposal below is for a six-man coaching staff,* including the head football coach, for a large high school (or small college). However, this proposal has been employed successfully in a medium-size high school by utilizing the junior varsity coaches as part of the total staff. The plan would then require keeping the two squads together for individual and group work, having the junior varsity games coordinated by the entire staff for home games, and assigning two coaches for away games for the junior varsity. The assignments are not all-inclusive nor rigidly fixed. Every head coach will have to tailor the plans to his own particular situation, and the suggested proposal may be easily modified to meet that end.

Assignments: Head Football Coach (Defensive Secondary)

Field Coaching
 1. Overall supervision of offense, defense, and kicking game.
 2. Specialty: defensive secondary (for example).

General Duties
 1. Total organization.
 2. Game plan coordinator.
 3. Practice plan.
 4. Notebook coordinator.
 5. Scholastic check.
 6. Faculty relations.

---

* See Chapter 6 for an illustration of a typical practice schedule involving a six-man coaching staff.

7. Public relations.
8. Administration.
9. Equipment (inventory and budget).

Specific Duties
1. Morale coordinator.
2. Quarterback meetings (game plan and strategy).
3. Personnel evaluation: staff and players.
4. Football clinics (assignments).
5. News letters (players—summer).
6. Discipline (overall).
7. Player counseling.
8. Parents.
9. Staff meetings.
10. Squad meetings.
11. Press, radio, television.
12. Banquet.

Collateral Duties
1. Total program.
2. Players' file.
3. Parents' clinic.
4. Booster club.
5. Travel, meals.
6. Scout squad.
7. Student body relations: pep assemblies, cheerleaders.
8. Officials' evaluation.
9. Summer employment.

Assignments: Offensive Coordinator (Offensive Line Coach)

Field Coaching
1. Offensive line.

General Duties
1. Offensive game plan (input from offensive staff);
   preliminary, final, evaluation.
2. Film: offensive line grades; opponents' film study.
3. Field equipment.
4. Team morale (offense).
5. Press box facilities—telephones, home and away games.

Specific Duties
1. Offensive practice organization (overall).
2. Summer letters to offensive linemen.

3. Offensive notebooks.
4. Administrative assistant.
5. Personnel evaluation.
6. Evaluate officials (coordinate and report).
7. Practice plan offensive line.

Collateral Duties
1. Morale and motivation (offensive line).
2. Counseling (offensive linemen).
3. Equipment (position).

Assignments: Defensive Coordinator (Defensive Line Coach)

Field Coaching
1. Defensive line.

General Duties
1. Defensive game plan (input from defensive staff); preliminary, final, evaluation.
2. Film: defensive line grades; opponents' film study.
3. Team morale (defense).
4. Team travel.

Specific Duties
1. Defensive practice organization (overall).
2. Summer letters to defensive linemen (secondary, head coach).
3. Defensive notebooks.
4. Personnel evaluation.
5. Practice plan defensive line.

Collateral Duties
1. Morale and motivation (defensive line).
2. Counseling (defensive linemen).
3. Equipment (position).

Assignments: Offensive Backfield Coach

Field Coaching
1. Offensive backs.

General Duties
1. Film: offensive backs' grades; opponents' film study.

Specific Duties
1. Strength coach (overall); winter, spring, and summer programs.
2. Offensive quarterbacks' training and meetings.
3. Offensive backs' practice plan.
4. Personnel evaluation.
5. Training room organization and maintenance.
6. (Junior varsity game coach, if necessary).

Collateral Duties
1. Morale and motivation (offensive backs).
2. Counseling (offensive backs).
3. Equipment (offense).
4. Scouting coordinator.
5. Offensive scout team.
6. Develop offensive game plan (with offensive coordinator).

Assignments: Defensive Linebacker Coach

Field Coaching
1. Defensive linebackers, including middle guards.

General Duties
1. Training rules coordinator.
2. Film: grade linebackers and middle guards; opponents' film study.

Specific Duties
1. Flexibility (stretching) coach; winter, spring and summer programs.
2. Defensive notebooks (position).
3. Defensive signal callers, training and meetings.
4. Personnel evaluation.
5. Summer letters to defensive linebackers and middle guards.
6. (Junior varsity game coach, if necessary).

Collateral Duties
1. Morale and motivation.
2. Defensive scout squad.
3. Assist in scouting.
4. Counseling (position).
5. Equipment (defense).
6. Develop defensive game plan (with defensive coordinator).
7. Visiting team arrangements.

Assignments: Special Teams Coach

Field Coaching
1. All special teams, offensive and defensive phases:
   Punting game.
   Punt return and block.
   Kick-off coverage, regular and on-side.
   Kick-off return, regular (middle and sideline) and on-side.
   Point-after-touchdown and field goal protection (and coverage).
   Two-point conversion plays and passes (with offensive coaches).
   Two-minute offense (with offensive coaches).
   Scout team kicking team.
2. Coach all receivers' passing game: tight and split ends, flankers, fullbacks, and tailbacks.

General Duties
1. Plan kicking game.
2. Film: grade kicking game; opponents' film study.

Specific Duties
1. Special teams notebooks.
2. Game film coordinator.
3. Audio-visual equipment: maintenance; recommend for purchase.
4. Request college films for off-season staff study.
5. Newspaper information (opponents).
6. Managers (coordinator).

Collateral Duties
1. Morale and motivation (gimmicks, locker room posters, and so on).
2. Kicking game scout team.
3. Counseling (position).
4. Equipment (kicking game).
5. Hi-lites and training films.

These duties and assignments are not all-inclusive, nor rigidly fixed, and every head coach should tailor the plans to fit his own coaching situation. Obviously if one does not have a six-man coaching staff he would have to double up on duties and responsibilities. In our illustration we have also specified the offensive and defensive line coaches as the co-ordinators. It may be that the head coach will want his offensive backfield coach and his linebacker coach as his coordinators. This is merely a matter of modifying the proposed plan and switching assignments to the coaches who have the coordinator duties and responsibilities.

Assignment of Administrative Duties

In addition to on- and off-the-field coaching assignments, there are many ancillary coaching details that require attention and follow-up and that are very time-consuming. The more follow-up details you delegate to your assistant coaches, the more time you have to supervise the overall program or to attend to essential or urgent matters. Administrative duties should be assigned to the assistants who are best qualified for handling them. Use your discretion to balance the work load of your assistants. You must be careful, however, that you and your assistants do not get so bogged down in administrative details and busy work that you cannot devote sufficient time to the players and their problems. Therefore, you must distinguish between what requires a coach's attention during the season and what can be postponed and attended to out-of-season. Some duties occur year-round, and all coaches will perform some of them. You as head coach should be kept apprised of your staff's activities, and you should get personally involved if a particular situation warrants it.

Examples of administrative details and duties to which assistant coaches are likely to be assigned are correspondence, grade checks, and counseling.

The Five "P's" of Success

"Prior Planning Prevents Poor Performance," are the five "P's" of success. In devising your football plan, you must consider all of the tasks and details that must be done to ensure success. Then as head coach you must assign these tasks and details to subordinates and others, and you must check to see that they are carried out. We have already outlined numerous tasks, duties, and responsibilities that should be assigned to assistant coaches in order to ensure the five "P's" of success. Let us now examine the evaluation of coaching staff members.

STAFF EVALUATION

Informal subjective evaluation is both inevitable and continuous. Judgments are made constantly about the performance of the players and the coaches, individually and as a team. Discussion here will be limited to the evaluation of the coaching staff, and in Chapter 4 ways of evaluating player personnel are discussed.

When you speak to a civic group, present or defend your point of view in a staff meeting, or explain and teach football techniques to your players, you are being evaluated subjectively by those to whom you are speaking. As you speak, your listeners are making judgments as to your knowledge of your subject, your manner of presentation, and so on. You are being evaluated subjectively as to whether you are a good teacher and a good coach. While few coaches are likely to consider this type of evaluation a threat, many *are* threatened by a written formal evaluation because they do not fully understand its purpose. It is a head coach's responsibility to inform his assistants of the *purpose* of staff evaluation in order to alleviate the uncomfortable feeling of it being used as a threat to their coaching positions.

Purpose of Evaluation

The objective or purpose of evaluation is to measure progress. Are we accomplishing the goals we set previously? Are there deviations between planned and actual results? Why? The key problem is to determine how significant these deviations are and what must be done to get back on track. It may be the goals were too lofty or unrealistic to begin with. Or it may be that coaching staff members, individually or collectively, are not doing their jobs for one reason or another. It may be that some of the methods, practices, techniques, or procedures are faulty, and these are causing the actual performance to deviate from the predetermined goals or desired performance. Or it may be there are only slight discrepancies, and minor adjustments and modifications by the head coach and his staff will correct them so that the football program is on course again. An important facet of the program to check progress is to evaluate the coaching staff on more than an informal basis.

Job Description Standards In the business world most workers upon being hired are given a job description listing their specific duties. When duties are added or their work assignments changed, they are always written into the employee's new job description. Many new employees are hired on a probationary basis; after a certain period of time they are formally evaluated in terms of their performance and job description, and only then do they receive a permanent appointment. When a worker is up for advancement in grade and/or salary, the worker knows his performance will be evaluated according to the standards set forth in his job description. Both the employee and the employer know how the employee will be evaluated. This is not so in coaching, however.

As an illustration, a job announcement may advertise the position of offensive line coach, with only a brief, general description of expected duties indicated. The new coach is *expected* to know all there is about offensive line play and ancillary aspects of coaching. The new employee may be an outstanding line coach and know much football, but it is very unlikely that he knows all that is expected of him, nor how his new head coach operates, unless the new line coach is given written detailed job specifics, such as those outlined and discussed in this chapter. Inevitably the offensive line coach will be informally evaluated, and he is likely to be judged on the basis of a job related activity that he was expected to do but perhaps did not perform. Or it may have been *assumed* he knew how to do some phase of his job, when in fact he did not know. Or perhaps the head coach *expected* the offensive line coach would do a job one way, but the assistant did it differently. While some of the details of his new coaching position will be obtained by word of mouth and by learning on the job, if each coach were given a list of his duties, responsibilities, and tasks, he could perform his new assignment well that much sooner, and the program's goals and objectives would be likely to be realized sooner, too. With written job descriptions, a head coach is in a better position to measure a subordinate's performance against specific standards.

Objective and Subjective Means of Evaluating   When evaluation is done in terms of measuring the employee's performance against the standards outlined in his job description, the rating is objective. Subjective rating looks at *degrees* of performance, how well or how poorly the employee measures up to the standards. If degrees of performance are not included and the employee is evaluated in terms of *yes* or *no*—he performed or failed to perform the responsibilities in his job description—then this is strictly an objective evaluation.

However, in evaluating professional people such as teachers and coaches (as compared to other workers who make their livelihood in the trades or by other means, and who are formally evaluated) many intangibles such as role skills and personality traits are usually included in the evaluation. Obviously these involve personal judgments, are more difficult to evaluate *accurately*, and are subjective rather than objective in nature. Teachers, coaches, and others are affixed certain role expectations as professionals, which are clear and pose no threat to the individual being evaluated as long as he knows in advance the evaluation criteria. Where subjective means of evaluation are utilized, or where the role expectations are vague, there are more likely to be differences of opinion between the evaluator and the individual being evaluated. However, it is well to keep in mind the purpose of evaluation: it is the interpretation of the results that is most important. Is the individual doing his job? Is he contributing individually and collectively to the objectives and goals that have been formulated and to the success of the overall program? How can his contributions be increased and strengthened? How can his contributions be better utilized? The answers to these questions are what the evaluator, the head coach, is seeking as he attempts to fit all of the parts together in an effort to build a winning program.

If a head coach were to utilize those essential qualities of a *good* coach, listed in Chapter 2 in devising criteria to evaluate his staff, he would find some are *objective* but the majority are *subjective*. Subjective qualities are more difficult to evaluate. On the other hand, if a head coach were to include as his criteria *many* of the items outlined and enumerated in this chapter under "Assignments: Field Coaching; General Duties; Specific Duties; Collateral Duties," these are easily measurable since they are *objective* in nature. To accomplish the desired end, it is essential to devise a rating scale with criteria that are both objective and subjective in nature, such as is illustrated below. The objective is *not* the rating scale itself nor merely to evaluate the coaching staff. The objective is to measure the progress at year's end toward the desired goal. If the results are negative, then you as the head coach must adjust and regulate, exercising your control function as a football administrator to get your subordinates back on the right track and headed in the right direction. In some instances that control might mean replacing an assistant or reassigning and changing his primary and secondary duties. Many times a subordinate simply is not aware of his weak points; he frequently does not recognize or want to admit his shortcomings. However, as the basis for discussion, we suggest that the assistant rate himself separately from the head coach's rating. Then the two can meet privately and discuss both ratings of the assistant's performance, with the head coach utilizing good human relations techniques in order to motivate the assistant and recognize his needs, too.

Evaluation Criteria: Self-Evaluation and Head Coach's Evaluation

We are grateful to Athletic Director Frank Broyles, University of Arkansas' highly successful former head football coach, for permitting us to include some materials he utilized for staff evaluation. We have paraphrased and slightly revised Coach Broyles's evaluation forms and materials to conform to the format and context of this book. You may wish to rearrange and revise the questions and material to conform to your own wishes and particular coaching situation.

Each assistant coach evaluates himself on each question circling the number he feels most accurately describes his performance, using the following rating scale:

5 = outstanding
4 = above average

3 = average
2 = below average
1 = poor

On separate forms the head coach evaluates the performance of each of his assistants, using the same rating scale.

Each assistant meets separately with the head coach and goes over his own self-ratings and his supervisor's view of his performance. Discussing the pros and cons of the assistant's performance might result in changing some of the numerical ratings, but more importantly the evaluative process apprises the subordinate of his work performance and keeps him and the program on target. Each assistant knows where he stands, sees his strengths and weaknesses, and acknowledges those areas in which improved performance is needed. Obviously the ratings could be used for other purposes, too, such as for promotion, financial increments, dismissal, and so on, depending on one's coaching situation.

Coaching, discipline, academics, relationship with players and staff, improving professional knowledge and staff efficiency, personal image in the school, community, and state are major areas that Coach Broyles employed for staff evaluation, with up to half a dozen criteria under each. Obviously almost any aspect of a coach's job could be included.

DIAGRAM 3–1
Evaluative Criteria

Coaching
1. Do you make an effort to coach all players, not just the top ones? Example: Do you work with B-team personnel during scrimmages and after practices?

5   4   3   2   1   *

2. Do you make a point of trying to praise players for good things done rather than just harping about their mistakes? In simple terms do you try to motivate daily with positive psychology to instill confidence in the player? Players tend to dislike coaches who constantly criticize and never throw a "rose."
3. Are your drills varied to the extent they do not become boring and stimulate little learning?
4. Do you take full advantage of getting written material in the

---

* Note that the rating scale for grading and recording performance has been omitted from beneath all other questions for the sake of brevity and is included under the first question only for illustrative purposes.

hands of your players, holding meetings, giving tests, watching films, and so on that promote learning and understanding?

5. Are your meetings and practices run in such a manner that you do not tolerate anything that detracts from learning? Are you strict in not allowing your players to make mistakes, and do you demand mental discipline on their part?

6. Do you spend the hours on the job (office, meetings, and so forth) that are necessary to get the job done?

Discipline

1. Do you do your part in demanding that players follow the rules or guidelines which we have set up, or do you rely on other coaches in order to avoid involvement?

2. Do you fulfill assigned discipline chores to the fullest extent? Example: Do you carry out help sessions, counseling individual disciplinary problems assigned to you?

3. Are you constantly aware to make sure that *all* players assigned to you are not tardy or absent from practice, and if they are, do you find out why? Or do you just check the players at the position you coach?

4. Do you do your part in helping with team travel to see that our players are dressed properly and conduct themselves properly, so as to keep them as a team in the right mental frame of mind, as well as to promote a good public image?

5. Do you notify parents of necessary discipline we have had to impose on a boy you have recruited or coached? A well-written letter will suffice; only drastic problems merit a phone call.

6. Are you sensitive to diagnose disciplinary problems your players may be involved in before they actually surface?

Academics

1. Do you always know exactly which courses your players are enrolled in and what their status is from an academic and eligibility standpoint?

2. Do you follow up and get on top of class cutting problems when one of your players is reported to you?

3. Are you constantly trying to promote public relations with faculty and administration that will lead to their help? Notifications to us of players not doing well in their classes, or on some occasions giving a student that second chance, is often all that is needed.

4. Do you visit on a regular basis with each player assigned to you in regard to his academic and personal problems?

5. Do you keep in touch with parents of players who are academic risks and solicit their help in motivating their son?

Relationship with Players and Staff
1. Are you guilty of making unfounded statements in passing judgment on players that have an effect on other coaches and our staff's evaluation of a player?
2. Are you courteous to all players at all times?
3. Are you courteous to members of our staff other than coaches? to such people as secretaries, janitors, cooks, and equipment men? Human nature is in effect here and such attention makes them more productive.

Improving Professional Knowledge and Staff Efficiency
1. Do you read all literature sent out by the professional organizations you belong to?
2. Do you attempt to seek out new literature and knowledge?
3. Do you make contributions in staff meetings on new trends and ideas you have learned, or do you sit back and let others set the pattern for our offense, defense, or total program?
4. Do you use good judgment in not relating internal staff problems to people outside our department?
5. In conversation with friends and acquaintances are you careful always to speak highly of each of our staff members regardless of whether you agree with his teaching, philosophy, effort, or the like?

Personal Image in School, Community, and State
1. Do you at any time use alcoholic beverages to the extent that you present an image of yourself that reflects poorly on our program?
2. If you are a married man, do you uphold marital responsibilities that are expected of you as a teacher and a coach?
3. Do you keep your financial and business affairs in a state that is not embarrassing to you, your family, and our athletic department?
4. Do you present a satisfactory image to the public in regard to grooming and dress, particularly in representing our department at public functions?

Obviously the criteria you employ for evaluative purposes for your assistant coaches will depend on the coaching situation and the level of competition at which your institution's athletic teams participate. As an illustration, a tenured faculty member who has coaching responsibilities as part of his teaching assignment might object strenuously to being evaluated on some personal characteristics such as dress, grooming, or his handling of personal financial affairs; multiple teaching-coaching duties might prohibit his participating in the football program, other than actual on-the-field coaching, to the extent a head coach would want and expect. A head coach's expectations might never be realized in such a situation, and he might be able to do little about it. He can look at the "could be" or "should be" situation, but he must recognize the "as is" situation. The important point is that a head coach should attempt to build a "results-getting" attitude in his assistants, and he needs to aid them in developing self-reliance so they can achieve prescribed goals with confidence. The methods and techniques described in this chapter should aid in accomplishing that goal and consequently in building a successful football program.

In the next two chapters we will examine player personnel—assessing potential and evaluating performance—in building a winning program.

4

ASSESSMENT OF INDIVIDUAL PLAYER PERSONNEL

Trying to assess accurately the abilities and skills of player personnel is one of the most important aspects of a coach's job. In many instances it is one of the most poorly executed ones. Many coaches do *not* know the capabilities of their players. Many times determinations and selections are made solely on a prospect's height, weight, and speed, and on his estimated *potential* as a football player. In this chapter we will deal with measurable and observable criteria for assessing or appraising prospects, and in Chapter 5 we will turn to position criteria for slotting or aligning players.

EVALUATION: ALL WAYS AND ALWAYS

The evaluation of players should go on year-round, *all ways* and *always*, if a coaching staff is to get to know its player personnel and to assess their abilities and skills in order to build a winning football program. Many coaches fail to secure measurable data, other than height, weight, and speed, and make subjective judgments as to a prospect's potential. The various types of criteria that should be utilized will be discussed shortly, as will be *potential* versus *performance*. The latter is a measurable quality.

Record Measurable Results and Observations

When prospects are assessed or evaluated, the results should be accurately measured, recorded, and available for examination by the entire staff. Too many times coaches do not know *accurate* measurements such as height, weight, and speed of their prospects. Nor have they a record of such measurements so that proper assessment of player personnel can take place. There should be a cumulative book or fact sheet on *every* prospect so that evaluation of personnel is always up to date. In the junior high and high school football programs in particular, where the characteristics and needs between ninth and twelfth grade prospects, as an illustration, are very diverse, maintaining individual cumulative records is most important and beneficial. We include below the types and kinds of records that can be maintained by a coaching staff at any level of competition to assess each prospect's potential as a football player (Diagram 4-3), his offensive (Diagram 5-1) and defensive (Diagram 5-2) skills, and his ability at his position. Separate checklists for each position are also included in Chapter 5, in addition to methods for evaluating player performance (Diagrams 5-3 and 5-4). You can modify or utilize these materials to suit your own coaching situation, to aid you in securing factual objective data for assessing potential and grading performance.

Personnel Boards   Just as business and industry utilize visual control boards for production, inventory, programming, scheduling, and sales performance, a football coach can utilize such devices for personnel alignment. Personnel boards are easily made and are relatively inexpensive. You can use simple pegboards with nails and/or hooks, hook and loop boards, card insert boards, and flannel boards, or you can turn to the more expensive commercially manufactured metal and magnetic boards, all of which serve the same purpose and function. Diagram 4-1 illustrates an offensive personnel alignment board, and Diagram 4-2 a defensive board, which were designed by the author and are utilized by several college coaching staffs.*

The important point is that some device or means should allow all coaches to view the names of all the available player personnel at one time, and thus be aware of each prospect's name, position, height, weight, speed, and class (and age, for the junior high and high school players). For instance, if each prospect's name is written on pressure-sensitive white tape, colored felt-tip pens can be used to illustrate class, such as red for seniors, black for juniors, blue for sophomores, and green for

---

* For specifications and directions on how to construct personnel boards, see Donald E. Fuoss, "Personnel Alignment Board," *Scholastic Coach,* January 1966, pp. 50, 52.

DIAGRAM 4-1
Offensive Personnel Alignment Board

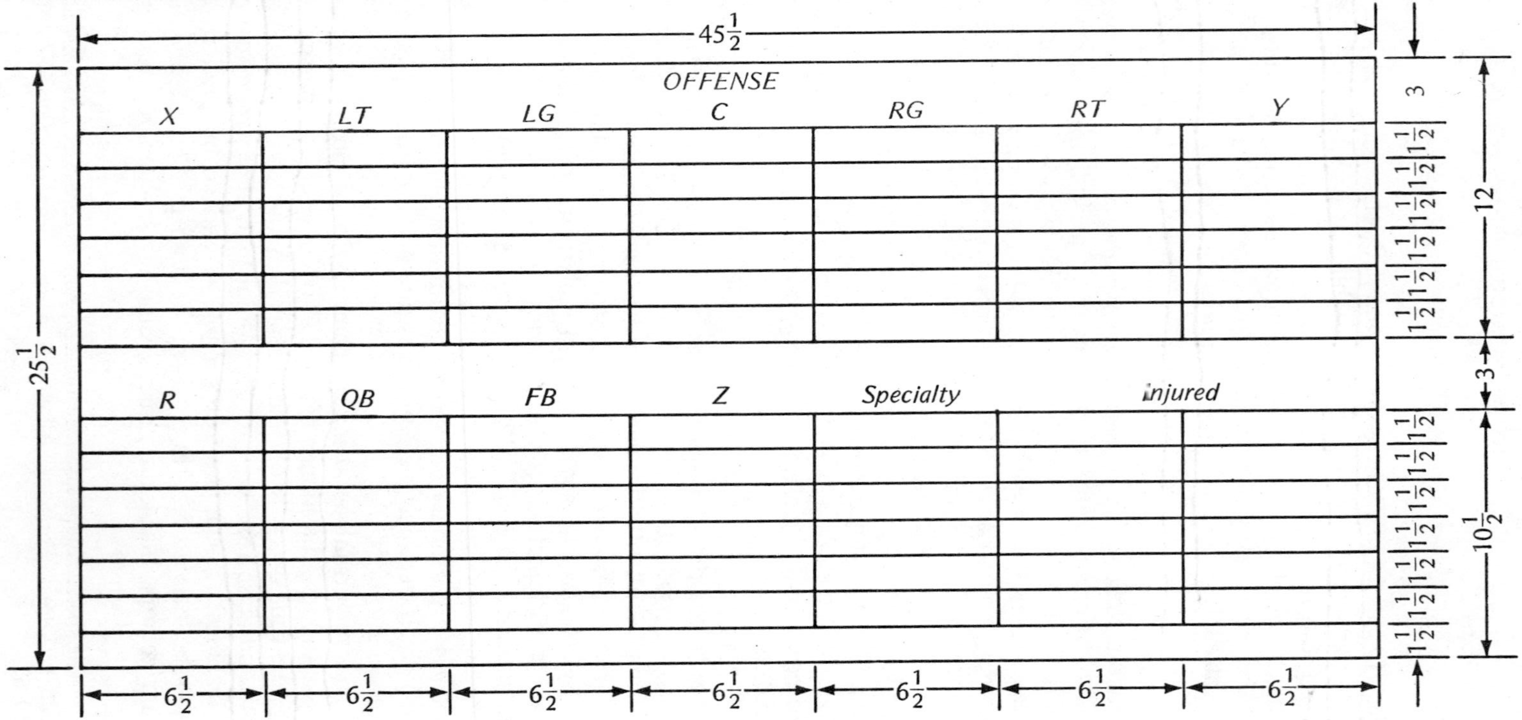

DIAGRAM 4–2
Defensive Personnel Alignment Board

DEFENSE

LF	LT	LLB	MG	RLB	RT	RE

LC	SS	FS	RC	Specialty	Injured

freshmen. Height, weight, and speed (and age) can be recorded for every player below his name tab, so that all of the coaches can view all of the squad members slotted offensively, defensively, and on special teams.

At the conclusion of the football season, and in preparation for the next season, the pressure-sensitive tape should be removed, new name tapes cut and lettered in the appropriate colors, and personnel boards made ready for continual evaluation and assessment of player personnel. When individual pertinent data changes, as may occur over the summer months, the boards are brought up to date prior to the beginning of the new football season. The players' names are moved up and down on the board as warranted by such circumstances as practice performance (Chapter 6) and game films (Chapter 7).

Year-Round Assessment and Evaluation of Players

Over the course of the year, formal assessment and evaluation of player personnel goes on before, during, and after the season. Informal evaluation takes places every time you observe or talk with a prospect.

Post-season Assessment   From the termination of the last football game of one football season until the pre-season call-out of another, post-season player assessment and evaluation take place. Your coaching staff is aware of the players who will be graduated or not returning and the positions which they vacate. Initially you will be thinking in terms of returnees and the other underclassmen who were regulars filling the vacated positions. In all probability some players will have to be shifted to new positions in an effort to get a tentative line-up of personnel at offense, defense, and on specialty teams. If the losses are too great in number and/or the personnel is too inexperienced, you may have to make minor or major adjustments in your coaching staff's philosophy of offense, defense, and/or the kicking game. It is unlikely a coaching staff would make a complete overhaul of its offense, defense, or kicking game; it is more likely that some parts would be retained, others abandoned, and still others added. As an illustration, if your graduating senior quarterback was tall, slow afoot, but threw well from the pocket on dropback passes, it is unlikely you would retain this feature of your passing attack if your upcoming quarterback is short, quick afoot, and runs the sprint-out well. Logic dictates you feature the run-pass sprintout option over your previously featured dropback passing attack. While a head coach need not make a final decision on such matters immediately after the season, common sense dictates that planning for different types of objectives will mean assessing the skills of *all* returnees in an effort to locate the eleven *best* athletes, then the *next* eleven *best*, regardless of position. This necessitates viewing the performance of players in the game films;

however, utilizing films *after* the termination of the season for this purpose rarely occurs.

During the season, the players should have been graded during the film study (see Chapter 5). These grades should be reviewed, and each position coach should view his players again in an early and late season film. Each should attempt to assess the skills and performance of the personnel at the positions he coaches. In addition all of the coaches should study the players at *other* positions, too, and the film grades of *all* players should be made available to your coaching staff in an effort to identify the best twenty-two athletes. If spring practice is impossible and no further film study of personnel is available, it is not necessary to finalize line-ups on the personnel board at this time. There are other means and opportunities to assess the abilities of your personnel, such as the off-season conditioning, strength, and flexibility programs, including the summer program, and in counseling with the student-athletes during the period until the next football season.

Many high school football coaches in particular do not grade their players' performance during the season, nor do they view their football films in the off-season to study their player personnel; they do not conduct off-season conditioning, strength, and flexibility programs; they do not have summer programs for their prospects; and they probably do not maintain close contact with their players after football season. Where no initial evaluation of personnel takes place until pre-season football practice, these coaches are already behind their competitors who continue with a year-round assessment and evaluation of their personnel.

Pre-season Assessment   Where you are viewing a prospect for the first time, especially where you must rely on "walk-ons" and/or you do not have a good "feeder" system, your initial determinations are made mostly on the results of skill and agility drills and practice performance. A method of organizing the practice schedule so that all coaches can evaluate all personnel, as well as how to select appropriate drills, will be discussed in Chapter 6. A method of evaluating and grading players' performance in films will be discussed in Chapter 5.

For the returning prospects who have been assessed and evaluated in the post- or off-season, pre-season is merely a follow-up on the part of the coaches to determine if their individual and collective assessments of players have been valid. Has a returning player improved his strength, flexibility, or conditioning in the off-season, or has he fallen off? Is he taller, heavier, quicker? Or does he have too much weight for his height; is he slower? Is his attitude better or poorer than it was the previous year? Does he really want to play football? Is he showing improvement? Is he carrying out his assignments and doing his job? The coaching staff seeks the answers to these and other questions as they go about slotting and aligning players.

In-season Assessment   Once the season gets underway, most of the evaluation will be objective in nature because games will be filmed and players' performance should be graded. Subjective evaluation by the coaches occurs on a daily basis as the players go through their practice schedule and drills, but the major emphasis will be how well a player performs and is graded in a game. During the daily practice sessions, however, players should be moved, at their positions, to different teams (up to first, down to third, etc.) so their performance can be evaluated (see Chapter 6).

Professional Talent Scouts' Guidelines

While scholastic and collegiate football coaches cannot recruit like the professional football teams, let us examine only the criteria the professional talent scouts employ to evaluate prospects. Since all things are relative at our respective levels of competition, the following information should prove helpful to *all* football coaches.

We are indebted to professional football for the original evaluative criteria for player personnel used in Chapters 4 and 5, although it is impossible to identify the exact sources of information, since much of the material is fairly common and is used by practically all of the professional talent scouts and coaches. Then, too, the origin of material has become clouded as much of it has been modified over the years, including that made available to and adapted previously by us and others for our own use. However, we are grateful to Coach Milt Von Mann, Special Scouting Assignments, Cincinnati Bengals, formerly with the Kansas City Chiefs, for permitting us to include his guidelines for the characteristics of an athlete in this chapter and his criteria for scouting positions in Chapter 5. The comments preceding and following Coach Von Mann's guidelines, however, are our interpretation of the subject matter.

In assessing player personnel, Coach Von Mann and other talent scouts all stress the point of *finding the athlete first*, then fitting him into the most desirable offensive or defensive position. The following guidelines describe the characteristics of an athlete.

EVALUATING CRITERIA IN ASSESSING
FOOTBALL PROSPECTS

Coach Von Mann includes guidelines for evaluating prospects in the following areas: speed, agility and balance, strength, toughness, desire, quickness and explosion, size potential, character, aggressiveness, pride, and reaction time. The authors have added others.

Speed

For the proper placement of personnel, it is imperative that you have *accurate* times for all of your players. Speed may be checked in 40-yard sprints against the watch for backs and wide receivers, and 20-yard sprints for down linemen. Some highly successful coaches are now using 10-yard sprints to establish quickness in coming off the line of scrimmage.

A common mistake in evaluating players is to judge them merely in relation to the other squad members. Only if you time them accurately in shorts or sweats and also in full gear will you be able to place players in positions where they can utilize their speed to the best advantage for the team. As an illustration, if you have two tackle prospects who are both good-sized men, but one runs a 5.2 second 40-yard dash and the other is timed at 5.6 seconds, you should probably align the slower tackle on offense and the quicker one on defense. While all things are relative in your own conference or calibre of play, it is a fact that a 10-second cornerback is not likely to cover a flanker with 9.7 seconds speed. While most football teams are likely to have only a few of the former, and very few or none of the latter, timed speed helps a coach determine where to place his player personnel.

Football Speed   Webster's New Collegiate Dictionary defines "speed" as "the act or state of moving swiftly; rate of motion," which still does not tell us a great deal about "football speed." However, the true measure of football speed is quickness in an immediate area. It is not how fast a player can run fifty or one hundred yards. For a defensive lineman, it is the quickness with which he moves from tackle to tackle, or the quickness of a secondary defender to rotate on flow his way from an inside safety position to cover the flat; that is *football speed*. If either defender lacks the speed necessary to carry out the duties and responsibilities of his specific position, then both he and his team are at a disadvantage.

Considering Speed out of Context   Many coaches have a tendency to consider speed and size out of context with a prospect's other attributes, especially if he possesses unusual speed. Speed should not be considered as a separate entity, as blazing speed by itself for a football prospect may be of little value. As an illustration, a prospect's unusual speed may be only in a straight line but falls off considerably when he must cut and evade and run a weaving course. Or a greater detraction would be a prospect who lacks "heart" to hit or get hit, despite his blazing speed. On the other hand you may have a hitter or striker who lacks the speed to get to the opposition to block or tackle. Therefore, speed should not be taken out of context—it is only one of a number of attributes that should be considered in assessing football players.

Running Styles   Merely for the sake of discussion among coaching staff members, the following common terminology may be employed to describe the running styles of prospects:

1. The fluid or smooth runner who seems to glide.
2. The floppy runner with arms and legs loose.
3. The compact runner with tight arms and upper body.
4. The stiff runner with no knee bend.
5. The laborer runner who works and strains.
6. The long strider.

In Chapter 5 we will see that players with certain running styles are better suited for some positions than others.

Agility and Balance

This characteristic is a combination of quickness and ease of movement, which enables a player to be exceptional in balance and maneuverability. The development of body control, agility, and the ability to react quickly and correctly are as important as the proper development of offensive and defensive fundamentals. Without the required skills, a player will be unable to execute the necessary fundamentals. If a player is unable to control his own body, he will not be able to control his opponent.

As a coach, you can evaluate agility and balance in your personnel by the following observations:

1. Change of direction or position from coach's hand signal.
2. Sled drills, spin drills, hit and recovery drills.
3. Back's and end's ability to change direction, cross over.
4. Follow-through on one-on-one block.
5. Pass protection blocking, hit and recover.
6. End's ability to regain balance when held up or "bumped" by linebackers.
7. Balance in tackling and blocking drills.
8. Back's ability to regain balance when hit.

In judging agility and balance, you should observe how quickly a prospect gets up from the ground. The agile prospect will sort of snap or bounce up to his feet and continue moving to block or pursue. The less agile prospect is likely to roll over and push up with both hands in a mechanical, somewhat stiff, and uncoordinated effort to regain his balance.

Strength

Many football prospects with good physical size are not strong. You are looking for the prospect with the physical strength to defeat an opponent. The following are ways to observe strength:

1. Ball carrier's ability to run through tacklers and get extra yardage.
2. Pass blocker's ability to keep from being overpowered.
3. Defensive lineman's ability to overpower the blocker and get to the passer.
4. Defensive lineman's ability to defeat a double-team block.
5. Offensive lineman's ability to drive out a defensive man in a one-on-one situation.

It is a common fallacy to correlate strength with physical size. From outward appearances you might expect the "body beautiful" type of prospect to possess great strength, and the "little guy" to lack strength, whereas the situation actually may be the opposite. Therefore, strength and physical size should be assessed separately. Neither prospect may have the "heart" to hit, which will be discussed shortly and which rules out a football prospect regardless of his body size or strength.

Toughness

Coaches speak frequently of being mentally and physically tough. The latter is certainly more evident and easier to evaluate than the former. Taking into consideration that the football season is long, and that a successful coach must build for the entire season and not just for a single game, the following observations may be made of each prospect in order to determine his mental and physical toughness:

1. Is he susceptible to injury?
2. Does he recover quickly from injury?
3. Does his efficiency drop noticeably because of minor pain or bruises?
4. Does he need prodding by the coaching staff?

Mental Toughness   The pain threshold among your players will vary. All experienced coaches have had players who were chronic complainers about their physical ailments, real or imagined, but who played in spite of them. Coaches have had players with a very high pain threshold, who played when hurt and who may even have tried to play with a broken bone. Conversely, an experienced coach is also likely to have had the *hypochondriac*, a person characterized by depression and fancies of ill health, or the *malingerer*, someone who pretends to be sick or injured, especially to avoid duty or work. While no coach should ever knowingly play a boy who is injured, and never one who was likely to be injured further, there are prospects trying out for the football team who are always "hurt." They really do not *want* to play, but they would like to be considered a part of the squad, enjoying all of the rights, benefits, and privileges of a squad member. To permit such members to remain on the squad after they have been pronounced 100 percent medically fit for scrimmage is to do a disservice to the game of football and to the other squad members, especially those "winners" who do "suck it up" and play with discomfort and pain.

Mental toughness also means how a prospect reacts to pressure and criticism. How does he react when he blows an assignment, misses a tackle, is physically whipped or beaten by his opponent? How does he respond to coaching when he is corrected or criticized? While a prospect may respond because of pride, desire, or competitive spirit, he may put so much pressure on himself that he does not perform well. He may not be tough enough to accept criticism or prodding. Or he may collapse and be unstable when the going gets rough because he lacks mental toughness. He may just lack "heart."

Desire

Great desire to excel on the part of a mediocre football prospect permits him to get the job done many times over a more skilled performer with less motivation or desire to excel. Desire is defined by Webster's as "conscious impulse toward an object or experience that promises enjoyment or satisfaction in its attainment." Some ways of observing this characteristic are:

1. The eagerness and persistence with which he attacks his job.
2. The intense desire to carry out an assignment successfully.
3. The relentness, emotional drive of a player when engaged in competition; his instinctive urge to dominate.

"Heart"

"You can't win without 'heart.'" "No one can 'look into the heart' of another person." "Ability comes in any size." "Football players come in any size." "A football coach cannot perform a 'heart' transplant!" These are all football truisms.

If a prospect lacks "heart"—that is, desire and courage—despite his size, quickness, and strength, he will not make a good football player. Without desire and dedication to football, the best physical qualities are inadequate. With sufficient desire, however, a prospect can play even with limited ability. Desire is a difficult factor to measure in evaluating a prospect, although methods of observing it have been listed above. Many times coaches end up judging a football prospect solely on his physical qualifications, and many "little guys" who are short on the physical qualifications never get the opportunity to play. Other "little men" with great desire and determination have made significant contributions to the success of outstanding football teams at all levels of competition merely because some coach saw their "heart" and gave them the opportunity to succeed. A premier football coach, the late Vince Lombardi, made the following statement relevant to the subject:

> Every time a football player goes out to ply his trade he's got to play from the ground up—from the soles of his feet right up to his head. Every inch of him has to play. Some guys play with their heads. That's O.K. . . . But more important, you've got to play with your heart—with every fiber of your body. If you're lucky enough to find a guy with a lot of head and a lot of heart, he's never going to come off the field second. (Washington State Coaches Association, Clinic Notes, 1966–67)

Quickness and Explosion

The ability of a player to move his feet, arms, and body quickly is one of the characteristics of a good athlete. The following are ways to observe quickness and explosion:

1. Quick movement of the feet.
2. Quick delivery of a blow.
3. Quick offensive and defensive start without command.
4. Quick movement in any direction.
5. The ability of a player to explode through an opponent and retain leverage, balance, and follow-through.
6. The ability of a defensive lineman to explode into and neutralize the blocker and yet maintain a good football position.
7. A tackler's ability to explode through a ball carrier.
8. The ability of a defensive back to explode through a receiver when "planing" the ball.
9. A tackler's ability to explode through a ball carrier.

Getting Off on the Snap   This ability will vary with the individual, but getting off on the snap is essential in having a fine offensive, defensive, and special team unit. This skill can be developed and improved with snap and ball movement reaction drills, which must be done quickly with the emphasis on the point of anticipation.

Size Potential

By size potential we mean a player's potential to reach the minimum height and weight requirements for his position in order to be an outstanding competitor in a given league or calibre of competition.

In a contact sport such as football, a good big man will generally beat out a good little man, especially if each has both desire and determination. While it is not advisable to exclude the "little guy" merely because of lack of size alone, a coach may be forced to limit the number of small men on his squad. If a coach has a choice between a big man and a little man, especially at a line position, inevitably he selects the bigger of the two prospects because a small lineman simply cannot physically defeat a big lineman. While there are always exceptions, the possibility of winning is greater with a player who has reached size potential already, than it is with a small-sized player, unless the latter has other exceptional qualities, namely speed and quickness.

Conversely, coaches must be careful they are not blinded by size, as we already pointed out with regard to speed. In these two areas in particular, if a prospect has good physical size and/or excellent speed, coaches have a tendency to envision his excellent potential and frequently overrate him. Potential versus performance will be discussed shortly.

1. Is the player lean because of participation in another sport (like wrestling)?
2. Has the prospect reached his maturity of growth? Some boys reach their maturity of growth at a very young age.
3. Does the prospect have a large bone body structure?
4. Linemen will usually gain more weight than backs, although this is not always true.
5. Try to project the weight potential according to the requirements of the position, that is, tackles are generally larger than guards, ends are generally leaner than tackles, and so on.
6. How large are the prospect's parents?

High school and small college football coaches who do not actively recruit football prospects with scholarship aid generally are compelled to work with all prospects, with the hope each prospect will develop, mature, and acquire the necessary skills to make a contribution to the success of the football program. A football coach at a large high school might not have to follow this procedure, depending on the calibre of his competition and the number and size of boys who are trying out for his football squad. A large or major college or university football program that gives scholarship aid simply will not recruit many physically small football prospects, perhaps one per year. Those selected usually have blinding speed, and in practically every case the small-sized prospect is a running back or possibly a flanker, never an interior lineman.

Height and Weight Have one person, trainer or coach, measure the height and weight of all the prospects so there is consistency, uniformity, and accuracy. This task might be assigned to the coach who is responsible for keeping the personnel board up to date.

When measuring the height of a player, his heels should be against the wall, toes out. Otherwise the player may curl his toes under and push up. A draftsman's tool should be used to get a prospect's true height by squaring it with the wall and the top of the player's head.

When a prospect is being weighed, he should stand in the middle of the scale, not forward or at the rear of center. Obviously the scale must be checked for accuracy so as to secure valid weights.

Character

Character is a combination of mental qualities in football, including the ability to inspire and lead others to perform more effectively. Some traits of a person with this inherent quality are:

1. He leads by example, and not by talking.
2. He has the poise and confidence to calm down his teammates under adverse conditions.
3. His teammates have the utmost confidence in his ability to perform in a "clutch" situation.
4. He is a good student.
5. He is a leader and prominent in student government and other school activities.

The importance which we attach to character is best exemplified by some thoughts of the late Vince Lombardi. He felt that character results directly from mental attitude and is more important than intellect. He believed that leadership requires sacrifice, self-denial, humility, and a perfectly disciplined will—all of which mark the distinction between great and lesser men.

Aggressiveness

Aggressiveness is the willingness and readiness to hit, the bold and energetic pursuit of a goal. The following are ways to observe this characteristic in a prospect:

1. Pocket pass protection for offensive backs and linemen.
2. Full speed in head-on tackling.
3. A defensive back playing through a blocker.
4. Loves contact!
5. Rough on the blockers protecting the passer.

As we pointed out previously, a lineman in particular must be aggressive. He must dominate. He must control his opponent and the line of scrimmage in his immediate area. He should love contact!

Pride

Pride is identifiable in a player when he displays a burning desire to win and the willingness to pay the price in hard work and sacrifice. Some ways of observing pride in an athlete are:

1. Does he fight harder when the going gets rough?
2. Does he perform extra work to correct a weakness?
3. Does he accept responsibility rather than offer excuses?

Pride and desire go together. They are almost inseparable. The desire to excel and the pride and satisfaction of getting the job done, whipping your man on either offense or defense, are essential to being a part of a winning football team. A well-known football axiom is, "You can't win without pride and morale."

Reaction Time

This is the superior quality of instant counteraction to the movement of an opponent. Ways to observe reaction time are:

1. A defensive lineman's ability to react to a trap block.
2. The ability of an offensive lineman to adjust a block to an opponent's moves.
3. A defensive back's ability to react to a receiver's final move of his pattern.

4. An offensive back's ability to react and change his direction as a ball carrier or blocker and to use his blockers properly.
5. The ability of a defensive player to recognize a fake quickly and to pursue immediately and effectively.

Football Intelligence

Football intelligence should not be confused with the broad general term of intelligence. Many individuals who are "book smart" may not be "football smart." The ability to think on one's feet, so to speak, and to make split-second decisions and reactions, are things that can be taught by training and repetitive drill. Some prospects never conceptualize the entire picture, seeing only their own position and speciality as isolated entities. Not so with the prospect who has football intelligence or "smarts." He will probably be a leader, too, and while a coach cannot bestow leadership on another, only opportunities to display leadership, the more individuals on a squad with football intelligence and leadership characteristics, the greater are that squad's chances of winning.

Diagram 4-3 illustrates a format for evaluating the characteristics described above, using a rating scale, in order to obtain a composite grade for each athlete-football player. In the next chapter we will illustrate how to evaluate personnel by positions offensively (Diagram 5-1) and defensively (Diagram 5-2).

POTENTIAL VERSUS PERFORMANCE

The prospects whom coaches have to work with at the high school and small college level, where players cannot be recruited, are far from the top athletes and ideal prospects whom the professional football and major college coaches recruit for their teams. For the latter two groups of coaches, the football players have proven their worth through performances that have been graded and evaluated. Through the recruiting process, these coaches can be highly selective of the football players they choose. Not so, however, with the high school and small college coaches, who must rely on limited feeder systems and walk-ons to build their teams. These coaches in particular must place a high premium on a player's potential, since performance is difficult to evaluate until *after* the prospect comes out for the team.

Evaluate Potential Realistically

It is for this reason every effort should be made to garner pertinent factual information, apply evaluative criteria, and try to secure valid opin-

DIAGRAM 4–3
Rating Scale for Evaluating Prospects

Characteristics	1	2	3	4	5	Use the Following Rating Scale:
1. Speed						1 Outstanding
2. Agility						
3. Quickness						2 Above Average
4. Toughness						
5. Desire						3 Average
6. Strength						
7. Size Potential						4 Below Average
8. Coordination						
9. Aggressiveness						5 Poor
10. Pride						

Offensive ability _____

_____

Defensive ability _____

_____

Best position and why _____

_____

If player is rejected, indicate why _____

_____

Rate prospect on offense _____
Rate prospect on defense _____

Use the following *rating scale:*

1.0–1.6 Star	2.9–3.4 Prospect
1.7–2.2 Starter	3.5–4.0 Questionable
2.3–2.8 Make the League	4.1 Reject

ions on all player personnel. Too many coaches assess only potential and give measurable qualities but a cursory examination. These same coaches many times tend to stay with a prospect who they feel has potential, but who never does develop into a consistent football performer. Perhaps the coach does not want to admit that he made a mistake in misjudging the prospect's ability. Or perhaps personnel is too thin and the coach has no other choice than to keep working with that prospect, hoping potential will develop into performance. However, a prospect may look, "smell," and even act like a football player on occasion, without ever quite developing into a stable, consistent football performer. He has *potential*, but he is not a football player. Don't make the common mistake of neglecting replacement of a "potential" player. Too often a coach fails to substitute for a player with potential because he keeps expecting him to perform satisfactorily. Not infrequently a coaching staff will continue working for several years with a player who has potential, generally one who has been "eyeballed" because of his size and/or speed, hoping he will develop into a football player, while ignoring the development of other prospects. The good looking prospect with potential may graduate from high school and/or college, still possessing the same potential he has always had and which the coaching staff has never been able to develop. In another case, a prospect may not have varsity game experience by his senior year of competition, and it may be highly questionable whether he should be retained on the squad if he is not a regular or the first back-up player at his position.

Consistency

On the other hand the prospect who performs, especially one who does so with consistency regardless of his other attributes, has proven he is capable of doing the job. You should remember that height, weight, and speed are tempered by the overall ability of the individual. In the final analysis, the evaluative criteria should be the consistency with which he does what is asked of him. As an illustration, regardless of all of his attributes and limitations as an offensive guard, how consistently does a player carry out his blocking assignment? He may be small or have good size, quick or slow afoot, use outstanding or poor techniques in blocking, but with what degree of consistency does he block his defender from pursuing the ball carrier to the point of attack? He may grade 100 percent on technique, but if he fails to carry out his blocking assignment, he grades zero on performance. Conversely, his techniques may leave much to be desired and his technique grade is zero, but if he eliminates his defender he receives 100 percent for performance. Performance is the sole criterion for determining efficiency as a blocker and team player. This subject will be discussed in greater detail in the next chapter.

"Winners"

Some people object to labeling individuals "winners" and "losers." However, we maintain that one's *attitude*, which influences one's actions, determines the category in which he places himself. The prospect who has great desire to excel, loves the game, plays with enthusiasm, suppresses his personal desires for the good of the team, will not quit and never accepts defeat, gives his very best and has a fierce competitive spirit, has got to be labeled a "winner." Such an individual's playing skills may be limited, but he is a better prospect than the individual who possesses many physical skills but has a lethargic attitude and lacks competitive spirit. The more "winners" a coaching staff has to work with as players, the greater are the chances of accomplishing the goal of having a winning program.

5 ALIGNMENT OF PERSONNEL AND EVALUATION OF PERFORMANCE

Regardless of the level of competition, football coaches must be concerned with selecting personnel according to certain specifications. These specifications will vary with the personnel available to you and the system of football you utilize.

Initially we will discuss criteria and suggestions for slotting or aligning personnel, and later we will discuss methods of evaluating player performance.

ALIGNING OR SLOTTING PLAYER PERSONNEL

A football coach who is a consistent winner is one who successfully places each player where he can use his potential to the utmost, and where every prospect can make the maximum contribution to the success of the football team. While most experienced coaches have an insight or "knack" for recognizing and evaluating talent, personal convictions and feelings are not sufficient and are seldom reliable as the sole means of evaluating and slotting personnel properly.

Personnel Depends on System, and System Depends on Personnel

The selection and slotting of personnel are also based on the type of offense and defense you employ. As an illustration, if you favor a power attack, then logically you should have big, strong players who can use size to their advantage. However, if you wish to employ a pulling type of offense or stunting defenses, then you will probably have to sacrifice size somewhat for agility and quickness in order to have your players execute these skills effectively. Receivers, preferably tall and rangy with good speed, who can maneuver to get open and then make the reception, are essential if your offense is built around the passing game.

Conversely, if your line personnel are physically small, then you are not likely to be successful employing a power type of ground attack. If your linemen are big but slow afoot, then a pulling attack is not likely to be successful. However, a straight ahead power attack would permit your big lineman to utilize their bulk and size advantageously. If the receivers are short in stature, they may be able to catch the football, but if they are also slow afoot then your offense will be operating at a disadvantage if you try to exploit the passing game with this personnel. Therefore, the offense and defense a football team employs will be based on the personnel available to the coaching staff.

Suggestions for Slotting and Evaluating Personnel

In the previous chapter we presented evaluative criteria for assessing prospects (Diagram 4–3). In this chapter we will offer criteria and suggestions for selecting and slotting players for specific positions. Once again, we are indebted to Milt Von Mann, Special Scouting Assignments, Cincinnati Bengals, formerly with the Kansas City Chiefs, for permitting us to utilize his suggestions for scouting positions in football, which we have included in each section below as suggested checklists by positions. Talent scout Von Mann's concluding evaluation point for *every prospect* is as follows: "Be able to discuss his ruggedness, durability, and desire, with the head football coach." He is referring to the talent scout's discussion with the college coach, and to his own discussion with the professional football coach and team for whom he is working in lining up talent. It is interesting to note Coach Von Mann concludes each position evaluation inquiring about two tangible characteristics, ruggedness and durability, and one intangible quality, desire, all of which were discussed in detail in Chapter 4. All three characteristics are "musts" at every level of competition in order to produce winners. Professional football has an "average computer man" for each position, an ideal description that includes height, weight, and speed for each specific position. While you cannot do in college and high school football what the professional teams do, everything is relative in your own league or calibre of competition. However, you should utilize any source of information which will aid you in doing a better job coaching, regardless of the source and level of your competition.

REQUISITES: OFFENSIVE POSITIONS AND PERSONNEL

Material at the small college and high school level in particular runs in cycles, especially where the coach does not have a good feeder system and must rely heavily on walk-ons. As a result a coach must make his system fit the available personnel, which changes year by year as the cycle evolves. This is vastly different from a coach who can recruit players to fit his system. A common mistake is for a coach to fail to recognize his situation and to make a futile and persistent effort to fit players to *his* system when they are not capable of performing the appropriate skills. While there are advantages and disadvantages to every offensive system, none in modern day football operates effectively without a skillful athlete at the quarterback position. Therefore slotting or aligning a prospect in the quarterback position should receive top priority.

Quarterback Prospects

Quarterbacks come in all sizes, and how the quarterback is utilized in the offensive attack will depend on his skills. Your quarterback's ability as a runner and a passer should weigh heavily in your ultimate decision in building a running and passing attack and in selecting an offense, that is, a two-, three-, or four-back offense. Physically a quarterback should have quick hands and feet regardless of the offense employed. A quarterback's ability to set up quickly for a pass, to mesh quickly with his fullback on a ride, belly, or wishbone series, and to execute an option keep-pitch or an option run-pass requires a quarterback prospect with quick hands and feet.

If you are building a passing attack then your quarterback must possess a quick release, peripheral vision, and the physical durability, toughness, and courage to "hang tough" and not panic in throwing the football up for grabs when pressured by defenders. If he possesses these characteristics, it is likely he can be taught to read defenses and to adjust his strategy to defensive changes if he is calling the offensive plays. As a competent passer, a quarterback must be able to clothesline the football to his open receiver, and yet have a sense of touch without throwing floaters that are easily intercepted.

Regardless of his physical attributes and skills, however, his most important inherent quality is leadership. A confident leader at the quarterback position will make a team believe in its ability to be a winner. A quarterback who is courageous, mentally tough, accepts the challenge, and is capable of making the big play, leads by example, and others will follow such a leader.

Suggested Checklist for Quarterback Personnel   Ways to evaluate player personnel at the quarterback position are as follows:

1. Is he an extraordinary passer? Does he pick up secondary receivers quickly and readily?
2. Is he accurate with the long pass, the short pass, or both?
3. How is his ball handling, footwork, faking, and so forth?
4. Is he a good, natural leader?
5. Can he assume authority and command the respect of his teammates?
6. Is he a good ball carrier? Does he like to run with the football?
7. Does he stay in the pocket?
8. How does he react under severe rushing pressure?

Rating Scale for Evaluating Quarterbacks   See Diagram 5–1 for a rating scale that may be used by both high school and college coaches, as well as by professional football scouts and coaches, to evaluate quarterbacks. Diagram 5–1 will also show how to rate all of the offensive positions discussed in the following sections.

Running Back and Fullback Prospects

A running back must be capable of "breaking it all the way" from anywhere on the field in order to have an explosive running attack. If he is also capable of running good routes and catching passes, you will have a versatile, balanced offensive attack as his additional skills add another dimension to the offense.

As runners, however, you are seeking prospects with good body balance, leg strength, and drive, lateral quickness, the ability to break tackles, speed, durability, the ability to explode through the hole, and the ability to accelerate beyond the line of scrimmage. If your running back possesses these skills, you can build a formidable running attack.

If you utilize passes and the running back is not involved as a pass receiver or decoy, the running back as a blocker must be capable of picking up and blocking firing linebackers on passing situations. When the fullback carries the football inside, generally the running back is the lead blocker on a linebacker. Obviously if the running back is a hard-nosed blocker and/or a capable pass receiver, he adds another dimension to the offensive attack.

The fullback is generally the "workhorse" in the offensive backfield. He must possess durability, stamina, and be physically tough. Usually he is called upon to get the tough short yardage inside or to lead the play and cut down defenders on the sweeps. He should be a powerful runner who has the physical strength to establish an inside running game against any defense. In addition to the above qualities, a fullback should possess a quick start, good balance, lateral quickness, and body control.

As a blocker, he will be required to block on both the run and the pass. On inside running plays when he is not carrying the football, he is usually the lead blocker or is faking over the football. His role and position are ones of hit or be hit on every play!

The fullback's ability to catch the football, especially on short routes, adds another dimension to the offensive attack.*

Suggested Checklist for Running Back and Fullback Personnel   Ways to evaluate player personnel at the running back and fullback positions are as follows:

1. Be able to discuss thoroughly his type of speed. Does he have a quick explosive start?
2. What is his style of running? Classify as to speedster, power, deceptive, elusive, dancer, or some combination of these.
3. How does he run in the open? Does he fight for extra yardage?
4. Does he use his blockers advantageously?
5. Is he capable of breaking the big play and going all the way?
6. Is he a chronic fumbler?
7. Rate him as a pass receiver. Does he have good hands? What are his faking moves? Decoying abilities?
8. Rate his blocking ability. Is he tough and will he do a rugged job of blocking for the other ball carriers?
9. Can he block the end off his feet on off-tackle plays and end runs?
10. Can he handle a big tackle or end?
11. How does he block when protecting the passer?
12. Do minor injuries bother him?
13. Does he pass, punt, or place kick?

Receiver Prospects: Flankers (X and Z) and Tight End (Y)

The tight end (Y) is primarily a blocker, whereas the wideouts, the split end (X) and the flanker back (Z), are primarily receivers, depending on your offensive system and football philosophy. If the tight end

---

* For coaching the offensive backfield running and passing game, see Donald E. Fuoss, *Championship Football Drills for Teaching Offensive and Defensive Football* (Englewood Cliffs, N. J.: Prentice-Hall, 1964), pp. 147–173 (running game), 108–146 (passing game fundamentals, skills, and techniques). Also see Dee G. Andros and Rowland P. "Red" Smith, *Power T Football* (West Nyack, N. Y.: Parker Publishing Co., 1971).

is utilized as a receiver, usually he runs underneath patterns in combination with his wide receivers. Many times he is the "hot" receiver on the short dump pass when a linebacker fires, or he clears out an area for a wide receiver. Your tight end's ability to catch the football should be the determining factor as to whether he is utilized in pass patterns, although his routes will be determined by his speed. If he lacks speed, his deep patterns in particular will be ineffective. If he has hands like concrete, stiff and inflexible, and has difficulty catching the football, his effectiveness as a receiver is limited despite even outstanding speed. His value in running pass routes will be limited, too, for his function as a decoy receiver becomes readily apparent if your opposition charts and analyzes your passing statistics. All of these factors must be taken into consideration in building a pass offense, which will be discussed in greater detail in Chapter 8.

The split end and flanker back are usually the same body types physically, and they perform similar functions as receivers and blockers. In combination patterns the tight end (Y) and flanker back (Z) usually work together, and the split end (X) and running back (R) frequently are involved in combination patterns on the opposite side where a two-back offense or pro-set is employed. Both flankers must be capable of running all of the short, medium, and deep routes on the "passing tree," and catching the football in traffic, or when coming back toward the passer, or when running away from defenders.

However, there is much more to the passing game for a receiver than just catching the football once it has been thrown within his reach. Other very important factors include releasing from the line of scrimmage, executing the exact route called, using proper faking techniques, learning the value of good position when competing for the football with a defender, and carrying the ball once the reception has been made.

As a blocker, a flanker must master the stalk and crackback blocks, not being reluctant to block through defenders downfield who are likely to be pursuing. Therefore, they must possess the physical toughness to block aggressively and must not try to avoid contact.

Suggested Checklist for Receiver Personnel   Ways to evaluate player personnel at the X, Y, and Z positions are as follows:

1. Analyze his type of speed. Has he the ability to cut sharply either way when running at full speed?
2. Does he depend on his speed or his faking ability to get into the open?
3. Does he run good patterns? Is his timing good?
4. Does he run hard and decoy well when he is not the intended receiver?

5. Does he have good sure hands that can catch the ball clean, or is he the bobbling catcher type?
6. Is he better at long or short patterns? Does he fight to get the football on all occasions?
7. When closely guarded does he have the pronounced ability to come up with the tough catch?
8. Evaluate his ability to get away from an opponent who is trying to keep him from getting out for a pass.
9. Rate his ability as a ball carrier after he catches the pass.
10. Evaluate his blocking ability, both on the line and downfield.

Offensive Line Prospects

As we indicated at the beginning of this chapter, the physical size and skills of your offensive lineman will determine to a large extent your type of offensive attack. As an illustration, if your line prospects have bulky builds and lack speed generally, you will probably find it difficult to employ successfully a pulling type of offense where interior linemen must lead on sweep plays, which is usually accomplished from a three-point stance. Their lack of speed and skills and their heavy body builds may dictate a straight ahead power type of offensive attack. In turn this could dictate a four-point offensive stance for the interior linemen, in particular, which would inhibit further their agility and quickness and would probably minimize the use of an interior trapping game or passing from the pocket. While it is not impossible for linemen to do either from a four-point stance, you should study the advantages and disadvantages of both the four-point and three-point types of stance.

Interior line prospects need body control, balance, quickness, agility, and strength in order to block effectively and to protect the passer. The progress that is made in analyzing each lineman's potential, improving their individual and team skills and techniques, and molding the offensive line into a cohesive effective unit, will determine whether the offensive backs get the football beyond the line of scrimmage. It is impossible to move the football with any degree of consistency if a team does not have sound blocking techniques. The above fundamental ideas dictate the types of blocks linemen must use to handle their offensive assignments. Every coach must determine the fundamental requirements of every good blocking maneuver and teach these first. This subject will be discussed in greater detail in Chapter 6.

An offensive lineman must be able to recognize defenses, adjust their blocking techniques accordingly, get off on the football, react to the defender's reaction so that he can sustain his block and have the strength to defeat his opponent one-on-one. A player's skills will limit the extent of the offense. As an illustration, in order to run the quick traps, your guards must be able to pull and trap, and to pull out of the line and lead block on sweeps, bootlegs, and counterplays and passes. Obviously if your interior line personnel cannot execute these skills, you may have the plays and passes in your coach's playbook, but you would be deluding yourself to include them in your game plan.

Suggested Checklist for Offensive Line Personnel   Ways to evaluate your player personnel for the offensive linemen positions are as follows:

1. Discuss speed thoroughly with comments on initial charge, agility, quickness, coordination, and reaction qualities.
2. Evaluate blocking ability. Does he have a good initial charge? Is he a good position blocker?
3. Does he keep his feet and maintain contact?
4. Does he take pride in really driving his opponent out?
5. Evaluate his ability at close line blocking, trap blocking, downfield blocking, and pass protection blocking.
6. Can he pull and lead interference and do a good job blocking?
7. Has he been successful thus far because of his size and strength?

The Offensive Center   The offensive center is the key offensive lineman, and it is not a position to be filled as a last resort. He is the leader and director of your offensive line. A prospect should not be relegated to the offensive center position because he is too slow or too small to play anywhere else, a mistake common to inexperienced coaches. Your center controls the timing of your offense on every play, and timing is the essence of any offense. If your center does not execute the exchange properly he will cause his team's offense to falter through fumbles, miscues, and poorly timed plays. Since the center-quarterback exchange of the football on the snap-back frequently is the cause of fumbles, we will analyze the reasons for ball exchange fumbles in Chapter 8. The center must be able to make the long pass to the punter in punt formation, and to the holder's hands on placement and field goal attempts. In addition the center must be able to execute the basic fundamentals and most of the techniques of the other interior linemen.

Suggested Checklist for Offensive Center Personnel.   Ways to evaluate your player personnel for the offensive center position are as follows:

1. Can he make the long snap to the punter both fast and accurately? (If he is a good center prospect, but weak in making the long pass for the punt, you might use another prospect in punting situations.)

DIAGRAM 5-1
Rating Scale for Evaluating Offensive Personnel

PLAYER _____ HEIGHT _____ WEIGHT _____ SPEED _____

_____ FORTY YARDS _____ TWENTY YARDS _____

POSITIONS _____ YEAR IN SCHOOL _____

ATTITUDE _____ EFFORT _____ COACHABILITY _____

FOOTBALL INTELLIGENCE _____

SECOND
GRADED BY _____ EFFORT _____

Rate individual on each skill by circling the appropriate number: *5–Outstanding, 4–Above Average, 3–Average, 2–Below Average, 1–Poor.* (Do not mark if it does not apply or you cannot evaluate.)

RUNNING BACKS: FB—HB(R) (Circle one.)		QUARTERBACKS (Circle one.)	
Start quickness	5–4–3–2–1	Quick set up (quick feet)	5–4–3–2–1
Balance and agility	5–4–3–2–1	Release (delivery)	5–4–3–2–1
Inside running	5–4–3–2–1	Throw off balance	5–4–3–2–1
Speed for position	5–4–3–2–1	Throw short—accuracy	5–4–3–2–1
Power running	5–4–3–2–1	Throw long—accuracy	5–4–3–2–1
Elusive runner	5–4–3–2–1	Running ability	5–4–3–2–1
Blocking (run or pass)	5–4–3–2–1	Poise and judgment	5–4–3–2–1
Hands (receiver)	5–4–3–2–1	Leadership	5–4–3–2–1
Aggressiveness and		Second effort (desire)	5–4–3–2–1
toughness (throw		Avoid rush	5–4–3–2–1
body around)	5–4–3–2–1	Drop back passer	5–4–3–2–1
Second effort (desire)	5–4–3–2–1	Size for position	5–4–3–2–1

RECEIVERS: SE(X)—WB(Z)—TE(Y) (Circle one.)		OFFENSIVE LINE: G—T—C (Circle one.)	
Receiving in a crowd	5–4–3–2–1	Quickness off ball	5–4–3–2–1
Hands	5–4–3–2–1	Quickness of feet	5–4–3–2–1
Get open short	5–4–3–2–1	One-on-one run block-	
Get open deep	5–4–3–2–1	ing explosion	5–4–3–2–1
Agility and balance		sustain block	5–4–3–2–1
(change directions)	5–4–3–2–1	Pass blocking	5–4–3–2–1
Quickness on release	5–4–3–2–1	Reactions—adjustments	5–4–3–2–1
Running ability	5–4–3–2–1	Agility and balance	5–4–3–2–1
Aggressiveness (throw		Strength	5–4–3–2–1
body around)	5–4–3–2–1	Size potential	5–4–3–2–1
Speed for position	5–4–3–2–1	Speed for position	5–4–3–2–1
Size for position	5–4–3–2–1	Aggressive and reckless	
Blocking	5–4–3–2–1	(throw body around)	5–4–3–2–1
		Second effort (desire)	5–4–3–2–1
		Pulling ability	5–4–3–2–1
		Deep snap (center)	5–4–3–2–1
		Short snap (center)	5–4–3–2–1

2. Is he agile enough to pull out of the line and block a firing linebacker or a defensive end?
3. Does he have the same abilities as the other offensive linemen?

REQUISITES: DEFENSIVE POSITIONS AND PERSONNEL

It is a well-known fact that football games are won or lost in the line, and the player who establishes physical toughness or supremacy immediately will generally control a particular piece of territory. While there is a difference of opinion among coaches as to whether the defensive lineman should move on the initial movement of the player opposite him or on the movement of the football, it is agreed a defender should literally sprint or explode into the offensive blocker or stunt to his area of responsibility (if pattern defenses are being used), depending on the tactical situation and the philosophy of the defensive line coach. In any case, the defensive lineman must get off on the ball (or the movement of the offensive blocker) so that he is delivering a blow rather than catching the blocker's. Football is a game of contact, and especially in line play it is either hit or be hit. The defender must protect his area, fight pressure, locate the football, react properly, shed and release from his block, take the proper pursuit angle, and make the tackle.

Defensive Interior Line Prospects

If you employ multiple defenses, such as the Pro 4–3 and the Over 4–3, which becomes a 5–2 alignment, or if your basic alignment is the Oklahoma 5–2 and you move to a 4–3, you must play defensive personnel out of their regular positions. In devising defensive schemes this factor should be taken into consideration. You will, for example, have a middle guard drop off the line to become the middle linebacker when moving from the Oklahoma alignment to the Pro 4–3 front; or you will slide the defensive line from the 4–3 to a 5–2 front, with a tackle nose-up on the center. These adjustments necessitate additional teaching-coaching-learning skills and techniques, and they must be considered when evaluating and slotting your personnel.

Suggested Checklist for Defensive Line Personnel   Ways to evaluate your player personnel for the defensive line positions are as follows:

1. Evaluate his speed thoroughly relevant to his initial charge, agility, quickness, coordination and reaction qualities.
2. Does he have a quick, fast charge?
3. Does he come on a tough charge and raise havoc?

4. Can he control his opponent and diagnose the play?
5. Evaluate his tackling ability.
6. Does he have good pursuit qualities?
7. Does he have strong arms and hands?
8. Evaluate his ability to handle running plays directly at him, and to either side of his position.
9. How does he react to trap plays?
10. Has he been successful thus far mainly because of his size and strength?

Rating Scale for Evaluating Defensive Linemen   A coach may evaluate his defensive line prospects as illustrated in Diagram 5–2. Diagram 5–2 will also show how to rate all of the defensive positions discussed in the following sections.

Defensive End Prospects

A team can get into more trouble with poor defensive end play than with any other position except the defensive secondary. Being on the end of the defensive line, an end defender has the most territory to protect. A defensive end is usually charged with containment, keeping the play inside, and aggressively rushing the passer. He must be capable of taking on as many blockers as the opposition sends at him in their effort to try to control the corner. Therefore, a defensive end must be a good athlete because of the demands placed on playing that position. Outstanding performances by the ends will be important to the success of the defensive team. A defensive end should have the strength and toughness of an interior lineman, but he also needs the agility and quickness of a linebacker. In selecting your defensive line personnel, give the defensive ends your top priority after selecting your linebackers.

Suggested Checklist for Defensive End Personnel   Ways to evaluate your player personnel for the defensive end positions are as follows:

1. Rate his type of speed.
2. Rate his ability to rush the passer.
3. How does he handle running plays to the inside and to the outside?
4. Rate his ability as a crasher and also his techniques in covering the flat territory.
5. Is he a smashing tackler? Rate his roughness and agility.
6. Does he use his hands well against his blockers and control them, or do the blockers get to his body easily?
7. Does he diagnose and react quickly?

Linebacker Prospects

The real heart of any defense is good linebacking, and there never has been a strong defensive team with incapable linebackers. Your linebackers are your "search and destroy" defenders. They need a rare combination of abilities. They need physical size in order to stand tough against the run, and they need speed to cover the offensive backs on man coverage coming out of the backfield. In building a defensive unit, therefore, prime consideration must be given to the selection of good athletes for the linebacking positions. After that it becomes a matter of coaching.

Suggested Checklist for Linebacker Personnel Ways to evaluate player personnel for the linebacker positions are as follows:

1. Does he have the ability and knack to diagnose plays and react quickly?
2. Does he have a keen desire for contact?
3. Can and does he meet the play in the hole?
4. Evaluate thoroughly his tackling ability.
5. Can he effectively hold up the ends?
6. Rate his type of speed.
7. Does he have good pursuit qualities?
8. Can he cover the swing patterns quickly in flat territory and downfield?
9. Does he play outside or inside linebacker?
10. Can he play in the line on defense?
11. Does he call defensive signals?
12. Do you consider him strongest against running or passing plays?

Defensive Secondary Prospects

The evaluation and skills of your personnel, especially linebacker and secondary prospects, will do much to determine whether you play a three- or four-deep secondary, and what percentage of zone and man coverage you play.

Secondary defenders must be able to move and react, fight a receiver for possession of the football, and make tackles in the open field. These skills may be taught through repetitive drills. However, drills are of little significance and value if a defender lacks the burning desire to play pass defense and to excel in his secondary play. A good defensive back not only wants to intercept every pass that is thrown, but he wants

---

DIAGRAM 5–2
Rating Scale for Evaluating Defensive Personnel

PLAYER _____ HEIGHT _____ WEIGHT _____ SPEED _____

_____ 40 _____ 20 _____

POSITIONS _____ YEAR IN SCHOOL _____

ATTITUDE _____ EFFORT _____ COACHABILITY _____

FOOTBALL INTELLIGENCE _____

SECOND
GRADED BY _____ EFFORT _____

Rate individual on each skill by circling the appropriate number: *5–Outstanding, 4–Above Average, 3–Average, 2–Below Average* and *1–Poor.* (Do not mark it if it does not apply or you cannot evaluate.)

DEFENSIVE BACK: SS—FS—C		LINEBACKER: WLB—MLB—SLB	
(Circle one.)		(Circle one.)	
Quickness and		Instinct ability (find ball)	5–4–3–2–1
acceleration	5–4–3–2–1	Lateral movement	5–4–3–2–1
Quickness of feet	5–4–3–2–1	Change directions	5–4–3–2–1
Flexibility	5–4–3–2–1	Quickness of feet	5–4–3–2–1
Pursuit (second effort)	5–4–3–2–1	Strength	5–4–3–2–1
Tackling	5–4–3–2–1	Aggressive and reckless:	
Reactions to ball	5–4–3–2–1	(throw body around)	5–4–3–2–1
Back peddle	5–4–3–2–1	Size for position	5–4–3–2–1
Speed for position	5–4–3–2–1	Agility and balance	5–4–3–2–1
Ability to catch ball	5–4–3–2–1	Pursuit (second effort)	5–4–3–2–1
Agility and balance		Pass coverage	5–4–3–2–1
(change directions)	5–4–3–2–1	Speed for position	5–4–3–2–1
Aggressive and reckless	5–4–3–2–1	Effectiveness v. run	
Defeat blockers	5–4–3–2–1	(defeats blockers)	5–4–3–2–1
		Tackling	5–4–3–2–1
		Hands	5–4–3–2–1

DEFENSIVE FRONT: MG—DT—DE

(Circle one.)		(Circle one.)	
Quickness on ball	5–4–3–2–1	Tackling	5–4–3–2–1
Quickness of feet	5–4–3–2–1	Toughness	5–4–3–2–1
Ability to get to ball	5–4–3–2–1	Aggressive and reckless	
Reactions	5–4–3–2–1	(throw body around)	5–4–3–2–1
Defeat one-on-one	5–4–3–2–1	Pass rusher	5–4–3–2–1
Lateral movement	5–4–3–2–1	Strength	5–4–3–2–1
Pursuit (second effort)	5–4–3–2–1	Size potential	5–4–3–2–1
Agility and balance	5–4–3–2–1	Speed for position	5–4–3–2–1

to make every tackle as close as possible to the line of scrimmage on running plays. Therefore, he must know well the responsibilities and duties of his position, and he must react properly with quickness and speed. Defensive football is reaction football, and a secondary defender's failure to react properly may mean that his teammates will be penalized six points. In no other phase of football is the penalty as severe as when a secondary defender fails to react properly on a pass play.

Suggested Checklist for Defensive Secondary Personnel Ways to evaluate your player personnel for the defensive secondary positions are as follows:

1. Does he love to play defense?
2. Evaluate thoroughly his type of speed.
3. Is he a good, sound, rough tackler?
4. Does he come up fast and meet the running play with power?
5. Can he cover man-to-man?
6. Does he fight aggressively for the football?
7. Does he pursue well?
8. Does he have sure hands? Is he a "ball hawk"?
9. Evaluate his skill as a ball carrier after an interception.
10. Does he return punts or kick-offs?

REQUISITES: KICKING GAME SPECIALISTS

Approximately 30 percent of the action in a football game involves some phase of the kicking game. Although a separate diagram is not included for rating kicking game specialists (with the exception of the center in Diagram 5–1), you should evaluate *all* of your available player personnel closely to locate such specialists. A prospect may lack a number of attributes that would make him a complete ball player, but he may possess some special skill, such as punting or place kicking, or exceptional speed, which could be utilized in covering or returning punts or kick-offs. He could still then make important contributions to team success. The lack of physical stature is not a deterrent if, say, a punter possesses leg snap and has good hands. A punt return and kick-off return specialist must have sure hands to field the football, and if he has quickness and speed to elude converging opponents, his diminutiveness may be an asset rather than a liability. To be in on the action on the kick-off or punt coverage specialty team, a specialist needs to have good speed and a "nose" for the football in order to break up a return before the ball carrier gets behind his protective wall. A place kicking specialist needs leg snap, too, and his holder needs sure hands. A kicking game specialist may lack physical size, but he cannot lack "heart," which might well be the most important ingredient to play any collision sport. Kicking game mistakes will be discussed in Chapter 10.

EVALUATING AND GRADING PERFORMANCE

While evaluations and judgmental decisions are made on the basis of potential, drills, and performance in game-like practice situations (Chapter 6), the most valid indicator of player personnel quality is actual performance in a scrimmage or game.

In Chapter 4 we discussed potential versus performance. Some players look like football prospects potentially, but they may never live up to expectations. A player may do well one-on-one in a drill, as an illustration, because it is staged and controlled and is only a single part of an overall teaching-learning evaluative situation. Where speed or size is involved, he may do well against his counterpart. His performance in a game may be something else.

Conversely, a player may not do well in a drill for various reasons, and his practice performance is poor. Yet his performance in the game may be good or outstanding. Only by carefully studying the players individually in game and scrimmage films can a coaching staff make a valid and reliable determination of player performance. The sole criterion should be, *did he do his job?* If the answer is yes, regardless of his technique or skill on a particular play, the player should be graded 100 percent for his performance. (A grading system will be discussed below.) Conversely, if a player did everything well technically but failed to carry out his offensive assignment of eliminating the defender from the play, or his defensive assignment of destroying the blocker and making the tackle, he did *not* do his job and he should be graded zero. A player can always be coached in the proper techniques.

Proper Use of Films

Most coaches today feel they cannot do a competent coaching job without their games being filmed, and we agree to the extent that coaches should be able to do a more competent job if they utilize their films properly. Some coaches view the films in a cursory fashion, and their players have little feedback on how their performances were graded. Films should be studied carefully for many reasons. They should be used to grade the players individually and to correct individual and team mistakes in preparing for the next opponent (Chapter 11). They should be used to grade effectiveness and correct mistakes in the offense (Chapter 8), defense (Chapter 9), and kicking game (Chapter 10). After grading your player personnel, you can determine accurately whether a player is getting the job done in terms of carrying out his assignment, and you can evaluate each player's techniques. You can determine whether you are playing your best personnel and whether they are slotted properly. You can also determine what must be taught, practiced, and coached during the week prior to the next game. Below we will discuss only evaluating or grading the player's performance.

Grading Assignment Performance

For illustrative purposes we are including *only* offensive assignment and technique performance, although the grading methods are equally applicable to defensive linemen. When a coach grades his offensive players, it is advisable to have the blocking categories broken down as follows:

    GM (Got Man)—means the offensive blocker eliminates his man from the play, in that he does not give the defender an opportunity to make the tackle; that is, *regardless of the technique employed* (correct or incorrect), the blocker knocks down his man, ties him up, walls him off, forces the defender to go behind (chase), not giving him a chance to get in on the tackle.

    MM (Missed Man)—means the offensive blocker goes after the proper defender; that is, applies his blocking rule correctly, but *regardless of his technique* (correct or incorrect), he is unsuccessful in eliminating the defender from the play, in that the opponent has the opportunity to make the tackle.

    MA (Missed Assignment)—indicates a *mental mistake* where the blocker either applies his blocking rule incorrectly (goes after the wrong defender) or does not attempt to block anyone.

    If an offensive player continues to bust assignments he simply cannot play for you, despite the fact he is a good blocker when he goes after the proper defender. In the final analysis *MA* will hurt the offense more than *MM*, although both count a zero in figuring blocking effectiveness. The reasoning is logical. A busted assignment frees a defender to make the big defensive play, which usually stops an offensive drive. When this occurs, there is also a good possibility of a fumble, an offensive turnover, and/or an injury to the quarterback or ball carrier. Usually the defender, many times a linebacker, comes through free with force and momentum and smashes into the offensive back before he gets possession of the football. The latter has little or no opportunity to protect himself since the defender's sudden presence in the offensive backfield is totally unexpected.

    Diagram 5–3 illustrates sample work forms that may be utilized to grade the effectiveness of an individual lineman (offensive center). Note how the player's blocking effectiveness drops off when he is graded down for *MA*. We will discuss grading technique performance, illustrated in the right-hand column (B) in Diagram 5–3, below.

DIAGRAM 5-3
Form for Grading Blocking Effectiveness: (A) Comments or (B) Techniques Performance

Player: D. SMITH   Position: CENTER   Opponent: STATE (10–6)

Play	Def.	Opport.	GM	MM	MA	(A) COMMENTS	Approach	Contact	Follow-through
24Pr.	05–2			1		Not set; poor exchange—fumble; dipped your tail.	1	1	1
23Pr.	05–2			1		Head behind M; he got T#1.	3	2	3
82	P4–3	No	–	–	–	No play; def. T o-s/pen.			
30Tr.	P4–3				1	Re-check your rule; block back, not 0; see me.			
Punt	odd	*	–	–	–	Low pass; punter hurried. Relax! Pass ball when ready.			
22Ts.	P4–3		1			Poor cut-off; M fell.			
G22Ts.	4–4				1	B.S.P., not ILB: re-check your rule; see me.			
37Dr.	G6–5	No	–	–	–	No; hard pinch on you.			
38L	G6–5		1			Exc. block on MLB. Techs. excellent, too!			
TOTS.	–	70	40	20	10	57% block effic. can't win; let's work to improve!			

(B) TECHNIQUES

(Numbers indicate errors in technique.)

Approach:
1. Movement—failure to get off with ball or starting count.
2. Improper angle or path of blocker.
3. Feet—stepping with wrong foot first; steps too long, etc.

Contact:
1. Poor initial contact—no "pop," too soft, etc.
2. Wrong shoulder; wrong technique.
3. Poor body position—back bowed, head down, etc.

Follow-through:
1. Failure to move feet.
2. Failure to sustain drive.
3. Falling to ground; feet in hole; other mistakes.

GM/Total Plays (exc.MA) = 40/60 = 67% (but not true %).
GM/Total Plays (inc.MA) = 40/70 = 57% blocking effectiveness.

* Punts not figured with totals (merely correct errors).

Grading Assignment and/or Technique Performance

The *technique* should *not* be figured in with, or have a bearing on, the totals when determining blocking effectiveness, although some coaches feel otherwise. In the (A) column in Diagram 5–3, space is provided for comments relevant to a player's technique execution. If the player who is being graded employs the wrong techniques, then this should be called to his attention when the player(s) and coach view the films together. In the practice sessions, the blocker should be coached and drilled to utilize the correct and proper techniques. In the final analysis, on every play either a player *GM* (gets his man), *MM* (misses his man), or *MA* (misses his assignment), regardless of the technique he employs. It is more important to be graded *GM*, even using the wrong techniques, than it is to be graded *MM* while adhering to all of the correct techniques. To grade a player unfavorably when he *GM* except he used incorrect techniques, and to grade him favorably when he *MM* but used the correct techniques, is an injustice to the player and is improper use of the grading system. No grading system is an end in itself, merely a means to an end. Its purpose, in this instance, is to aid both the individual performer and the team, and it is a means of evaluation for the coaching staff to do a better teaching job. Diagram 5–3 (A) illustrates one method of grading a player's technique performance, and (B) another method of grading technique execution.

Another relatively simple method of grading a player's performance is to mark a horizontal line (–) if the player satisfactorily performs all of the following: huddle break, hustles to the line of scrimmage, stance, alignment, take-off, and approach to the block. A vertical line (|) is awarded if the player gets his man. Thus, if a blocker performs all phases correctly and gets his man, he has a horizontal line with a vertical line through it forming a plus (+). If his performance is very poor, he receives a zero (0). One point is awarded for every vertical line (|); one point for every horizontal line (–); two points for every plus (+) mark; and zero points for every zero (0). By multiplying the number of times technique and execution were properly performed (possible two points; that is, a plus (+) for every play) by each of the above point ratings, you arrive at the total number of points graded. The total number of plays the player performed in the game is then multiplied by two and divided into the total number of points scored to get the efficiency percentage.

Techniques Factors and Rating Scale   You may focus on (B) techniques in Diagram 5–3, analyzing and grading approach, contact and follow-through. The numbers 1, 2, and/or 3 are recorded by the coach in each of the columns to indicate that the offensive lineman performed the technique or execution incorrectly. The spaces are left blank when the

DIAGRAM 5–4
Form for Grading Defensive Performance

Name: Jones   Position: LB   Game: TECH   Date: 10/12

Def.	Off. Play	Chances		Tackling	Errors	Pursuit	Bonus	Comments
W6–2	44	1	1	T2		Good		Met BC in hole
W6–2	60P	1	1				Inter.	Good job going to hook
5–3	40T	1	0		Wrong way	None		Accepted block
05–2M	11 OP	0	0					Fumble C-QB exchange
05–2M	12 OP	1	1	T2		Good	Rec. fumble	Good job, knocked ball loose and rec.
5–3R	39T	1	1	T1		Good		Shot gap-fired
05–2M	42 sp.	1	0		Over-ran	Poor		Missed tackle
W6–2	60P	1	0		Too tight	None		Up in line, out of pos.
G–8	42 sp.	1	1	T2		Good		Shot gap
Totals	9	8–5		4	③		2★	⁵⁄₈ = (62.5%)

player performs the technique correctly. The left-hand side of Diagram 5–3 remains the same, and the player's performance grade as a blocker is determined in the same way as explained previously. The items listed in column (B) are by no means all-inclusive.

There are other methods of grading offensive performance; for example, a grading system from 0–5, with 0 being awarded for a missed assignment, 5 for an excellent assignment, and most of the scores falling in the 1–4 category. The scores are averaged and each player is given a numerical rating as well as a percentage rating. The offensive team must collectively average 3.0 or higher and 70 percent or better on blocking assignments to show a potential winning performance.

Diagram 5–4 illustrates a form that may be used to grade defensive performance. The same suggestions discussed above for grading offensive performance should be adhered to. Under *Tackles* indicate T1 (solo) or

T2 (assisted with tackle), where a defender has a chance to be involved in the play. No grade is recorded when a defender is out of the play, nor are these plays figured in the total for percentage purposes. The *Errors* column includes missing the tackle, getting blocked, and making a mental mistake, such as wrong alignment, wrong area on pattern defense, wrong coverage, and so on. Since defensive pursuit is important, it is generally a good idea to include a column so that it can be noted in particular as "poor," "incorrect angle," "chasing from behind," and so forth. A *Bonus* column is for noting the big defensive plays, pass interceptions, fumble recoveries, blocked punts, and the like. Quarterback sacks are recorded under the *Tackles* column, with a notation for recognition. Once again, a defender's technique should not be graded down unless you are using a form similar to Diagram 5–3(B), modified for defensive grading.

Self-Evaluation

Since coaching is a race against time, a coach may employ player self-evaluations, in which each player grades himself. In many cases, a player will prove to be more critical of himself than his coach is. The main objective is to let the players see their mistakes, make them understand *why* they made those mistakes, and develop a workable plan for eliminating their errors and improving their play.

An arbitrary rating scale must be set up for grading so that the percentage figures have meaning and can be interpreted. Most coaches feel an individual rating of more than 80 percent is excellent and might be classified as championship performance; anything below 60 percent is a poor performance; 60 to 69 percent is considered fair; and 70 to 79 percent generally is a winning performance.

6 ORGANIZATIONAL PLANNING AND PRACTICE MISTAKES, AND HOW TO AVOID THEM

Your practice schedule and plans during the season should be well conceived and highly organized in order for optimal and effective teaching-coaching-learning to take place. Everyone should be working under a structured schedule so that daily objectives are being met and each practice session is a beehive of constructive activities. "Coaching is a race against time," and "Time lost on the practice field is never regained," are two coaching axioms that will become all too obvious to you if you don't have good practice plans and schedules. In this chapter we will suggest how to plan, organize, and conduct practice sessions during the season in order to accomplish your objectives. Planning and preparing for the football season actually begins in the off-season, which is the period of time from the termination of the last football game of one season until the beginning of practice of the following season (see Chapter 12).

STAFF MEETINGS: PLANNING AND ORGANIZATION

Staff meetings are a necessity, despite the fact they are often criticized for being too many or too few, or too long or too short! There is no formula for the right number or the length of time of staff meetings. Yet productive staff meetings are a necessity in order to develop well-planned, detailed, productive practice sessions.

Establish a Time for Staff Meetings

You must set aside a time *exclusively* for coaching staff meetings, when *all* coaches can attend, in order to conduct football business. How wisely the time is utilized depends on you, the head football coach. Your own particular coaching set-up will dictate the *best* time for staff meetings: it may mean meeting at different times on different days, and it may not always be for the same length of time, in order to accommodate all of the coaching staff. Long staff meetings involving all of the coaches can be minimized if you divide your staff into offensive and defensive specialists. Then separate offensive and defensive staff meetings are necessary, but full staff meetings will not be so lengthy. As head coach you attend all meetings.

The Purpose of Staff Meetings

The reasons you meet are to plan, organize, coordinate, evaluate, and schedule activities and personnel, in working toward the development of individuals into a cohesive team in a joint effort to reach a common goal. The development and gradual implementation of the proposed game plan into the daily and weekly practice plan, as illustrated in Diagram 6–3, will be discussed in detail in Chapter 7.

Also, you meet to "coach the coaches" before the coaches coach the players, although most of the coaching techniques discussions should be finalized and agreed upon prior to the pre-season football practice sessions (Chapter 12), so that you can be reasonably certain all of the staff members will be teaching the same football techniques. This does not always occur, and the failure on the part of a head coach to coach his coaches *first* is a serious mistake.

It is not enough for a head coach to have firmly in his mind what he *hopes* to accomplish with his team on a given day. Unless *all* members of the coaching staff have a full knowledge of the day's objectives, there will be confusion not only among the members of the coaching staff, but also within the team ranks. Note the different objectives in the illustrations of practice schedules in this chapter. The coaches' meeting is the foundation on which all team organization rests, it is an essential feature of coaching procedure. Staff meetings are mandatory, a very important "must"!

Staff Meeting Suggestions

The following suggestions may help you have productive staff meetings.

1. One assistant should be designated to serve as recorder, to ensure the subject matter discussed and the decisions reached are accurately recorded.

2. One assistant should be designated as in charge of the audio-visual equipment and films (Chapter 3); his responsibility is to have projector and films set up for viewing prior to staff meeting time.

3. An assistant coach is responsible for the personnel boards (Diagrams 4–1 and 4–2), which should be current. When personnel is discussed, this assistant will be responsible for moving players' names up, down, and off the board (injuries, for example) in the depth charts so that all of the coaches will know the personnel involved in the drills, rotation, and all phases of the practice schedule. (All coaches should copy the players names on 5″ by 8″ cards printed up in outline form like the personnel boards. Along with the practice schedule each assistant carries this organizational material with him to the practice field.)

4. The offensive and defensive coordinators (Chapter 3) are responsible for presenting valid and reliable information and data (statistics) on the upcoming opponents' defensive and offensive attacks. Some of this information will be provided by the scout squad coach, and other information must be compiled from film exchange. Data must be compiled prior to staff meetings, as decisions will be made (practice plans, game plans) in staff meetings after the data has been analyzed.

5. Limit the discussion to "football-talk" or football related items, and conduct the meetings in a business-like manner.

6. Do not permit interruptions, telephone or otherwise.

7. Standardize your football terminology; terms like rollout, sprintout, double-team, drag pattern, bootleg, and so on, do not have the same connotation to *all* coaches—nor to all players! It is not unusual for coaching staff members to mean the same thing but use different terms. Unless vocabulary is standardized for teaching and discussion purposes, confusion and misunderstanding are likely to occur.

8. By adopting a standardized form, format, and routine for each day's practice, the basic information can be filled in quickly, thus minimizing time in staff meetings. Working out the details

of the practice schedule and preparing for implementing the practice plan will consume most of your time.

Advantages of a Well-Planned, Organized Practice Schedule

An inexperienced coach is likely to assume that a practice schedule retained in his mind is adequate. Some experienced coaches feel, possibly because of multiple coaching-teaching duties or for other reasons, that they do not have time or that it is not necessary to prepare a written practice plan. However, you will obtain the best returns on your efforts if you put on paper your complete practice plans. Situations often arise during the course of a practice session that may cause a coach to forget one of the most important parts of his mentally-fixed practice schedule. Other advantages of a well-devised and thorough practice schedule are:

1. It provides the secure feeling of being prepared.
2. Budgeted time pays greater dividends.
3. It builds confidence, morale, and enthusiasm, as your players can quickly sense whether or not your coaching staff is well organized and prepared.
4. It creates a favorable environment for coaching-teaching-learning.
5. It allows for checking the practice plans against the master plan. By checking the written records it is possible to determine quickly what has been neglected or overlooked. Always retain a corrected file copy.

PRACTICE SCHEDULE PLANNING AND ORGANIZATION

Regardless of the level of competition and the particular coaching set-up, the following suggestions and guides on practice schedule organization should prove helpful.

Take Time to Devise a Good Practice Plan

Spend considerable time and thought on devising a good practice plan, and then follow it. Detail the assignment for each coach for every minute of practice. Allot about twice as much time on planning practice and preparation as on the practice itself. It may be advisable to work against a master schedule or checklist that includes *all* of the various phases of football which must be covered adequately. If you organize your practice schedule around your offensive plays and your defenses, perfecting these will generally ensure victory.

Assign Coaching Areas, Duties, and Responsibilities

Make certain that all of the coaches and managers have a copy of the daily practice schedule and that each one knows his duties and responsibilities. The schedule should then be followed without deviation. The time for planning is *before* practice. On the field the objective is to carry out the established plan. Detail the assignment for each coach for every minute of practice. It is important to designate where each coach will be stationed and which phase of the program and activities he should teach and supervise. It is also important for the team manager(s) to know *before* practice what equipment will be needed on the field and where it should be placed for immediate accessibility and use. Usually an assistant coach is assigned the responsibility for field equipment and managers' assignments, the latter including practice and game assignments (Chapter 3).

Post the Practice Schedule

It is advisable to post the daily practice schedule, along with the pre-practice and post-practice drill schedule (if you use them), in the locker room for all the players to read before they go out on the practice field. One of the biggest problems in coaching is to find sufficient time to work on improving a player's individual weaknesses. Yet a few minutes of individual instruction before or after practice will help solve this problem. A similar difficulty is getting players to work on their own, without a coach's supervision, on their individual weaknesses before or after practice. Posting the practice schedule, along with the pre- and/or post-practice drill schedule, will help to alleviate these particular problems. Also indicate by teams, positions, or otherwise *who* will participate *where* in *which* activities. One of the most important and time-consuming tasks of the coaching staff is to organize the practice sessions so that every player is participating in meaningful activity every minute of the time.

Determine Available Player Personnel, Alignment, Rotation

Since each player is assigned to a specific activity during every minute of the practice period, it is important to know which players are not going to be at practice on a certain day or cannot participate in certain activities, such as the scrimmage. Prepare a master sheet showing which players will miss a certain afternoon's practice because of late laboratory classes, injuries, illness, and other reasons. The remaining players can be assigned to teams wearing different colored scrimmage vests, which they can pick up as they come on to the field after checking the posted practice schedule and scrimmage assignments in the locker room. Also the players can move quickly from one activity and area to another if they have read the schedule before they come on to the field.

Adhere to the Practice Schedule

Start practice on time; stop practice on time; adhere to the schedule for all activities. Emphasize player participation and not coaching lectures. Players learn by doing, not by being told what to do. Active participation is better than passive reception. Repetitive drill is very important. However, correct performance is the most important coaching point.

Give Adequate Consideration to All of the Fundamentals

Give adequate consideration to all of the basics of the game—running, blocking, tackling, passing, receiving, and kicking. Analyze each player's job in the game and then see that he spends a proportionate amount of time on each phase in practice. It is not systems or plays that win games, but players who execute the fundamentals better than the opposition. Sharpness in fundamentals is the winning edge in athletics. It is not necessarily *how much* you teach your players, but *how effectively* you teach them. Select practical and effective drills that will develop individual and team fundamentals, techniques, and skills under game-simulated conditions. Develop agility and reaction by repeating the situations in your offense and defense where these skills are necessary.

Adhere to Laws of Learning and
Sound Principles of Teaching

Successful coaches may employ widely different procedures. No one system or method is the correct one for every coach. What proves to be successful for one coach may be unsuccessful when tried by another coach. But while there is no one all-winning system, a great majority of successful coaches adhere to certain basic principles. Probably the most important basic element in coaching is one's approach to teaching. Therefore, knowing and using the laws of learning and sound principles of teaching should prove beneficial in obtaining desirable results.

Coaches commonly work with athletes that come from all segments of society. This would include the poor as well as the rich, the bright, the dull, the average, the overachiever, the underachiever, the underprivileged, the over-privileged, the mistreated and the over-protected. The coach needs to recognize that all of these characteristics and backgrounds are factors that can affect the behaviors of the athlete, yet not all are under the control of the coach. Therefore for effective learning it is essential that the coach direct his energy and resources in his teaching to controlling only those variables that are truly controllable. These are reinforcement, motivation, retention, and transfer.

Reinforcement   Reinforcement is the coach's response to the player's efforts as they relate to the task required by the coach. It is the decision of the coach whether to reward positively, neutrally, or negatively the performance of individual ball players. It is also the decision of when such rewards or reinforcement are given, since the timing of the selected reinforcement is as important as the kind. Social rewards such as verbal statements may be more effective than tokens (tangible rewards, stickers, certificates, etc.), which tend to become inflationary.

Motivation   Motivation is the desire of the individual player to perform a task or tasks required by the coach. The coach needs to control the level of difficulty of the task assigned so it is attainable by the player. The coach also needs to make the assigned task interesting to the players, and to create a comfortable feeling tone by providing an appropriate reward for successful completion of the task and by controlling the level of tension, or anxiety. If the coach is able to control the variables of motivation, successful performance by his players generally follows.

Retention   Retention is extremely important to coaches and deserves attention. Research done on learning curves, or forgetting, shows that 80 percent of new learning is lost or forgotten in the first 24 hours. Therefore, it is essential that coaches plan for this in their construction of practice plans or skills to be taught to the players. The coach needs to remember that massed practice is utilized for rapid learning and distributed practice is needed for maximum retention of skills learned. In other words, to learn a new skill the coach should provide many repetitions at the first practice session, with other practice sessions in the future, reviewing the skill and its components, distributed over a longer period of time to ensure maximum retention.

Transfer   Transfer occurs when a player makes use of techniques learned in practice and applies them to new learning or game situations. It is important that the coach recognize that learning transfer can be positive or negative, and that negative transfer should be avoided if possible, since it causes confusion and makes new learning more difficult. As a general rule, for techniques that are similar, emphasize similarities; for those that are dissimilar, emphasize differences.

The old adage that practice makes perfect is untrue. Practice makes permanent, perfect practice makes perfect. If a coach plans and organizes his practices well and controls the learning variables as much as possible, he can feel comfortable knowing that he and they have done everything within their power to ensure successful performance.

Practice Schedule Breakdown Suggestions and Guides

As a point of departure, allot approximately 50 percent of the practice time to offense and 50 percent to defense, with the various phases of the offensive and defensive kicking game receiving their 50–50 apportionment. Another general type of breakdown allots approximately 50 percent of the practice time to defense, 35 percent to offense, and 15 percent to the kicking game, depending upon a coach's particular philosophy and the importance he attaches to the offensive, defensive, and kicking games. A further breakdown would be to allocate approximately 25 percent to individual, 30 percent to group or combination, and 45 percent to team work, if this particular plan of organization is employed. You analyze each player's job in the game and see that he spends a proportionate amount of time on each phase in practice.

Typical Early Season Practice Schedule   A typical football practice schedule in competition may be divided into four periods as follows: specialty, individual, combination or group, and team work (Diagrams 6–1 and 6–3). The drills you use would be designed and selected to fit into this type of practice schedule organization. You can modify this (or any) plan according to your own particular circumstances.

Diagram 6–1 illustrates a typical early season (morning) practice schedule when you are likely to be involved in "two-a-days," with the squad members in shorts, T-shirts, shoes, and helmets. Note the heavy emphasis on the *teaching* of fundamentals, where six coaches and all prospects (approximately eighty candidates) are involved. While the players have been placed on teams, much emphasis is placed on giving every player an opportunity to be evaluated individually by the coaching staff.

When practicing twice a day in early season, it is better to have the prospects dressed out in light gear in the morning sessions, in which you stress teaching fundamentals, skills, and techniques, including offensive plays and defensive alignments; then have the players dressed in their

DIAGRAM 6–1
Typical Early Season Morning Only Practice Schedule

Date: Friday, August 29
Practice No. 6 (A.M.)
Gear: Shorts, T-shirts, shoes, helmets

	Offense	*Defense*
TEACH	*Vs. 40, Pro & Okla.* 23–24 Power, 123–124 Power G23–24 Power, G123–124 Power 81–82, 181–182	40 and Pro (plus adjustments to flexed end)
8:55 (20 min.)	Squad Assemble On field: Exer-Genie —————————— Defensive teams—defensive coaches Offensive teams—specialties	

9:15 (5)	Stretching (Finley) (Same as no. 1) All coaches check line up	DT—OT BP	G—C/M CP	LBS—DE GW	X/Y BW	2/5 QB/4 JF	R/3 F/F GC

9:20 (10)	Agility and sprints (Conditioning) (Same as no. 1)	CB—off. linemen JF—off. backs BW—flankers	RP—def. linemen, Es, Ts GW—LBers, and M GC—secondary

	INDIVIDUAL	
9:30 (20)	Stance fundamentals, etc. Ball handling, cuts, blocking Line and Y—CB Backs—JF Flankers—BW	Stance, alignment, techniques, reactions Responsibilities, use of hands, etc. Es, LBers—GW M, Ts—BP 4 Deep—GC

	COMBINATION	
9:50 (20)	Line—CB Huddle, spacing, alignment, blocking, assignment Flankers—Cuts and assign—BW Backs—Ball Handling, etc.—JF	Def. line—BP and GW (Rotate LBers) Def. backs—GC (Rotate LBers)
10:10 (5)	*Water Break* 4 Areas: Off. line—CB; Off. backs—JF, BW Def. line—BP; GW, Def. backs—GC	
1st 10:15 (10)	*TEAM OFFENSE* 1–2–3 v. 3 Def.	*TEAM DEFENSE* 1–2 Def. v. 4 Off. (6 min.–4 min.)

Diagram 6–1 (Cont.)

2nd 10:25 (10)	1–2–4 v. 3 Def.	2–1 Def. v. 3 Off. (3–7)
3rd 10:35 (10)	1–2–3 v. 2 Def.	1–3 Def. v. 4 Off. (7–3)
10:50 (15)	Punt protection and coverage 1–2–3 Off. v. 3 Def.	Punt return (Rt./Lt.) 1–2 Def. v. 1–4 Off
12:00–12:30	Lunch	

regular full gear for the afternoon or evening practice sessions.* Otherwise they are likely to be worn out physically and mentally from practicing in heavy gear twice a day, and their learning and performance generally leave much to be desired.

Typical Early Season Scrimmage Practice Schedule   Diagram 6–2 illustrates the type of practice you would have in early season about two weeks before your first game. It is a logical follow-up to what you have been teaching in the pre-season practice sessions. Your primary purpose is to evaluate your teaching methods and personnel and not to prepare specifically for your opening game opponent. You should continue to evaluate your personnel to determine if you have aligned and slotted them properly. Film this practice session, if possible, to aid the coaching staff in making determinations about personnel. Each candidate's performance should be graded. It is not advisable to scrimmage your best players (1 Offense versus 1 Defense) against each other, because of the possibility of sustaining injuries. It is recommended that you use officials with "quick whistles" and simulate game-like stuations, as illustrated in Diagram 6–2.

After this scrimmage, you can commence to concentrate specifically on getting ready for your opening game opponent. Select demonstration or scout squad members to simulate the opponents' offensive plays and defense against your first two defensive and offensive teams, respectively, in long and short yardage and goal line situations, as illustrated in Diagram 6–3. The demonstration squads' contribution and importance to the overall program will be discussed shortly.

---

* Even beyond the number of practice sessions required by federation rules where players are restricted by regulation to dressing only in shorts, T-shirts, shoes, and helmets.

DIAGRAM 6–2
Typical Early Season Practice Scrimmage Session

Date: _____
Practice No.: _____ (P.M.)
Full gear (scrimmage session)

3:00	Squad assemble in stadium Stretching (B.P.) (Same as no. 1)		
	Scrimmage—Defense: Okla., Pro, 40, 60 Goal)		
3:05–3:20 (15 min.)	1 Off. v. 2 Def.	1st–10	3 Down zone
		1st–10	4 Down zone
3:20–3:35 (15)	2 Off. v. 1 Def.	1st–10	3 Down zone
		1st–10	4 Down zone
3:35–3:45 (10)	3 Off. v. 3 Def.	Scrimmage—Chains Down/Distance	
3:45–4:00 (15)	1 Off. v. 2 Def.	2nd Long (7+)	3 Down zone
		2nd Long	4 Down zone
4:00–4:15 (15)	2 Off. v. 1 Def.	2nd Long (7+)	3 Down zone
		2nd Long	4 Down zone
4:15–4:25 (10)	3 Off. v. 3 Def.	Scrimmage—Down/Distance	
4:25–4:40 (15)	1 Off. v. 2 Def.	Goal line offense 4 Downs	
4:40–4:55 (15)	2 Off. v. 1 Def.	Goal line offense 4 Downs	
4:55–5:00 (5)	1 Off. v. 2 Def.	2-minute offense—	35 yd. line 50 yd. line 35 yd. line

Typical Mid-season Practice Schedule　　Diagram 6–3 illustrates a typical mid-season Tuesday practice schedule. The format is similar to Diagram 6–1, although the emphasis is now on preparing for the upcoming opponent. Note, however, the continuing emphasis on working on offensive and defensive fundamentals and techniques, and the physical conditioning of the squad. Tuesday and Wednesday are usually heavy work days with *controlled* hitting and some scrimmage. Monday practice sessions are usually limited to getting out the "kinks" from last Saturday's game and recognizing the upcoming opposition's best offensive plays (favorite, scoring) and defensive sets (which must be blocked). Thursday is a day

DIAGRAM 6–3
Typical Tuesday Mid-season Practice Schedule

Date: Tuesday, October 7
Practice No.: 42
Game: Eastern

	Offense	*Defense*
TEACH	Our best plays v. Eastern's Split 6 and stunts	Start stunts v. Eastern's favorite play and passes Def. the option, 80's and 90's passes; play action passes
	Work on offensive and defensive fundamentals and technique—aggressively	
3:00	Squad on field. Kickers, specialty men practice your specialty first. All others go thru horizontal ladder and running ropes 3 times	
3:15–3:20 (5 min.)	Stretching (CB) (Same as no. 1)	
3:20–3:23 (3)	Agility drills Fumble drill, Backs; Flankers, Rag drills	Def. linemen/LBers over bags and Def. reactor

INDIVIDUAL

3:23–3:40 (17)	v. Split 6 Off. line—1-on-1 pass blocking—CB Off. backs—Techniques —JF Flankers —BW	Techniques sec.—GC Stop 25–26 Pick (X) Ts/M—BP LBs/E—GW

COMBINATION

3:40–3:57 (17)	v. Split 6 block stunts Off. line Off. back	BP—One line GW, GC—Perimeter and pass (Rotate lines)
3:57–4:00 (3)	Sled—7-man sled Off. backs—Bull sled	Tackling—Tackle ball drill and tackling upright dummies
1st 4:00–4:15 (15)	*TEAM OFFENSE (v. Eastern's def.)* 1–2 v. 3 Def.	*TEAM DEFENSE (v. Eastern's plays)* 1–2 v. 3 Off.
2nd 4:15–4:30 (15)	1–2 v. 3	1–2 v. 3
3rd 4:30–4:45 (15)	1–2 v. 3	1–2 v. 3

Diagram 6–3 (Cont.)

4th 4:45–5:00 (15)	1–2 v. 3	1–2 v. 3
5th 5:00–5:15	F.G. protect. and coverage—live	6–2 Punt return rush Okla. Red
5:45	Get together. Announcements. Dismissal.	

for "healing" (no scrimmage) and firming up the game plan. Each day a different phase of the kicking game is taught and reviewed, as is illustrated in Diagram 6–3.

Typical Day-before-a-game Late Season Practice Schedule Friday's practice plan deviates completely from the format set for the other weekdays, in preparation for Saturday's game. Such a practice is generally short and limited to polishing and timing out various phases of your game plan. Some coaches merely have their players walk through offensive plays and defensive alignments and stunts in various areas on the playing field, such as in the scoring and danger zones. Generally the session consists of briefly reviewing offensive sets and plays attacking the opponents' defensive alignments, and showing their favorite plays against your planned defensive alignments and stunts, as illustrated in Diagram 6–4.

Specialty Period The specialty time segment is devoted to the development by each individual of his particular specialty. Passers work on their throwing, while punters and place kickers work on their kicking specialties. Receivers handle the punts, and ends practice catching the ball. Interior linemen work on pulling, trapping, or whatever other phases of their game have become specialties for them. The same specialty development applies to offensive backs and defensive secondary men and linebackers.

Some coaches prefer to have their specialty work period at the conclusion of practice after the team work. The punters, place kickers, passers, and receivers remain for their specialty work, while the other squad members go to the showers. There are various reasons why some coaches prefer this procedure, one of which is to commence practice with a brief squad meeting and then have all players go on to the field together.

Other coaches prefer to have the specialists report first and have the other players come on to the field after they dress. While the punters, passers, place kickers, and receivers are working on their specialties, the

DIAGRAM 6–4
Typical Day-before-a-Game Late Season Practice Schedule

Date: Friday, November 28
Practice No.: 78
Game: Tech—THE BIG ONE—LAST PRACTICE
Gear: Blue game jerseys and pants, helmets

PRACTICE IN STADIUM

3:15	All squad members in stadium. No one will go out early. Wait in locker room or outside door. WE WILL ALL GO OUT TOGETHER.	
3:25	Stretching: Co-captains (Same as no. 1)	
1st 3:30 (25 min.)	*TEAM OFFENSE* Polish, timing, sharpness 1 v. 2 demonstration	*TEAM DEFENSE* v. favorite plays 1 v. demonstration passes and tendencies 2 v. demonstration; check assignments Also v. 2-point plays
3:55 4:00	Get together. Announcements. Dismissal.* * Centers, QBs, receivers, stay out for five minutes of passing.	

remaining players report to their position coaches and commence working on their individual weaknesses or some other specialty phase of their game.

Warm-up or Flexibility Stretching Period   We have not mentioned the warm-up period previously as a separate phase of the practice schedule since warm-ups might be handled in several different ways. Generally there is a pre-practice warm-up period prior to the work on individual weaknesses and specialties. In the pre-practice warm-up, the players loosen and stretch their muscles on their own, although they may be under the direction of a coach. A second method is for the position coach to direct and supervise the warm-up exercises as part of the individual work at the beginning of the individual period. A third method is for the warm-up period to be placed after the specialty period or the pre-practice work but before the individual period, as illustrated in Diagrams 6–1 and 6–3. After the whistle has sounded at the end of the specialty work, the entire squad assembles together at one end of the field. An assistant coach or one of the players directs the warm-up exercises or drills, and other coaches station themselves between the rows of players and supervise them. In all cases, adhere to a prescribed stretching routine and sequence, worked out prior to the first practice session.

Individual Period   The squad may be divided up by positions with each coach directing the warm-up work, then progressing to agility, reaction, and conditioning drills at his position station on the field. Emphasis is then placed on developing the blocking, tackling, and running of each individual in order to develop him. Here the focus is on individual fundamentals and techniques by position. The position coach selects and directs drills that will teach and develop particular fundamentals and techniques, offensively and defensively. These drills should be decided on prior to the season (see Chapter 12).

Combination or Group Period   This segment of time in the practice schedule breakdown is devoted to small units or skeleton drills both live and dummy. As an illustration, one combination group might be your linebackers and defensive secondary versus the opposition's pass cuts. Another combination might be your defensive line versus the opposition's running game. Offensively another group of backs might be working on timing their plays and ball handling. A fourth group might be working on offensive line blocking versus the opposition's defensive alignments. Each group rotates and progresses so that the players are drilled both offensively and defensively. The size of the squad and the number of available assistant coaches determine the number of work groups, progressions, and the rotation of personnel. This progression type teaching gives individuals a clear view of the overall picture and still permits the coaching staff to concentrate on coaching the individual within the group.

Team Period   The next progression is to the team period, where the emphasis is placed on developing the team as a whole unit. This is necessary in order to polish the timing of plays, to check offensive assignments and defensive alignments, and to put the individuals into game-simulating situations. There are limitations on the progress a team can make in individual and group work because many players will react quite differently in a game situation. How well they have mastered the fundamentals will show up in team drills. The objective here is the general all-round development of the team in working together as a unit. Regardless of the outstanding skills of your individual players, it is difficult to win if they do not work together collectively as a team. On the other hand, teamwork will often overcome definite limitations of individual players and develop a team into a winner.

   In brief, the practice schedule is organized so that the fundamentals, skills, and techniques are *taught* in the individual period; *practiced* in the group or combination period; and then woven into overall offensive and defensive *team effort* and tested under game-simulating conditions during the team period.

PRACTICE TIME AND PRACTICE SESSION PLANNING AND ORGANIZATION

It makes little sense to spend considerable time devising a practice plan, then have little or no opportunity to implement the plan fully during the allotted practice time. Coaches and players must be present in order to carry out the plan. You should take corrective disciplinary action if players or coaches are tardy or absent from practice without justifiable excuses. Every effort should be made *in advance* to prevent this situation from occurring; don't be forced to revert to corrective action *after* it has occurred. Since all of the players and coaches should be accounted for in the schedule for every minute of the practice session, tardiness and absences force makeshift adjustments in the practice plan. Such adjustments are not only disruptive from the organizational standpoint, but they may also make it impossible to accomplish the desired objectives of the scheduled practice.

Football Practice: The Coaches

Some coaches prefer having a squad meeting where the players and coaches meet together before going onto the field together. Other coaches do not call the squad together until after a pre-practice period on the field. In the meantime the players come on to the field as they are taped and dressed, in order to practice their specialties. There may be a brief squad get-together on the field prior to the warm-up exercises, or afterward, depending on the format devised by the head coach. Little is accomplished by the players, however, if they are on the field before their coaches arrive. And if coaches come late to practice, players tend to hang back in the locker or training room rather than to come on to the field and practice their specialty or work on strengthening a skill or technique in which they are weak. You should assign one coach to hurry the players out of the locker and training rooms and on to the practice field. Other coaches should already be on the field to supervise players whose schedules permit them to report early to practice. By the stated practice time, all players and coaches should be ready to commence to follow the written, posted practice schedule.

Football Practice: The Players

While working up practice schedules, you should account for *all* players at *all* times in *all* activities, excluding only those who are being treated and/or excused from active participation in the practice session due to injuries. Therefore, in advance of the practice session, all players are slotted and involved in the personnel rotation for individual, group, and team work. Should a player be late for practice or fail to come to practice, then adjustments can be made accordingly. The assistants should report to the head coach at the beginning of practice the names of individuals at the positions they coach who are not present. As head coach you should coordinate personnel changes and notify those assistants who are involved, so they in turn know which players they will be working with. Otherwise, if coaches try to make changes on their own, the situation gets more complicated and the practice plan and schedule deteriorate. The coaches end up taking players from each other, and the players you want to be coached may not be. The drills and activities tend to lose their meaning, and the time schedule goes out the window. Therefore, make player personnel changes quickly at the beginning of practice, moving players up where possible, so that the entire practice schedule is not disrupted. You can alleviate much confusion by careful planning initially.

Late and Missed Practice Policies   It is important that your players understand your practice policies: especially that a player *must* be at practice and on time or he does not play. It is impossible to win without players, but your chances of winning are greater if you work with the players who are reliable, who attend practice regularly, and who accept coaching. If players will not adhere to these principles, and you try to build a winning program with unreliable players, you are not going to accomplish your personal and professional goals. So enforce your policy or rule when a player is late or cuts practice, and tardiness and absence are not likely to become problems.

Organizing the Disorganized Demonstration Teams   Having one or more assistant coaches responsible each week for the performance of the scout or demonstration teams will aid tremendously in getting your varsity ready for its upcoming opponent. These performers, usually selected by the head coach and staff, should understand their role in building a winning program. If they are made to feel it is a "rat" detail and they are there merely because they are the "tail-enders," not good enough to perform on the varsity, their emulation of the opposition and their contribution to getting the varsity ready to play the upcoming opponent will be poor. In order to ensure performance and presenting a good picture, the players should be selected according to their positions rather than just selecting an offensive and defensive team of eleven bodies. The position coach can make the best determination; do not just select a mixed bag of offensive and defensive reserve players.

In an effort to present a true picture of the imminent game, the reserves who become the scout squad performers must feel, act, and look like the upcoming opponent, if possible. In order to do this, your coach must sell these reserve squad members on their contribution and value to the total program. To assist the performance of the demonstration team, the coach or coaches who are assigned this responsibility must do a good job organizing their work. The total Monday practice should be spent working on the opponents' formations and "bread-and-butter" plays, as defensing what your opposition does best ensures a greater chance for victory. You must stop your opposition first in order to have a chance to win.

To get the best available picture, encourage the scout squad performers to go full speed and give a 100 percent effort. The scout squad coaches should draw up the opposition's favorite formations and plays against your team's defensive alignments, illustrating the blocking assignments on flash cards. By coordinating in advance with the defensive coordinator the defensive set and the offensive play, the scout squad will observe on the flash cards their blocking assignments versus the defense they will face. When working with the defensive scout squad, the procedure is reversed with the offensive coordinator specifying the alignment, adjustments, and stunts he expects the offensive team to face in various field and down-and-distance situations.

Football Practice: The Plan

Regardless of the type of plan, when the whistle blows or the horn sounds signaling the beginning of the structured practice session, the practice schedule that has been set up should be religiously adhered to. All coaches have the written plan and know which personnel they will be working with. All field equipment is available and is in designated places, usually an assistant coach's assignment delegated to the managers. No player should be permitted to come on to the field without his full equipment, nor give the erroneous impression he is ready for "combat" when he is not taped and suitably protected. The team physician determines whether a player has medical clearance for practice and games. The player does *not* make that decision. It is the player's responsibility to be taped, ready for what the practice plan calls for, unless he has been ruled out of rough work by the team physician in advance. Obviously if a player is injured during practice he does not continue to take part in any further contact work.

The managers should have extra equipment available so that if equipment breaks or is torn, changes can be made quickly. Once again, all of this must be planned for in advance.

During the practice sessions, depending on whether the head football coach is involved in actual coaching or is free to move around and observe others, he should observe and evaluate the performances of his players, the teaching methods of his assistant coaches, and their adherence to the practice plan. It is well to carry a pencil to jot down observations, comments, deletions, and additions. Later you should evaluate the effectiveness of the plan and the practice session, the coaches, and the players, as will be discussed shortly.

Practice Plans and Practice Sessions

In pre-season planning and in the practice sessions, the objectives are to identify the hitters in the available personnel; to condition your squad physically; to teach the fundamentals and basics of football; and to teach and implement your system of offense, defense, and kicking game. The foundation of your football program is laid during pre-season, which generally does not conflict with school and teaching activities since it is frequently held prior to the beginning of the academic school year. However, you must be exceptionally well organized in order to utilize effectively the available time; it is possible to practice-teach-coach twice a day on the field, with player and staff meetings before, between, and/or after the practice session(s).

As pre-season football practice period draws to a close and you approach your first game, as well as during the playing season, your objectives and practice plans differ from your early pre-season ones. While you are trying to bring your players along throughout the entire season, after the first game the coaching staff should know the hitters on the squad. Physical conditioning, on the other hand, must be maintained throughout the season although it will not be as extensive nor take up as much practice time as during pre-season. Fundamentals and basics should be taught during the entire playing season although the amount of practice time devoted to teaching depends on how well the basics are being executed. As the season progresses, more time is generally devoted to combination and team work, as you polish and refine your system of offense, defense, and kicking game, and as you get ready each week to play your upcoming opponent. The latter includes implementing your game plan into your practice plan and sessions. Although a coach is likely to follow a general format, the length and intensity of the practice sessions change, both in pre-season and during the season. Several coaching errors or mistakes include:

1. The failure to continue teaching fundamentals and techniques.
2. The failure to maintain conditioning.
3. Too much scrimmage and/or always going live.
4. The failure to practice game-like situations.
5. The failure to teach and enforce adherence to the rules.
6. Too much time spent on practicing plays and gimmicks, usually too much offense; too many defensive alignments and stunts,

usually too much defense; and too little time spent on the kicking game.

Selecting Appropriate Drills   The selection of a particular drill, and the amount of time you devote to it in your practice schedule, should be decided by looking at the *purpose* of each drill and asking, "Are we going to use what this particular drill teaches?" "How much are we going to derive from this particular drill?" And "How much are we going to use what this drill teaches in a game—skill, fundamental, technique, or segment of the game of football? In order to answer these questions, a coach must analyze thoroughly his own offense, defense, and kicking game. Various purposes of drill are:

1. To teach coordination of eye, mind, and body.
2. To develop confidence and poise.
3. To evaluate and align personnel.
4. To improve fundamentals, skills, and techniques.
5. To create game-like situations in practice.
6. To practice the way you are going to play the game.

A football drill should not be an isolated entity. While a particular drill may be isolated from the overall game for the purpose of strengthening a particular phase of football, it is actually a segment of the game. You should employ drills to improve a particular fundamental, skill, technique, or segment of the game of football. The drills you select must fit with your own particular theory, objectives, methods, and philosophy of football and coaching. You must devise drills that will thoroughly cover the essentials of your system of football.

EVALUATION: PRACTICE SESSIONS AND PLAN, PLAYERS, AND COACHES

At the conclusion of the practice session or at the staff meeting before the next day's practice plan is drawn up and finalized, the coaches should evaluate what was and was not accomplished at the previous practice session, and the head coach should secure his assistants' input for drawing up the next plan. The new plan could include few or many changes, with reasons for and against changes.

Practice Sessions

Despite the best made plans, at times practice sessions do not go well. Players may be dragging, have no hustle, spirit, or enthusiasm. They may be missing assignments, causing broken plays, fumbles, interceptions, and blocked punts. There may be a series of injuries caused by freaky circumstances, not by contact work. Players and/or coaches may be carping at each other. The environment is not right for learning, motivation, or winning. It is important to know why. It is also important to have a plan to combat this situation, because too many sessions of this nature make it impossible to build a winning football program.

On the other hand, the practice session might have been outstanding. Why? What caused the difference? Creating a favorable environment is very important. As head coach you are expected to be a leader, to motivate, and to create a winning environment.

Practice Plan

It is important to evaluate whether the coaching staff accomplished the objectives of the practice plan. Much time and effort have gone into planning the practice. Were its objectives or goals reached? Why or why not?

Despite initial careful planning, must you now modify or change plans? Frequently coaches try to teach too much offense, defense, or strategy, but the players do not comprehend and execute to expectations. The practice plan may have to be altered considerably.

As you implement your game plan into your practice schedule, you should observe whether the players are comprehending and executing the plan. You may have to delete parts of the plan during the week, because you are trying to teach too much. The day prior to your game you may have to delete even more from your anticipated game plan simply because you have not been able to teach all of it during the week. It is important to analyze why this has occurred.

Players

Player evaluation goes on all the time. Each day you should have some idea of the progress, if any, of every player on your squad. It is a gross mistake to slot a player and leave him there without further evaluating his performance, or put him there and just hope he gets better. A player either gets better, makes no progress at all, or falls off in his performance. Why? Players should be challenged. Which players are competitors? Which are front runners? Who are your leaders? followers? Who are the stable or unstable players? Who are your winners? quitters? Which ones need encouragement? Which ones are having problems and need your help? What are you going to do about them? Player evaluation is *all ways and always!*

Coaches

Were the coaches able to teach what they intended to teach when the practice plan was formulated? Why or why not? Did their actions and conduct contribute to a good or poor practice session? Did they teach and correct, or did they shout and criticize? Did they give "seminar talks" or did they have the players actively engaged? Was it necessary for them to deviate in any way from the schedule? Why? Were they enthusiastic and encouraging, or were they dragging and sarcastic?

If the head coach is not engaged in the actual field coaching, he has a better opportunity to observe what occurs during the entire practice session. It is suggested he keep a pencil handy to record remarks, make notations of changes and proposed changes, and so on, during the practice session. Many times immediately after the practice sessions, when the coaches are going off the field and/or are in the coaches' locker room, you can give and receive feedback to and from your staff on their day's work. Since it is likely that you will play the game like you practice, it is important that you practice the way you want to play the game. No detail, however small, should be overlooked.

7 GAME PREPARATION, ORGANIZATION AND HOW TO AVOID MISTAKES

In making the game plan the coaching staff must first establish its basic overall philosophy. Basically, the coaches devise a particular game plan from one of three approaches: a conservative field position–establish the run approach, a more wide open–take chances approach, or a middle-of-the-road combination. The ideal plan is affected by many criteria, some of which will be explained below.

DEVISING THE GAME PLAN

By the use of competent scouting and film breakdowns, a coaching staff will arrive at a definite profile of the strengths and weaknesses of its opponent. Your team's strengths and weaknesses should be matched against the strengths and weaknesses of the opposition in order to determine your best chance of winning. In order to win, your team must dominate in two out of three of the following basic categories: defense, offense, and/or the kicking game.

A team with a superior offense and kicking game would probably choose ball control maintaining good field position to allow its defense to bend some and to play on the long end of the field.

A great defensive team with a good kicking game can also play field position but allow the offensive team to be a little more wide open because they will get the ball back for the offense.

Devising Your Offensive Game Plan

In devising your offensive game plan, you and your staff must decide *how* and *where* your team is going to attempt to move the football and the manner in which you are going to put points on the scoreboard.

By Running   In an effort to establish your running attack, you must determine whether your team can run the ball inside and/or outside. After analyzing defensive alignments and the opposition's personnel slotted in those alignments, you must determine which blocking patterns are likely to be the most effective. Basically, you are seeking ways to establish the *triad* of getting the football to your best ball carrier behind your strongest blocker(s) attacking the weakest defensive player(s) or the weakest segment of the defensive alignments.

By Passing   In an effort to establish a passing attack, you must determine whether your team can complete passes in front of secondary defenders in the flats and/or over linebackers, or which receivers can beat secondary defenders deep. In formulating your passing game plan, you must answer the following questions in order to make your determinations of whether you are going to attempt to pass short and/or deep:

> Do we utilize play action, sprintout run-pass action, semi-sprint action, or dropback pocket passes? Which ones?
>
> What can we do to ensure the best protection?
>
> What is our opposition's pass–rush ratio?
>
> What is their basic front?
>
> Are they primarily a reaching defense, or do they dog and blitz often? Tendencies? On which downs do they come and how frequently?
>
> Do they utilize basically man-to-man or zone coverage?
>
> Do they predetermine rotate to flanker and/or field, or do they rotate on backfield flow? middle? Hash: short side? long side?
>
> How do they adjust to changing sets?
>
> How do they adjust to short and long motion strong side (trips)? weak side (double wing)? middle? Hash: short side? long side?
>
> Do they have predictable down-and-distance tendencies?
>
> Do they have tip-offs we can read, such as positive "cheats" on certain alignments? Do they ever fake the dogs and blitzes, and not come, or do they cheat up and then come? Do they disguise their dogs and blitzes well? Do they come immediately or late? Do they scrape off with flow?
>
> Where are the weak links in their defensive chain?

Diagram 7–1 illustrates a finalized relatively simple offensive game plan. Others are more detailed and complicated showing zones of the playing field and specific offensive plays to be utilized on each down (by using colors) based on the opposition's defensive tendencies. The coach in the scouting booth has a copy of the offensive game play, as does the offensive coach on the sideline, so they can communicate with each other and the head coach especially after the opposition's pattern of defensive play begins to become apparent.

Devising Your Defensive Game Plan

In the formulation of your defensive game plan, initially you must go on your opposition's *established* offensive tendencies, which have been charted and analyzed from scouting and/or game film(s). You must then answer the following questions and devise your defensive game plan accordingly:

What must we stop?

What are their bread-and-butter plays? field, down-and-distance, and formation tendencies?

Whom do they go to in the critical run situation?

How do they like to get the football to him?

Whom do they try to throw to in the must-pass situation?

Identify his best routes: short, intermediate, and/or long.

Does the quarterback "freeze" on the primary receiver, or can he pick up the secondary receiver and use his flare control?

Can we pressure and panic the quarterback? How? Hot receiver?

Are there any giveaways by substitution or alignment(s)?

What must we do defensively in order to win?

Diagram 7–2 illustrates a finalized defensive game plan, which is more detailed than the offensive plan illustrated in Diagram 7–1.

On the upper left-hand side are listed the opposition's favorite plays in each zone of the field coming down the page from their own danger zone down to their scoring zone. The notations in the middle section beside each zone remind the defensive coach or signal caller of defensive calls, which are on the bottom half of Diagram 7–2. The opposition's run-pass tendencies are listed at the top right-hand side.

Devising Your Kicking Game Plan

There are numerous factors to analyze in the overall offensive and defensive kicking game. Offense includes the punt and punt coverage, rushing and returning the punt, kick-off alignment and coverage, returning

DIAGRAM 7–1
Illustration of an Offensive Game Plan

Game: State v. Tech
Note: Check and determine as quickly as possible:

1. What are their basic defensive fronts:
   V. RT/LT =   ?   V. Slot =   ?
   V. RD/LD =   ?   V. Special =   ?
2. When are they in *4–4 compared to 4–3?* Down distance or sets?
3. How and when are they in *man coverage?*
4. Who are the *inside LBers keying?*
5. Who are the *outside LBers keying?*
6. Are the *guards keying* guards or FBs' feet?
7. Are *LBers running through?* How and when?
8. Can we *screen?* When and how?
9. How about *squib pass?* (Pass from squib punt)
10. How about *end around?*
11. How about *fake FG screen?*

Running Game

V. 4–4: Run normal attack—favor short side option and 18–19 for outside game. No traps in middle if stacks on grds.

V. 4–3: Run powers and middle traps—favor short side. Also 30–31.

V. "Gap stacks": Traps away from—30–31 away from—pwrs towards.

V. 6–2: No 70 series—favor pwrs, middle traps, and 30–31.

V. 7–1: No 30–31. Otherwise normal attack. No middle traps if pure stack on center.

Passing Game

3 Deep Zone:
1. All hook
2. Option passes
3. Side line patterns

Pure Man Coverage:
1. FB counter passes
2. 52–53 pass "pick"
3. Cross patterns

Man with Two Free Safeties:
1. FB counter passes
2. 52–53 pass "pick"
3. Cross patterns

Man with One Free Safety:
1. FB counter passes
2. 52–53 pass "pick"
3. Cross patterns

Goal Line and Short Yards

RT/LT: 26–27, 56–57 Pr(Grd), 52–53, 52–53, Pwr

RD/LD: 58–59, 56–57 Pr(Grd) 52–53, 52–53Pr, 9, 52–53 opt., 52–53 pass "pick"

SLOT: Pwr RT or LT, Pitch to slot

Two-Point Plays

1. LO = 52 pass GL "pick"
2. Left Slot = Pitch right
3. Fake FG Screen

DIAGRAM 7–2
Illustration of a Defense Game Plan

TEAM: Central Washington   DATE: 10-14

GOAL	26 PWR – 26 PWR – 25 PWR – 25 PWR – 26 PWR – 25 PWR –	– 26 PWR – 40 TRAP	No gamble No blitz No big plays —20	*Tendencies* *Downs*

First				
				RUN 78% PASS 22%

Second
PASS   59%
RUN   41%

Third
RUN   70%
PASS   30%

Fourth
K.G.
PUNT RUN   2
PUNT PASS   3

Main defensive grid:

GOAL	26 PWR – 26 PWR – 25 PWR – 25 PWR – 26 PWR – 25 PWR –	– 26 PWR – 40 TRAP	No gamble No blitz No big plays —20	
	28 PITCH – 26 PASS 28 PITCH – 25 PASS 26 PWR	– 29 PITCH	Play conservative —35	
	28 PITCH – 41 TRAP 28 PASS 40 TRAP		Attack some on first down —50	
	28 PITCH 26 BLAST 41 TRAP 28 PITCH		Attack some on first blitz; some 3rd and long (poss. 2nd and long) +35	
	48 PITCH 41 TR 56 PWR 26 BLAST 26 BLAST 56 PWR		+35	
	26 PWR 20 BLAST 20 BLAST 25 PWR 26 NEAR 56 PWR		+20 Attack in man coverage	
GOAL			*Put out fire*	

1. *Best Basic Defenses:* 4 BASE 4 FLEX STR 4 TIGER	5. *Pressure Defenses (Pass Rush):* 44 – WHIP 47 – THUNDER 47 – LIGHTNING	9. *Automatic Defenses:* COVER 2 RED COVER 2 TRIPS
2. *Best Run Defenses:* 44 43 WIDE AND SHORT	6. *Maximum Coverage Defenses:* 48 – 5 BKS 49 – 6 BKS	10. *Unusual Formations:* TRIPS R and L
		11. *Formation—Set Tendencies:* 60% PRO—RUN and PASS 20% FLK ALL PASS 10% RED and TRIPS ALL PASS
3. *Best Short Yardage* *Defenses:* 6 – 5 IN	7. *Play Action Situations:* ANY 2nd INSIDE —30 TO +30	12. *Motion Adjustments:*
4. *Goal Line Defenses:* 6 – 5 NORMAL 6 – 5 IN 6 – 5 OUT 6 – 5 PLUG	8. *Screen and Draw Situations:* 2 and LONG 3 and LONG	13. *Two-Point Play:* SPRINT PASS WK 1 REC. SIDE

the kick-off, point-after-touchdown alignment and protection. And the defensive kicking game includes the all-out rush and the safe rush, field goal alignment, protection, and coverage, and defending against the field goal by the all-out rush and the safe rush. Each of these areas takes time to study and analyze, and probably this particular phase of football is neglected more than any other. There are numerous reasons for this, which will be pointed out later in Chapter 10, but one is the lack of importance many coaches attach to the kicking game. As a result they expend all of their available time in working on their offensive and defensive plans to the detriment of their kicking game, which receives little more than cursory attention and preparation. When mistakes occur in the kicking game, usually they nullify well-laid offensive and defensive game plans since not infrequently kicking game mistakes are not only costly but also demoralizing to a team. In preparing your kicking game plan, your staff should answer the following questions and prepare accordingly during the week prior to the contest:

Is their center's pass strong and accurate on punts and extra points?
Does their holder have good hands?
How many steps does their punter take? Is he slow? Does he "mold" the ball and then step, or does he "mold" the ball as he steps?
Does he panic?
Analyze the protection both in terms of design and personnel.
Are there chinks in their punt protection that can be exploited?
Can we block their punts? Where? How?
What is their punt coverage? Who is their safety?
Do they release immediately, or do they sustain their blocks and release slowly?
Who are their head hunters and first individuals coming downfield?
Do they run specials off their offensive kicking game? Run and/or pass?
Can we break a big return? Where and how?
When we punt how and where do they load up?
What are their return patterns?
Analyze their individual(s) who handle/return punts: good or super, why? Should we punt to, away from, or out-of-bounds? Does he try to field the ball all or most of the time, or does he fair catch or stay away from it? Does he ever let it bounce, and then try to pick it up and run? Does he handle the ball inside the 10-yard line, fair catch, or let it go into the end zone? Does he fair catch well under pressure?

Similar questions would be included relevant to their alignment and coverage on the kick-off, including the depth and hang time of the ball by their place kicker, so as to devise your strategy for returning the kick-off; analyzing their kick-off return patterns and receiving personnel in particular, asking questions similar to those asked above about their safety man handling punts; field goal attempts, distance, accuracy, and defending against the field goal; and other phases of the overall kicking game. If you want to have a definite kicking game plan, then you must take time to secure answers to these and other questions pertaining to your opposition's overall offensive and defensive kicking game.

Have a Plan for Half-time and After the Game

In addition to making up your offensive, defensive, and kicking game plans prior to the contest, you must also have separate plans, well-thought-out in advance, for half-time when you are ahead or behind and for after the game when you win or lose. While today's players are not likely to be hoodwinked by a coach's oratory, for the most part most players believe what a coach says until they have reason to suspect he is not telling the truth or until they label him as a phony or not genuine. The important thing for a coach to remember is that once he says something, he cannot retract it and his players expect what their coach has said will happen, will indeed happen. If it doesn't, problems and doubts are inevitable.

At Half-time   Despite the fact that a game is measuring up to or surpassing your expectations and you are two or three touchdowns ahead at half-time, you must be careful that your players do not become overconfident and complacent in their thinking and playing in the second half. Therefore, you must plan in advance what you are going to say so they do not let down in their individual performance and coordinated team effort in the second half. In football no one can predict what a safe lead is: some teams have discovered in the second half that a three touchdown lead at half-time was inadequate.

There will be occasions when nothing appears to go right and you may go in at half-time down two or three touchdowns. Once again, you must have a plan of what to say to your players. If the opposition has superior personnel, there may be little you can do other than encourage your players not to give up and to continue to do their best. If they perceive no hope or encouragement from the coaching staff, their performance in the second half may be considerably less than in the first half.

However, there are occasions when your personnel is equal to or perhaps superior to that of your opposition and unexpectedly your team may be down two or three touchdowns. What you say at half-time in this situation is especially important, because now it appears you have not done a good job in preparing your team to compete against a team with inferior or equal personnel. It makes little difference that that deduction may be unfair; for whatever reason, the players have not been performing individually and as a team to their expectations. They need a lift at half-time in order to get back in the game the second half of play. A contingency plan is necessary, and in all probability it is likely to be more psychological than strategical and tactical.

After the Game   There will be occasions when your team wins not so much by its own efforts but by the opposition defeating itself through its own mistakes. There are also occasions when your team does a super job and wins, or does a super job and loses. Then there is the situation, the hardest to face, when you have superior personnel but your team loses. You must have a plan for talking with your squad members in each of these situations, mindful that how and what you say is likely to have a direct bearing on your players' performance for the next games.

Playing Percentages

In order to build confidence you must play percentage football and not gamble needlessly. This means when you are in three-down territory, you punt on fourth down and short yardage instead of trying to make the first down back in your part of the field by running or passing. When you cannot move the ball forward in order to sustain possession, especially early in the game, you turn over the football by punting it to the opponent's part of the field. Now, at some point in the game in a similar situation, in order to try to retain possession either to maintain your team's momentum or possibly to win the game, you *do* try for the first down in your part of the field. It is important that you have planned out ahead of time what you are going to do in such situations, as you do not want to get caught not knowing immediately or guessing what you should do. In a closely fought game, a big play of this nature can change the outcome of the contest. Usually if the offensive team makes a critical fourth down and short yardage play, it gets a big psychological lift and sustains momentum. The failure of the offensive team to make the big play means surrendering possession of the football immediately to the opposition near or in four-down territory. Not only has the opposition increased its chances of scoring by 25 percent by possessing in four-down territory and not having to punt on fourth down, but also the team that fails to make the first down on fourth down usually has a psychological letdown when they go on defense. Not infrequently the opposition tries to score immediately with a big play, and should they be successful they can turn a tightly fought game into a rout. Also, they can force you to deviate from your game plan as you now try to play catch-up football, gambling more frequently instead of playing percentage football. The important point is to have practiced your fourth down and short yardage play in advance so that when the situation arises your players have confidence in their ability to make the first down. And your defensive team must continue to play well not feeling the game is lost if your offensive team fails to make that first down and loses possession of the football to the opposition.

Motivation versus Preparation

Motivation during game week is highly important, but it is not a substitute for sound preparation for the game. It is of little value to talk about "fighting the good fight" if the players have not been prepared physically and drilled technically in blocking and tackling in fighting the good fight. The psychological lift occurs *after* the execution of a strategy or tactic that has been practiced and prepared for in advance. The mere motivation of wanting to run the football at the opposition on fourth down, rather than give up possession by punting to them, is of little value if a team has not practiced for this situation. Even then they may be unsuccessful in their attempt for numerous reasons, but their chances of success are greater if they are prepared for this situation rather than merely psyched up for it. Consistency is brought about by establishing emotional maturity through preparation on the practice field and through meetings and film study.

Your opposition   A team that underestimates an opponent is usually reflecting the attitude of its coaching staff in squad meetings and practice sessions during the week of the game. Usually a combination of underestimating an opponent and overconfidence occurs in preparation for nonconference opponents and/or conference teams with unimpressive win-loss records. Each member of the coaching staff must guard against indifference or merely going through the motions, as alert players will note these tip-off behaviors. If the coaches are not emotionally ready or up for the game, the players will not be emotionally prepared for the contest either. Some coaches overestimate the strengths of their opponent to their players hoping to prevent overconfidence. Such a ruse is not recommended. Only established factual information concerning opposing personnel and team performance should be given to your players; we consider any attempt to motivate your players by falsifying information about their upcoming opponents to be unethical and of little or no value.

Building Pride   It is impossible for a team to win consistently without pride and morale, and these should be cultivated and nurtured by a coaching staff. The importance of pride is best exemplified by statements made by Darrel Royal, highly successful former head football coach at the University of Texas. In personal conversation with one of the authors, he said, "Pride is what causes a winning performance. The primary task of a head coach is to plant, fertilize, groom, and develop that pride." On another occasion Coach Royal stated, "Pride is like good paint, it covers a lot of rough spots."

Goal Setting   One of the game's winningest coaches, Bud Wilkinson, has been quoted frequently as asking his players, "How good do you want to be? The staff can bring out your maximum potential if you really want to be that good." Coach Wilkinson's statement implies individual goal setting, and the coaching staff then assisting the individual to achieve those goals. Coach Wilkinson has spoken frequently of the importance of having an individual goal of giving 100 percent on every possible play, in order to get team consistency. This eliminates "quitting down" and the inconsistency that result when several players rest on a particular down. They may give 100 percent for several more downs, but in the meantime several others are resting on a quitting down. Should a point of attack be directed at a player who is resting because of his all-out physical effort on previous downs, his failure to carry out his offensive assignment may mean he or a teammate gets hurt or his team loses the football. Defensively his inconsistency may result in a long gainer or a score for the opposition. Individual goal setting should include giving 100 percent effort whenever a player is in a game, even when it hurts physically or psychologically to do so.

Do Not Forget the Basics

In planning for the game the coaching staff must not get carried away with the strategy and tactics while forgetting to spend time teaching and drilling the basics. The game plan is successful only if your team is fundamentally sound and can execute the plan. If your players cannot execute the fundamentals well, the best devised game plan will collapse.

"What If" Syndrome

Despite the fact that a coach have a plan for everything, you must be careful that you do not waste time and energy practicing for the "what ifs." Specifically, this means "what if" they do something like run unusual spread sets, or put their remaining back in motion so that only the quarterback remains behind the center, or use a huddle muddle play, or have their center on the end of the offensive line, or utilize a forward pass off a lateral pass to a flanker, and on and on. Your plan should be *not* to panic but to call time-out immediately in order to show your players the necessary adjustments on a blackboard on the sideline. In making your game plan, first defense their bread-and-butter plays in order to take away their favorites. Adjust as necessary to the "what ifs" that arise, although they may never occur during the course of a game. Standardized rules for covering eligible receivers, including double-wing and triples to one side, and motion, are basic preparatory measures, which are usually taught before the first game so they should not be considered unusual. Occasionally reviewing rules for covering the un-usuals should suffice for adjustments to be made quickly. Once the ele-ment of surprise is taken away, the opposition usually reverts to its basic alignments and favorite plays.

DEVIATING FROM YOUR GAME PLAN

While there may come a time during the course of a game that you must deviate from the game plan you have prepared and practiced in order to win the contest, exercise restraint *not* to abandon your game plan too soon and start "grab-bagging" in an effort to get points on the score-board. It is not likely that your opposition will deviate too much from what they have done previously, and upon which you have formulated your game plan. Your final plan represents the best thinking and plan-ning of your staff over the course of a week's time. You have put in long hours devising your game plan and practicing it. To abandon it early in the first half merely because your plan is not materializing to your ex-pectations is foolhardy. Your plan has not even had time to succeed or fail. To abandon it and attempt to pull another out of your hip pocket is illogical and irrational. Plans may be adjusted, but seldom would you jump successfully to a totally new strategy. When you try to do that, usually you are gambling and not playing percentage football. As an illustration, to start throwing the ball from all over the field without hav-ing a good passer, competent receivers, adequate protection, or good passing strategy favors the opposition and is playing the gambling game of football.

Playing Today's Game or History?

One adjustment that must be made during a contest is to reality. You must remember that your present game plans have been based on past performances, both the opposition's and your players'. If the opposition is not following their past performance script, then you must make ad-justments in your game plan. As an illustration, if you have devised your defensive game plan to stop an outstanding passing attack, but now the opposition's quarterback is injured and his backup replacement does not throw the ball well, it is foolhardy to stay with pass alignments and coverages if the new quarterback has switched to a running attack. Conversely, you may have an offensive player injured, say an outstanding passing quarterback; it is unwise to stay with the offensive game plan if his backup cannot execute as well as the injured player. You must make poised and not frantic, massive changes in the defensive and offensive game plans under such circumstances. While you may be reluctant to change, you must recognize the reality of what the opposition is doing in the game. Some coaches have difficulty getting the feel and tempo of the game being played and tend to stay with history rather than recognizing and adjusting to reality.

Hidden Factors

In analyzing statistics, for both devising the game plan and reviewing the game played, you may frequently overlook mistakes and errors that have been made. There are hidden factors that often mean the difference between victory and defeat. In order to win, first you must not beat yourself through your mistakes and errors. Your team must also be able to capitalize on the mistakes and errors of your opposition.

Offensive Illustration   In devising your offensive game plan if you run the triple option offense, you may choose *not* to run the pitchout back in your part of the field, from your goal line out to your 35-yard line. Once beyond your own 35-yard line, however, you will run the pitch off the option. In reality then, from your goal line out to your 35-yard line your quarterback is instructed either to give to his fullback or to keep the football himself, and never to pitch out to his trailing back. Your intent is to guard against a fumble in your part of the field where, if the opposition recovers, they are in four-down territory immediately. If they recover the fumble at their end of the field, they have a longer distance to go to score, and they only have three downs to make their ten yards until they get to approximately your 35-yard line. Many coaches do not run the triple option because of the high incidence of fumbles and possible turnovers.

Defensive Illustration   From a defensive standpoint you may devise your game plan to play reading defenses and few stunts when you have the opposition backed up deep in its own three-down territory. Stunting at that end of the field may cause as many problems for the defensive team as for the offensive team. When a team stunts, pursuit angles are generally poor if the offensive point of attack is away from the line of direction of the stunt. If a defender is walled off and does not get to his area of responsibility there is a void in the defense. Not infrequently a relatively simple play such as a hand-off will turn into a long gainer as a result of a void in the defense.

The above are but two illustrations of game plan preparation where you work to avoid your team making possible mistakes and errors. Coach Bud Wilkinson has shown that more than 80 percent of football games are won by the team that makes the *fewest turnovers*. Therefore, game plan preparation should do everything to prevent turnovers from occurring.

GAME WEEK PREPARATION AND ORGANIZATION

Practice organization was discussed in Chapter 6, and illustrations of typical practice schedules were included. It is advisable to follow the same format each day of the week so that, for example, the players know that Monday is a day of light work, game films, and scouting reports; Tuesday and Wednesday may be heavy work days in your plan; Thursday is polish; and Friday is a light walk-through practice (if the game is on Saturday). Some coaches have their players report on Sunday for treatment of injuries, sweats, stretching, loosening up, sprints, films, depending on their particular situation. At the high school level Sunday practice is probably the exception rather than the rule. Game films are not as quickly processed and as readily available for viewing at the high school level. Most college coaches have their game films by late Saturday night or early Sunday morning. If a coaching staff does not receive game films until Monday, obviously their work schedule will be altered from that of the staff who can view its game film on Sunday.

Game Films

As we indicated previously, game films should be viewed, performance graded, and feedback provided to each individual. The earlier in the week this is done, the better. It may be necessary, however, for coaches and players to view the film and grade performance together. It may be possible for a head coach at the high school level to show the films during homeroom periods (if he has a *football homeroom*). Or a projector may be set up in the coach's office, and players can come in on their own to view the films during study periods. Or show the game films to the players late in Monday's practice session prior to receiving the scouting report. It is of questionable value to continue showing last week's game films beyond Tuesday noon for teaching purposes as Tuesday's practice should be geared to getting ready for the upcoming opponent.

Scouting Report

The scouting report should be basic, short, and factual. It will be easier to read (and more likely to be read) if it is typed, but it need not be. It is advisable to prepare and distribute to each player a three- or four-page report on the upcoming opponent. The depth chart of personnel should not go beyond two deep, and should only include name, height, weight, age, and class. A single page of possibly three or four favorite running plays and three or four favorite passes, the opposition's bread-and-butter offense, is all that is needed. Add a single page of defensive alignments, personnel, and stunts, and a concluding page of kicking game diagrams of alignments and personnel. The initial scouting report is merely an orientation for the players and should not be a dissertation. The oral scouting report should be given by the scout in fifteen to twenty minutes time.

It is not necessary to give your players all of your opposition's offensive and defensive tendencies by formation or alignment, field position, and down-and-distance. They will not remember them. The coaching staff may not have all the statistics broken down early in the week when the scouting report is given. You will teach and practice against your opposition's tendencies during the week as you implement your offensive and defensive game plans.

If you have time and if your squad members are split into offense and defense, it may be more advisable for the scout to give separate reports to each group of players, and not bother each group with the part of the report that does not relate to them. Your defensive players need not be concerned about the opposition's defense, nor your offensive unit about the opposition's offense. Your players should be encouraged to study during the week the report distributed to them by your scout coach.

Football Homeroom

Much teaching can be done at the high school level if a coach has a football homeroom. Just as each day's practice schedule follows a set format, each day's football homeroom during the season should follow a prescribed teaching format.

The Drive Sheet Breakdown   Monday is the most logical day to discuss the previous game and probably the best way to do this is to discuss the drive sheet breakdown. Such information can be compiled during the game by an assistant or a manager on the sideline who is familiar with your offense and defense. Basically, that individual compiles a play-by-play of the game offensively and defensively. Over the weekend you can chart a meaningful profile on a simulated football field showing the following: how and where your team received possession of the football, what your team did with the football during that drive, how and where your team gave up possession of the football. From this, as an example, you might realize your team had possession of the football a total of nine times during the game, five times the first half, four times the second half, but you only scored once in each half, winning 14–13. In the first half your team did not score until its fourth possession, which was acquired by recovering a fumble on your opposition's 30-yard line. Your team then drove thirty yards in six running plays, with your quarterback scoring on the keeper off the triple option. In the second half your team intercepted a pass on its own 30-yard line for its third possession. Your team then drove seventy yards on nine running plays and three passes, the last being a 20-yard pass for a score. You can also breakdown how and where you gained possession on the other seven occasions you had the ball and how and where you gave up possession since you did not score. It is possible to glean much information from the drive chart offensively and defensively that can be used for teaching and coaching purposes. Diagram 7–3 illustrates a defensive drive chart.

From experience as high school coaches we have found that covering a different specific phase of the kicking game each day on the blackboard during the football homeroom period, and covering the same phase of the kicking game later that afternoon in practice resulted in better execution, fewer mistakes, and more effective teaching-coaching. Depending on the length of the periods, it is also possible to teach and review your upcoming opposition's offensive sets and favorite plays and passes, and their defensive alignments and stunts. Many coaches cover the information mentioned above in short pre-practice meetings with all of the squad members before the players take the field together for the afternoon's practice session. If you utilize football homeroom time to cover such material, pre-practice meetings are unnecessary and you have that much more time on the practice field to teach-coach.

Your Game Plan Versus Your Opposition's Tendencies

You need not have your complete game plan finalized early in the week, but you do need to familiarize your players early with your opposition's favorite plays and passes off their favorite offensive sets, along with the defensive alignments, stunts, and coverages you are expecting from having scouted them. It is best to diagram this information with felt-tip pens on large cards so that scout squad members can simulate the opposition offensively and defensively. This entails good planning and organizing by the offensive and defensive coaches, along with the scout squad coach,

DIAGRAM 7–3
Defense Drive Sheet

Date: 10–7				Game: Central Washington	
Down	Distance	Yard Line	Defense Called	+/−	Comments
1	10	−30	44 BASE	0	Sam backer too close
2	10	−30	44 RUSH	+ 1	Exc. job
3	10	−31	41 STAR X	INTC	Exc. play—Bucky Hargrove
1	10	−29	50 SAM	+12	No contain by end
1	10	−41	51	+ 0	Good job—Mike
2	10	−41	44 BASE	+ 5	No reaction front
3	5	−46	44 FLEX STR.	INTC	Exc. rush and cover
1	10	+49	44 FLEX STR.	+ 2	Slow off ball
2	8	+47	44 BASE	+ 4	——
3	3	+43	44 BASE	+ 0	Exc.
4	3	+43	Punt Block	+35	Good rush

so that what the scout squad does enables your players to get a picture of what the opposition does. Each card and play is numbered so that the scout squad demonstrators are following a script that every coach has at hand, coordinated by your offensive and defensive coaches, who are testing your defenses and offensive blocking patterns and plays, respectively, versus the opposition's tendencies from their favorite sets and alignments. While all of the action will be at full speed in order to get a good picture, only parts of it will involve live tackling. Most of it will involve "thump"—defenders will pursue the ball carrier but not tackle him. The football should be moved from hash to hash, and up and down the field to get a truer picture of the opposition's tendencies. These sessions must be carefully controlled so as to avoid injuries.

By Wednesday, the game plan should be set. However, if there is not good execution and/or comprehension by the regulars, certain segments of the game plan may be deleted by Friday. While the battle plan is refined and polished, deleting segments if necessary, additional plays, alignments, strategy, tactics, *should not be added* beyond Wednesday. Nothing should be retained for the game that has not been practiced or performed to satisfaction.

Controlled Practice Sessions—Limited Scrimmage

A common coaching mistake is to leave the game on the practice field; that is, poorly organized coaches scrimmage and have "meat" practices rather than teach and coach. Tuesday and Wednesday should be heavy work days, in which coaches supervise and control small group contact work. Scrimmage may be limited to both ends of the field where, for example, the offensive team is working live for five to ten plays coming out of their danger zone or for five to ten plays attempting to score from their scoring zone. Your defensive team is facing the offensive scout team in similar situations under similar conditions. Your coaches should make it clear which plays are live and which are "thump."

Few coaches practice punt coverage, which includes tackling, punt returns, punt blocks, kick-off coverage, and kick-off returns, live, because extended study reveals the incidence of injuries is much higher in these segments of the kicking game than in any other offensive or defensive segment of the game. With twenty-two players spread out over the field and with peelback blocks being utilized on pursuers in order to open a running lane for the ball carrier, more serious injuries occur. Therefore, many coaches do not practice these phases live, although punt protection must be practiced live *excluding* actually blocking the punt or crashing into the punter if punt protection breaks down. The patterns and necessary spacings in the coverages and returns may be practiced full speed, but blocking and tackling downfield beyond the line of scrimmage should be excluded. It is important that all the coaches supervise and control this carefully so that all players understand there is no live blocking or tackling downfield during practice sessions.

Squad and Player Meetings

Typically a squad meeting is held sometime just before the day of the game. A high school coach is of course more limited in bringing his players back at night. Basically, a coach may wish to meet his squad on Friday night before Saturday's game in order to go over the final game plan, assignments, and scouting report, to view film, or merely to build the cohesiveness of the squad. He may or may not want to follow-up with a bed check. A coach's situation may be such that he cannot bring his players back at night, but he can have a short squad meeting after Friday's practice, which is typically short anyway. Such a meeting is highly recommended, depending on the coach's situation and preference.

Offensive and Defensive Quarterbacks   Each coach must decide whether he is going to train his offensive and defensive quarterbacks to call the offensive plays and defensive alignments, stunts, and coverages, respectively, or whether he is going to send in this information by substitution or wig-wag his signals from the sideline. If the quarterbacks are handling calls, then the coach must set up sessions to train and drill his offensive and defensive signal callers during the week. If the coach calls signals, then he controls the plays and defensive alignments by messenger or by hand signals. If he utilizes hand signals, then the signal callers must be taught to read them. Although the easiest method is to send in messages by substitution, a coach may not have his best eleven players on the field at all times when he does this. The second easiest method is by wig-wag, or hand, signals, although some coaches feel this is unethical. To train and drill the offensive and defensive signals callers requires much time.

Regardless of the method utilized, we suggest a coach follow it 100 percent. To permit a player to call some plays, and then have the coach step in to call others, can create problems in the coach-athlete relationship. This mixed method is also ineffective. A coach has better control of a game if he calls all of the plays, and the most effective way to do it is probably the wig-wag system. Regardless of the method, it is likely offensive and defensive signals callers will have to view their opposition via film exchange during the week of the contest anyway in order to recognize defensive alignments, understand tendencies, recognize offensive sets, and so on.

Practice the Day before the Game

Assuming Friday is the day before the game, the Friday practice session should be short. It is impossible to review everything, nor should a coaching staff attempt to do so. Many coaches review tendencies, offensive sets, and defensive alignments, and repeat how their game plans have been formulated to counter or take advantage of what the opposition is likely to do. Many coaches also review several phases of the kicking game, generally walking through their offensive and defensive patterns. The main emphasis is on team unity and cohesiveness, and on the reassurance that you have prepared well as a staff and team for the upcoming game. A coach must be careful his players do not stay on the field too long, especially the passing and kicking specialists who at times have a tendency to practice too much the day before the game. While a team meeting is recommended after practice or that evening, this is a situational matter. Under no circumstances should anything be added to the game plan. In fact a quick review by the staff may reveal that certain plays, stunts, coverages, or the like, should be deleted from the final game plan. (Diagrams 7–1 and 7–2 illustrated the finalized version of offensive and defensive game plans.)

GAME DAY PLANS AND GAME ORGANIZATION

Probably one of the best methods of evaluating the ability of a head football coach to plan and organize is to observe his behavior and that of his assistants on the sideline, and to observe his players on the sideline and field during a game. Some players have difficulty getting into and out of the huddle and up to the line of scrimmage properly; they have probably been told what to do but perhaps not drilled properly in how to do it. The same principle applies to sideline and game organization. Some head coaches make things happen as the result of good planning and detailed organization. Others do not know what is happening, and their bench and sideline indicates confusion, disorder, and the lack of organization. The game day plan will vary with the coaching situation, whether it be a high school or college, a day or night game, but there are certain areas of organization that remain constant for all.

Pre-game Meetings

It is advisable to limit the number and length of meetings on game day to a minimum. Some coaches put off until the game day meeting what normally might be covered in a Friday night meeting. This information was discussed above. The real purpose of the game day meeting is merely for players to touch base with their coaches on any last minute questions they might have. It also gives the coaches a chance to check out their players as some start getting pumped up too soon before the game. After the players are taped, most coaches have their players stretch out and rest in the gymnasium or locker room, observing a quiet time to get it all together. At a predetermined time the players will start to dress out with the exception of shoulder pads and shoes.

Squad Meeting Typically there is a brief squad meeting approximately forty minutes before going on the field for the pre-game warm-up. This short meeting is where the head coach may note any changes or make comments on anything he considers to be significant to the game or personnel. The attempt is not to get the players pumped up too early but to continue to bring them up slowly so that they all are concentrating fully on the task at hand.

Coaches' Final Briefing—Morning of the Game　A staff meeting earlier in the day is desirable for a final check to determine everything has been or will be taken care of in order to play the game. By game time everything should be operational, and each coach and player should know his function. Coaches will have the appropriate copies of their phase of the offensive, defensive, and kicking game plans (Diagrams 7–1 and 7–2), and current offensive and defensive personnel depth charts. Only a defensive personnel depth chart (Diagram 7–4) is included here, for illustrative purposes. These plans and charts should be placed in clear plastic waterproof envelopes for the appropriate coaches on the sideline and in the scouting booth.

At the coaches' final briefing on the morning of the game, staff members should go over a checklist of *all* phases of the game plan, as is illustrated in Diagram 7–5, taking into consideration appropriate courses of action that will be followed in each situation. We express our appreciation to John Ralston, former general manager and head football coach of the Denver Broncos, for granting permission for us to include in Diagram 7–5 the material he utilized in his coaches' final briefing, pre-game checklist on mornings before games.

Pre-game Details

Field Organization　Know before going out on the field which is your bench. Which end of the field do you have? Where is your pre-game warm up area?

Pre-game Drills　After the squad meeting the players will continue to dress, finishing so the specialists may take the field for a twelve-minute period before the rest of the squad joins them.

After the entire squad is assembled, stress togetherness in a five-minute stretching and calisthenics period, followed by a five-minute drill unique to each group, for example, pass skeleton backs and receivers versus linebackers and secondary personnel.

The last part of the pre-game drill usually consists of two offensive teams running dummy plays against the first defensive unit from the 10-yard line in to the end zone. The remainder of the defense stands out of the end zone. The defensive coach can send in messengers or flash

DIAGRAM 7-4
Personnel Depth Chart for Purposes of Substitution

DATE: 10-14   GAME: CENTRAL WASHINGTON

FRONT

L. End	L. Tackle	R. Tackle	R. End
Stevens	J. Rousseau	J. Michelletti	Henry
Meeks	M. Heaslip	Goddard	McJunkin

LINEBACKERS

SAM	MIKE	MAC	WILL
Di Palma	D. Mossbacher	J. Eckhardt	S. Reese
B. Gunnion		Edens	M. Kyle

BACKS

LEN	SID	COVER VIII (Fifth Back)	COVER IX (Sixth Back)	FRED	RON
L. Young	B. Foltmer	S. Bootman	D. Gayaldo	C. Carter	B. Hargrove
B. Morris	S. Bootman	B. Van Dorn	N. Constanza	D. Thomas	J. Collins
R. Traversi	M. Constanza			K. Williams	

SPECIAL SUBSTITUTIONS

40 to 50			To Goal Line			Special		
Heaslip	for	Michelletti	No	for	change	None	for	this week
Eckhardt	for	Rousseau		for			for	
	for			for			for	

hand signals to the defensive signal caller so the latter can call alignments and coverages just as will be done during the game.

Last Minute Instructions   The squad will then return to the locker room for a final equipment check, to take care of their personal needs, and to receive last minute instructions. Care should be taken here not to permit this period to drag too long.

DIAGRAM 7–5
Pre-game Check List, Morning of a Game

I. WHAT TYPE OF GAME DO WE PLAN ON?
  A. Conservative—field position—establish run
  B. Let it all hang out—possession—take chances
  C. Or more or less in the middle
  D. Considerations
    1. Are we favored?
    2. Are they favored?
    3. Game a toss-up?
II. CHECK COMMUNICATIONS: OFFENSE—DEFENSE— KICKING
  A. Press box information to sideline
  B. Sideline information to players on field
  C. Penalty decisions from sidelines to playing field
III. SUBSTITUTION—CHECK THOROUGHLY BY POSITIONS
  A. Know percentage of time each player to play
  B. What situations plus chain of events would cause us to change our QB?
IV. WHAT TWO MUST SUCCEED IN ORDER TO WIN TODAY? (Two of three have to be dominant in order to be successful.)
  A. Offense
  B. Defense
  C. Kicking
V. EXAMINE END-OF-GAME OFFENSE AND DEFENSE
  A. Two-minute offense and defense procedure
  B. How to play last minute of game (Offense)
    1. Time-outs left?
    2. Position of ball?
    3. Need three or seven points?
    4. Communication on time-outs?
    5. Substitution?
    6. Conserve time or run clock down?
  C. How to play last minute of game (Defense)
    1. Time-outs left?
    2. Position of ball?
    3. Scrambling QB—pocket QB?
    4. Strength of blitz and prevent defense?
    5. Do they need three or seven points?
VI. SCORING COMBINATIONS—KNOW EXACTLY
  A. Take safety?
  B. Where are we kicking from?

C. Field goal or touchdown? Run through some situations that may exist during game.
D. Two-point play—when to use? Rule of Thumb: four minutes left, six minutes left.
E. How important is it that we score first?

VII. GOAL LINE PROGRESSION OF PLAYS "GOING ON" (OFFENSE/DEFENSE)
A. Review all situations
B. Order of plays offensively or calls defensively: six yards and in, four yards and in, two yards and in
C. Third and one to go; fourth and one to go

VIII. GOAL LINE PROGRESSION OF PLAYS "COMING OUT" (OFFENSE/DEFENSE)
A. Review all situations
B. Order of plays offensively or calls defensively: first and ten on the 1, first and ten on the three, first and ten on the five

IX. SHORT YARDAGE SITUATIONS (OFFENSE/DEFENSE)
A. Aware of play action pass?
B. Aware of "go for broke play"?
C. Plays going to outside?

X. BLITZING (OFFENSE/DEFENSE)
A. Check thoroughly—calls to counter—situations to use

XI. AUDIBLES
A. Review exact procedures
B. Get out of bad play?
C. Throw over top?

XII. KNOW SCORES OF OUR CONFERENCE OPPONENTS DURING GAME
A. Will we take a tie?
B. Must we win?

XIII. KICKING GAME
A. Go after them—punt block—on-side kick—plays from punt formation
B. Conservative—field position—punt cover—return
C. Assign coaches to watch kicking game (during game)—coach this area for exactness

XIV. MOMENTUM CHANGERS
A. List in order
B. Do you want to start game with big play?

XV. PRE-GAME WARM UP
A. Uniform change-ups—no pads—helmets, etc.
B. Know area on field to warm up
C. Review warm-up procedures and assignments

XVI.   HALF-TIME SEATING AND COMMUNICATION
    A.   How much time for half-time—total
    B.   Check physical layout—blackboards—training room—coaches' room
    C.   Three distinct time blocks—how much time for each?
        1.   Players care for themselves as coaches get together —changes
        2.   Coaches' and players' question and answers—changes
        3.   Summation—head coach
XVII.   BENCH PROCEDURE
    A.   Proper seating—all personnel (trainers, doctors, and so on)
    B.   Check procedures—going on field—coming off
XVIII.   TOSS OF COIN—WHAT GOAL TO DEFEND?
    A.   If wind is a factor? rain? cold? muddy field?
    B.   Would it affect choice of goals?
    C.   Possession primary! Strength of defense and kicking will determine
XIX.   POST-GAME THOUGHTS
    A.   What if we win? Statements to press—to players
    B.   What if we lose? Statements to press—to players

Source: John Ralston, General Manager-Head Coach, Denver Broncos. Used by permission.

Check Field Phones   The first duty of the managers or a designated coach on arrival in the stadium should be to check the condition of the field phones and to make certain they are operable. If they do not function and cannot be repaired, then a contingency plan must be arrived at for communication purposes. It is a helpless feeling, at an away contest in particular, to learn of a communications breakdown between the scouting booth and the field. However, expect it, and prepare a backup plan.

Coin Toss   The choice accompanying the coin toss will be affected by weather conditions and the condition of the playing field. Your team's strengths and weaknesses versus those of your opposition, taking into consideration wind and weather factors, are the criteria for choosing a particular alternative.

Equipment Storage   Before the team comes out onto the field, the managers should have all the necessary equipment in position on the sideline. The team physician and trainers should establish a place for injury care in advance. Have all equipment available on the spot and be sure players know where it is.

On the Sideline during the Game

Bench Organization   Have designated places on the bench for offensive, defensive, and special teams personnel, and a special place near the field phones for the offensive quarterback and defensive signal caller. Have a plan for the key substitute or messenger both offensively and defensively.

Set the bench up so the coach in charge can communicate with his players when they come out of the game. Give him a chance to make any necessary adjustment or correction to ensure the information is properly comprehended.

Who Instructs Whom   To whom do your players report when they come off the field? Do they head for the water and the trainer, the head coach, or their specialty coach? Good organization will not leave this to chance, and your players should be instructed whom to report to. While the head coach has the prerogative of stopping any player as he comes out of the game to query him or to give him information, more effective coaching allows the players to report directly to their specialty coach. Each coach should have a small portable chalkboard in order to illustrate and discuss changes and adjustments, with individual players in his group. Many times this may not be necessary, and the coach merely waves off the players to their designated area on the bench. Often, however, a coach wants to convey information to a player whom he cannot locate on the sideline. Unfortunately, if the ball changes possession quickly due to a turnover, the player may return to the game without having received instructions from his coach.

Bench Discipline   You want to organize your bench and have it disciplined, without stifling the emotional involvement of the players. Assign each player a designated area and keep him in that area. Encourage them to have the pride in being available on the right spot at the right time yet emotionally concerned with the game on the field.

One or more player(s) may have to be in different spots in different situations defensively and with special teams. Set the standard, educate them, and sell poise and pride to accomplish bench discipline.

Substitutions   Who is responsible for making substitutions? Who gets the punter and special teams up and ready? Who has the field goal unit ready? Who substitutes the fifth back in the prevent defense? In the organized chaos of the sideline these duties must be detailed, otherwise the chances of having too many or two few plays on the field become highly probable.

In evaluating personnel on substitutions, you should ask yourself: Are we getting whipped somewhere? whipping someone? Anyone losing poise? Anyone fatigued? Anyone injured? Answers to each of these questions are critical in making key substitutions and correct calls.

Captains' Decisions   Regardless of whether your game captains are appointed or elected, they should be trained to make proper, competent decisions so as not to make critical mistakes. The training of the offensive and defensive captains will be discussed in greater detail in Chapters 8–10.

Press Box Organization and Sideline Coordination   The coaches in the scouting booth or press box must constantly be on top of what is occurring during the game. To be effective they must be well prepared and organized in their work. The primary job of the coach in the booth is to observe what is occurring offensively and/or defensively and to relay factual, specific information to the individual(s) on the sideline phone(s), probably an assistant coach, such as the offensive or defensive coordinator, or the head coach, depending on the situation and the particular hook-up. It may be that the offensive plays and the defensive alignments, stunts, and coverages are being called from up in the box and relayed to the sideline to be sent in by substitutes or by hand signals. Typically the plays originate on the sideline, although the sideline coach on the phone may ask the coach in the booth for assistance in calling plays. There should be a clear understanding on the part of each coach to eliminate unnecessary talk, which destroys concentration. Also, one coach's attempt to "help" another by offering suggestions without being asked usually creates more problems than it solves. As an illustration, if there are two phones to the field and the offensive coach in the booth starts talking with the offensive coach on the sideline trying to help the defensive coaches who are trying to stop a drive, this interference can only heighten the anxiety and add to the confusion as different instructions are coming to the head coach and possibly the players from coaches upstairs and on the sideline. Each coach should know his specific duties and responsibilities and should not help out unless asked to do so. No one who is untrained should be in the scouting booth with the coaches unless that individual can assist in some capacity. Having too many people in the booth can cause as many problems as having too few. If your scouting booth staff is too small, it simply cannot secure all of the necessary information when they must observe and record, too. Too much is happening too quickly—it is not possible for one person to see everything going on involving all of the offensive and defensive players. One person can watch his team on offense or defense concentrating on the football at the critical point of attack, but he cannot view what all of the players are doing. We describe below how two coaches can assist each other, each with specific assignments.

The ideal situation is three coaches in the scouting booth or press box with phones to their offensive, defensive, and special team counterpart coaches on the sideline. The head coach on the sideline has a toggle switch to any of the three lines. While this is the most expedient system, few high school coaches have more than one bench-to-booth phone communications line. In that situation, two coaches in the booth can assist each other the following way.

Watching for Changes   Your scout booth coaches should try to determine if the opposing team has made any changes or adjustments in their tendencies from the previous game that you scouted and charted. If the opposition's tendencies are holding up, your original game plan need not be changed. If you determine they have gone away from their previous tendencies, then changes in the game plan must be made, especially if your team is not moving the ball and/or is not stopping the opposition. In order for two coaches in the pressbox to secure factual information on the opposition, they operate as follows when your team has the football:

> *Offensive coach:*   watches ball, backfield action, and is responsible for play calling;
> watches offensive line blocks and blocks and picks up any defensive stunts;
> watches defensive secondary and charts defenses and corresponding offensive plays.
>
> *Defensive coach:*   watches all defensive fronts, stunts, and is responsible for checking all substitutions by opposing team's defense;
> watches defensive corner support and is assigned to watch particular players who may be hurt or possibly not playing well.

When the football goes over to the opposition, your coaching booth assignments for your two coaches change as follows:

> *Offensive coach:*   watches play, picks up routes of receivers on passes;
> watches offensive blocking scheme and is responsible for substitutions by opposing team's offense.

> *Defensive coach:*   watches ball, blocking scheme, and is responsible for calling defenses;
> watches end and corner support and charts plays and corresponding defense.

Accuracy of Information   Information that is communicated to the bench must be accurate. It must be sorted and matched versus the history that went into making up the game plan. Record similarities, establish patterns, get the breakdowns and recommendations to the proper coach on the sideline. Remember information from the box to the sideline is of no value unless it reaches the players in the game. Be sure it is conveyed to the players as stated not as an interpretation of what sideline coaches think you said.

Well-recorded information may set a pattern of your opponents' play, which will allow you to be a play ahead, not just anticipating and not a play behind.

The Phones Should Never Be Left Unattended   When hand held or table phones are utilized, it is not unusual that a coach on the sideline will leave a phone unattended in order to take care of some detail or talk to a player. A manager, an injured player, the backup quarterback, a defensive signal caller or someone else should be assigned specifically to the phone at all times so that if a coach puts down a phone someone else monitors it immediately. Other than the communication system going out of order, it is most exasperating for a coach in the press box to want to communicate with someone on the field and find the sideline phone unattended. Conversely, while it is imperative the press box coaches get to the locker room quickly at half-time, if one departs before the end of the half in order to be in the locker room when the squad gets there, the other should remain in the booth on the phone until the second quarter terminates. A crisis may occur right before the half and a sideline coach requesting help from his colleagues in the scouting booth expects to receive a reply. When no one is in the booth, problems on the sideline are inevitable, and so are staff problems between the two coaches. Leaving your post is not responsible coaching.

Time-outs

The purpose of a time-out is to rest, get a mouthful of water, get organized, adjust equipment, get some advice or help on offense or defense depending on the situation at the time, and/or possibly discuss strategy with the quarterback or the defensive signal caller. What occurs during your time-outs?

Do you know what your players on the field are doing or talking about during a time-out, or do you assume they know what to do? Several may be bickering among themselves or one might be ripping up another teammate because he has missed an assignment, block, or tackle, dropped a pass, or has committed some other mistake. They may be doing just the opposite of what you want them to be doing if you have never informed your players of the purpose of time-outs.

As for the quarterback or defensive signal caller who comes to the sideline during the time-out, who talks to him? Sometimes every coach on the sideline may attempt to give the player advice, which may be in conflict with your advice. As part of your plan, your staff should know before the first game of the season who talks strategy with your quarterbacks and defensive signal callers. If a player needs help, you should give him something definite. Be a decision maker. You want to feel reasonably certain that your quarterback or defensive signal caller will believe you have made the right decision. While your decision or choice may be wrong, its chance for success is greater if the player believes in what you say. On the other hand, if you lack poise and confidence in making even a right decision, its chance for success may not be great if the player perceives that you have self-doubts or are hesitant and confused. If several coaches have talked with your quarterback or defensive signal caller, he may return to the huddle more confused than when he came to the sideline for aid.

Planning for Tactical Situations

Tactical situations that must be planned for in advance, and a staff must be on the alert for the following:

1. A sudden change from offense to defense or vice versa.
2. Scoring suddenly and having to make a decision on whether to attempt for two points or one. If a two-point play, pass or run?
3. In fourth and less than a yard situations *near* midfield, when do you *not* punt the football on fourth down but decide to attempt to go for the first down? Your play in this situation?
4. With a critical third down play coming up, when do you attempt the field goal or the touchdown on fourth down?
   Do you know the maximum distance range of your field goal kicker?
   If going for the field goal attempt, is the kicker up with his kicking shoe on?
   Does he have the kicking tee? Who makes the substitution?
5. Do you need to take a time-out to regroup?

Each of these decisions is necessary. Do you have a plan? Who is responsible for the decision and its execution?

Strategical Planning

While offensive (Chapter 8), defensive (Chapter 9), and kicking game (Chapter 10) phases of football will be discussed in greater detail, here are several critical situations that require long-range strategical planning; these are *musts*, which have to be accomplished either to win a game or to prevent an opposition from scoring or getting out of a hole. Obviously all must be practiced in advance, too, so they can be activated when necessary during a game.

Two-minute Offense   This situation occurs near the end of the first half or toward the termination of the game. Below are variables that must be taken into consideration:

1.   What is the field position?
2.   How many time-outs left?
3.   Are we ahead or behind? Do we bleed the clock or kill it?
4.   Do we need a touchdown or will a field goal win for us?
5.   If we score, do we need the try for point? If so, one or two points?
6.   What substitutions will we need? Who makes them?
7.   If ahead late in the game back deep in our danger zone, can we take a safety?

One coach who had never drilled his team in practice on taking a safety found that he wanted his team to give up a safety late in a game, which would have meant a 6–2 victory for his team. He merely yelled to his quarterback to "take a safety." The quarterback pretended he was going to pass, was tackled from the blind side, fumbled at the 2-yard line, the opposition recovered, called time, then scored and kicked the extra point, winning the game 7–6.

After a safety does your team know how and where to line up for the free kick or to receive the free kick?

Two-minute Defense   This is the counterpart of the two-minute offense. Whether on offense or defense, a team must be drilled to keep its poise and not panic. Below are variables that must be taken into consideration:

1.   What is our field position?
2.   How many time-outs left?
3.   Are we ahead or behind?
4.   What type of quarterback do we face? Dropback? Scrambler?
5.   How strong is our defense? Do we blitz or play prevent?

6. What substitutions do we make?
7. What do they need: field goal or touchdown? If touchdown, do they need try for point. If so, one point or two?
8. How do we bleed the clock? How do we kill the clock?

If a team is behind, the clock becomes the enemy, not the opposition. If a team is ahead, the clock becomes the ally. Therefore, the team ahead should try to bleed the clock using as much time as possible, and the team behind tries to kill the clock.

Each team's scoring zone and danger zone offense and defense require strategical and tactical planning, too. Each is considered briefly below.

Scoring Zone or Goal Line Offense (Going In)   You must have plans for when the ball is slightly beyond the 10-yard line and at varying distances between the goal line and the 10-yard line. In the former the objective is to get a first down and then the touchdown; in the latter you need to score as a first down is not attainable. Basically, you should know your best offense and your best back behind your best blocker(s) against the opposition's weakest or least experienced player from the 11-, 9-, 4- and 2-yard lines. You must also know your best third and one and fourth and one short yardage plays, and whether the opposition's coverage is man or zone.

Goal Line Defense Versus Opposition's Scoring Zone Offense   Ball or field position and the short yardage situations are the same as above, only your team is now defending their goal. You must know the opposition's tendencies from past performances so that you will know where they are most likely to attack. You must plan in advance to defense and stop what the opposition does best in this area. You must know whether where, when, and how you can overload and blitz.

Danger Zone Offense (Coming Out)   From the offensive standpoint your attack is most limited in this part of the field due to your poor field position. Basically, you are trying to run safe plays to attain several consecutive first downs in order to punt the ball beyond the 50-yard line. The possibility of sustaining a drive for ninety yards for a score is prohibitive, unless by chance your team happens to break a long gainer in the series. With the football back on your own 1-yard line, you must get to the 3-yard line in order to use spread punt to kick out of the end zone. If you are forced to close down offensive line splits or you cannot employ spread punt, your punt coverage is likely to be poor and unless the opposition fumbles the return they should be in excellent field position immediately. You may be forced to punt on third down to alleviate the all-out punt rush, which would mean only two downs to get out to the 3-yard line. When backed up deep in your own territory you have at best only three downs to make the necessary yardage before punting.

Danger Zone Defense Versus Opposition's Danger Zone Offense   Your objective is to force the opposition to punt the ball to your team so that you will receive possession in excellent field position. However, your objective is *not* to shut off the opposition for no gain on each play when you are defending the long part of field. Several first downs still will not aid your opposition to any great extent, as long as your team keeps them in the three-down zone in which they must punt on fourth down. You must guard against the long gainer, forcing the opposition to hammer away and possibly to mishandle the football or to gamble. Therefore, you must be most careful about playing tight short yardage defenses and man coverage too frequently. From scouting you should know their offensive running game tendencies in this situation, as well as whether they employ play action passes or attempt to throw long. Defend all of the field since your goal is to your team's back; do not play so tight and close to the line of scrimmage that it is impossible to cut off the long gainer if the ball carrier or receiver gets outside or beyond the defensive perimeter. Percentage football usually pays off for the defensive team in this situation.

HALF-TIME PLANNING AND ORGANIZATION

The half-time break is a time to rest, repair equipment, and make the necessary adjustments in the game plan from pre-game and the first half performance. Half-time procedures should be formalized.

Time Factor

Knowing the total time available is essential to proper planning. The duration of half-time is set by rules, but it will vary in length. Assign a manager to find out in advance the length of half-time so you can plan accordingly.

The manager should open the locker room early and should have included in his pre-game check the availability and presence of a blackboard and chalk. It is too late to start looking for chalk at half-time.

Players

When the players first arrive in the locker room they should take care of their personal needs, get equipment repaired or replaced, and sit or lie down. The managers can help the equipment attendant and trainer in these functions, freeing the trainer to adjust injury pads, tape, or retape players, and so on.

Staff

While this is taking place the offensive and defensive coaches should get together with their scouting booth counterparts in different areas of the dressing room to go over factual data and formulate an offensive/defensive and special teams plan for the second half. Typically the head coach is involved in the decision-making process.

Coaches should then meet with their players to answer questions, make adjustments, and present the changes for the second half. Splitting in smaller groups allows the respective units' members to go over the plan in greater detail and allows for more questions and explanation.

Head Coach

The third period of the half-time should be free for the head coach to make remarks that he feels are appropriate for the second half. He may be factual and unemotional or highly emotional. However, whatever his approach, it should be real—the head coach should be speaking not acting.

Do not bring your squad out too early. Have a manager check the field. Check with the official. You do not want to stand waiting for bands to clear the field.

POST-GAME PLAN

After the game the coach must have a plan of what he will say to his players, as well as to the press.

Closing the locker room to the public for a short time after the game allows you and your players to settle down before meeting the press, parents, friends, and other interested parties. It is prudent to select your words with care and not fall prey to "hoof and mouth" disease. If you have made an unwise statement you may regret having done so. Do not be overly critical of an individual or overpraise him, as the game film may not support your claim.

Remember: Whatever *we* do *we* do together. *We* win and *we* lose. Not I win and you lose. Keep it all in the perspective of we and us. Give praise and take blame. Be complimentary when winning and losing, but if losing get to work on correcting your team's mistakes and errors.

Check Injuries

Before leaving check your injuries. Be sure treatment is started promptly. Many players think something is minor and it well may be; however, getting treatment promptly may return a player to action much more quickly.

Compile and Check Statistics

These will be of aid in writing up a post-game evaluation. Consider your offense and defense, your opponent's offense and defense. How did you win? How did they win? Did the other team beat itself? Did you beat them? Did you beat yourselves? Did they beat you?

Each coach writing the same type of evaluation for his specialty will help in correcting mistakes for next week and for next year's game with the same opponent, too.

Know what they did offensively that hurt your team. Know what they did defensively that hurt your team. Where did you fail in strategy, execution, or personnel? All of these facts when properly evaluated, recorded, and utilized will help you to build a better football team.

8 OFFENSIVE FOOTBALL MISTAKES AND ERRORS, AND HOW TO AVOID THEM

While you may err in favoring and adopting an offensive system that proves ineffective because you do not have the necessary personnel to operate it, a greater error is not to have an offensive philosophy but merely a collection of plays from different offensive systems. While a coach should study football all ways and always, at some point he must come to some sort of agreement with himself and formulate a philosophy as to what he believes and what he will teach and coach offensively and defensively. Offensive football will be considered in this chapter, and defensive football discussed in the next.

Oftentimes when a novice coach accepts his first position his knowledge is likely to be limited to the positions he himself has played. The offense and defense he employs usually will be what he was most familiar with as a college and/or professional player. His administrative philosophy may come from what he liked or did not like as a high school or college player, and at best it will have many gaps, which can usually only be filled by experience.

From these basics through experience, attending clinics, reading books, studying the game, and exchanging ideas with other coaches, he will grow professionally and he will add to his football knowledge and expertise. After a time there will be some original facets he still does and believes in, others will have changed. In all of this the starting point is having a foundation on which to build, and a young coach might do well to examine himself and answer the following questions: "What do I know best?" "What can I teach best?" From that point on, it is merely a matter of filling in the gaps, adopting, adjusting, and discarding as he goes along. Times and events will bring changes but the parts are easy to fit together when he has a basic plan as a foundation.

OFFENSIVE SYSTEMS

There are many excellent offensive systems employed in modern-day football. Each is a complete package that may function on game day like a smoothly running machine scoring touchdowns. Some teams are run oriented and aggressively attack with the run. Others put the football in the air from literally anywhere on the field. Yet if another team were to adopt the total offense of one of these successful teams, they might be totally ineffective in running that particular offense.

What would cause this? A coach may be competent, well organized, manage his time well, have meaningful practices, yet not accomplishing the desired results of winning regularly. Some of the reasons and variables, which frequently are not considered by a novice coach or one with limited experience, are discussed below.

Personnel

The primary consideration of an offensive system is player personnel. Systems themselves do not win football games, people do. And the people facet needs complete study. You feel you know your players. You have weighed, measured, and timed them. You know their exact heights, weights, and speeds. You know how agile and quick they are. However, do they fit the slots and abilities required to play the particular offense you are utilizing or you anticipate using? Do you have the personnel necessary to make your offense effective?

The priority you establish for slotting your defensive people will also have a bearing on the people available for your offensive unit. If you load your defensive unit with quickness as opposed to strength, what physical qualities do your offensive personnel possess? With a big strong line, you might employ shoulder and power blocking; with a smaller quicker line your bread and butter might lie in the scramble and reach blocking scheme.

Quarterback Probably no one person will influence the style of play you employ as will your quarterback. This is especially true at the high school level since you cannot recruit or draft replacements.

Flexibility

"A coach should teach what he knows best" is an old, and true, axiom in coaching. However, a successful coach will adjust what he knows best to the talents of his people. Many offensive philosophies can be adjusted utilizing the same offensive sets with a slightly different offensive emphasis as personnel dictates. A classic example is found in John McKay's and John Robinson's USC Trojans over the years. Even though colleges can recruit players to fit systems unforeseen events often occur. Injuries, athletic ineligibility, and other unexpected events occur that force adjustments to be made. The Trojans have shown how these educated adjustments may be made without losing continuity in the program, as has been evidenced in the strong tailback attack, long a USC feature, coupled with an extremely well-balanced pass offense.

A Total New Concept?

A coach should be wary of going to a whole new style of play just because he *thinks* it would be the right thing to do. Each year coaches attend clinics and become intrigued by a new offensive concept that has been successful for some other coach. He may quickly evaluate his personnel, check his clinic notes, and put in this great plan that he hopes will lead his team to an undefeated season. Halfway through the season he may still be looking for his first win. Such an approach usually leads to disaster. Before going into a complete change, a coach must learn all that he can about every aspect of a new concept. He should study film, talk to coaches who have used and played against this offense. If possible, he should visit colleges where this theory has been a success and find out as much as he can before making a complete switch. The application of this principle applies to all areas from plays to blocking schemes to drills and strategy. In a complete switch many questions will arise the first year no matter how well prepared you are, but they may be somewhat minimized by a thorough study prior to the change. The coach must sell himself totally, then sell his staff and players on his philosophy. To do this he must have the answers, and these will not be found in brief clinic notes or in books.

After convincing himself and his staff, a head coach must then assign specific duties in the overall program to his assistants—they in turn must become experts if the offensive attack is to be effective.

As basic and fundamental as this sounds, there have been major college coaches at name institutions who switched from successful running attacks to passing attacks, or vice versa, and they and their staffs have not understood fully the total new offense they were adopting.

A major college coach, for example, recruited an outstanding passer with the idea of going to a wide open passing game. After several years of so-so seasons the coach reverted back to his running game, which had been and again became outstanding. In the final game of his senior year, the outstanding passing quarterback had been relegated to holding for extra points while a quarterback with limited passing ability successfully ran options and directed a running attack.

The opposite of this situation is also true: a college coach changed from a highly successful passing attack to the wishbone. After his team lost its third consecutive game at the start of the season, the coach switched back to a passing attack and his team won five of its last eight games.

Know What Your Offense Can and Cannot Do   Another important factor to consider is knowing what the offense can and cannot do. Take, for example, the wishbone: It *can* control the ball taking time off the clock making long drives for touchdowns. But does it have the flexibility to play catch-up without breaking the wishbone set? If you must break the set are you as effective? Have you practiced this phase sufficiently since you may be forced to break your offensive set late in the game when you are behind.

Weather

A consideration often overlooked by many coaches is the effect that their local weather might have in the consistency of their offense week in and out. This might only hold true in the selection of a pass-predominated offense in extremely rainy or cold areas of the country.

Learning: KISS (Keep It Simple Stupid)

Simplicity is essential but needs to be defined. The individual learning abilities and experience of the players, the teaching ability of the staff, combined with tradition, motivation, and many other factors will determine what is simple or complicated for your situation. Simplicity will vary from one program to another but one guiding caution would be this: what you and your staff feel is simple must be put into the perspective of the players. It is what they can execute that will win. No provision is made on the scoreboard for theory or what you have attempted to teach. What you have taught and what your players have learned will be reflected in the final score.

Avoid and Eliminate Mistakes   Keep to the basics if you cannot get your ideas across to your squad. Even though your offensive system may be outstanding you can only progress as rapidly as your players can learn. Players must play aggressively to win, and they will not be aggressive if they are confused or are uncertain in what to do. Football games are won by aggressiveness and execution. You must force things to happen; make the other team throw the interception, fumble, or push the panic button. You cannot accomplish these objectives when your players are making mental or physical errors.

Time

As the management of time is a factor in the total program, it is an important factor in offensive planning. As we indicated in Chapter 6, typically a larger portion of time is allotted to practicing offensive football than to the other phases of the game. No matter how large a time block is allotted, however, seldom will it be sufficient. Therefore the coach should study, evaluate, and eliminate any offense that prevents a maximum effort on the basics.

Master the Basic Attack

Repetition is essential to proper execution. Repetition builds confidence and self-assurance in the minds of the players. The elimination of doubt both mental and physical demands repetitive practice and drive, which take time. Therefore, any offensive plays that are not utilized, including gadget plays that are practiced but never used, should be eliminated. Anything that detracts from the basic execution of the offense should be eliminated.

Too Much Offense Most coaches probably have too much offense, which is like a false security blanket in that a coach wants plays for every situation. Timing and execution are the primary factors that make an offensive play successful. If you have seven running plays and seven pass plays in your offense, you must practice these diligently to get perfection and proper execution. If you have twice that number, as an illustration, you will *not* have sufficient time to practice all of those plays to perfection. Any play you do not have time to practice sufficiently will never be executed well. The team timing and execution will not be good enough to ensure consistent play. Therefore, even the minimal time you devote to that play is wasted time that can be utilized better elsewhere. Most coaches should decrease their number of plays in order to devote more time to increasing the execution of the plays that remain in their offense.

Confusion must be eliminated as a confused player does not play aggressively. It is much better to be able to execute a few plays well against all of the defenses you encounter than to have a whole repertoire of plays and not execute any of them well.

Consistency

Consistency in your offensive attack is essential to acquire winning results. It is important that the offense you employ gives your team consistency of ball control enabling it to stay ahead of your down-and-distance formula. Typically in the three-down zone where you will be punting on fourth down you must average slightly more than three-and-a-third yards per try; in the four-down zone, two-and-a-half yards per try. Consequently, this demands the elimination of the bad play. The bad play or the play that puts you in the hole may be eliminated only by the proper amount of repetition to master the techniques involved. Again, this takes time.

Penalties, fumbles, and pass interceptions are key factors in destroying the consistency of an offensive football team, and great effort must be taken to avoid these miscues and turnovers.

Eliminate Fumbles   If there is a fumble in practice between the center and quarterback, or when the quarterback is handing off or pitching out to another back, or between two offensive players trying to exchange the ball on a reserve or punt return, the error should be corrected immediately. In a game the mistake should be remedied as soon as possible after determining why the fumble occurred. It is of little value merely to blame a player for his mistake. It is equally of little value for a player to say, "My mistake," if no effort is made to determine why the error occurred and how it can be rectified.

A team simply cannot win if its players are indifferent about fumbles. They must be conditioned to the fact that when a player does fumble, either he is careless or he may lack courage. If it is carelessness, it must be corrected as a player with an indifferent attitude is not going to contribute much to team success. If it is fear, it is highly questionable whether he should be playing football.

Eliminate Interceptions   While it is virtually impossible not to throw interceptions on occasion, an effort must be made to cut down on them. An interception occurs because of poor throwing by the quarterback, poor pass protection by the linemen and backs, poor routes run by receivers, and/or poor passing strategy.

Pass interceptions are inevitable at times, despite the fact you work hard not to have them. If a team has an interception, as bad as it is, this is not the time to panic and abandon your passing game. A coach should, however, try to correct the mistake when an interception is thrown and try to instill even more confidence in the passing game.

While pass interceptions do not signal the end of the game, the responsible player cannot be indifferent. Such indifference will defeat a team.

Eliminate Penalties   On a single play, a key penalty in a critical situation can often determine the final outcome of a game. A mentally alert football team sustains few penalties. However, when a player is tired or tries to slough off and take the easy way in performing a technique, when he is uncertain of his assignment, or when he fails to concentrate 100 percent on his task or has a mental lapse, usually he will sustain a penalty for his teammates. Also, when a team is disorganized the incidence of penalties is more frequent.

The consistency and efficiency of the offensive attack is destroyed by fumbles, missed or broken assignments, interceptions, blocked punts, and penalties. The holding penalty, in particular, is especially disastrous. It is not only a violation of the rules and the spirit of the game, it is also a grievous error for a coach to fail to correct this particular violation. Very few coaches have a 15-yard gainer per attempt in their offensive attack to offset the penalty sustained by an offensive player who admits to his teammates, the opposition, officials, and spectators, that the only way he can handle his opponent is to hold him.

The above mistakes and errors occur many times because a player has not been oriented as to their importance. They also occur because of indifference, or because a player is not in the best physical condition and gets tired. It is better to work initially to prevent mistakes that draw penalties from occurring, than it is to have to work to correct those mistakes afterward. To do neither is poor coaching.

Offensive Balance: Run-Pass/Pass-Run

To be consistent, the offense must have balance between the running and passing games. This definition of balance determines the coach's philosophy of offense. Balance is not necessarily a 50-50 split but rather could be weighted in any degree in one direction or the other.

Basically there are two theories of acquiring balance in an offensive attack. First, establish a strong running game and use the pass to give the offense balance. The passing attack is usually based on play action passes. Second, build a strong passing attack that gains its balance from pass related plays, such as the optimal use of draw plays and various screen passes that correlate with the type of passes being thrown. As an illustration, if you employ straight dropback passes, basically your draws and screens are off of straight dropback action in order to simulate pass and to complement your dropback passing attack.

Each coach must have a feeling for some point of departure for his philosophy. Once this point has been established and weighed against his available personnel, the team's opposition becomes a situational variable that must be considered.

Strengths and Weaknesses: Offense versus Defense The various strengths and weaknesses of your opponents' defenses should be considered in the selection of your offensive attack for a particular game. The types of defense utilized by the coaches of the teams you play may be grouped in terms of similarities. Then you can establish what attack to employ to move the ball with consistency. Your opponents' overall personnel must also be considered in your master planning. In a league where you are totally outclassed by physical or program size, your only chance may be to go to a wide open offense. If your personnel is comparable, then you may choose a more conservative style of attack.

While the individual strengths and weaknesses of your opponents' players also will be considered in formulating each game plan, you must be cognizant of the fact that if you are forced to try to defeat your opponent "left-handed"—that is, trying to win by utilizing the passing game when your team is not proficient in these skills—you are gambling, not playing percentage football. Such a move is likely to cause more problems for your team than it does for the opposition, although on occasions you must try to utilize a different offensive approach if your personnel does not match up to your opponent's. There are those, however, who feel that a coach should always remain with what his players execute best because the chances of winning, although minimal, are greater than if the coach tries to win by changing tactics totally. Each coach must make this decision, and your opposition cannot be discounted. It is not the X's and O's on paper or the blackboard that counts, but it is the height, weight, and skills of each individual those X's and O's represent that is most important and must be considered offensively and defensively.

Overpredominant Running Attack The dangers inherent in adopting a predominant running attack usually are found near the end of the half and in the fourth quarter when considerable time is typically necessary to sustain a ground attack drive and the clock becomes your enemy. If your attack lacks balance, your team is behind, and you must try to defeat your opposition left-handed, your team must go away from what they do best. When you switch to another mode of attack, not infrequently your players will lose confidence quickly if the attack is not successful. You are now faced with the dilemma of neither mode of attack being effective, your players likely having lost confidence in both passing and running, and your team being now unable to execute and perform effectively in order to score.

Overpredominant Passing Attack   Few teams have ever won championships strictly with a predominant passing attack at any level of competition. Generally teams that rely heavily on the pass are handicapped by weather and/or their inability to run time off the clock by sustaining a drive and maintaining ball control when playing keep-away is essential to protecting a slim lead. When they are behind and must score to win, their opposition need be little concerned about defensing a nonexistent running attack, save draws, which means the percentage lies with the defenders not the blockers. Defense can dig in and come on tough pass rushes knowing that your offense favors throwing the football. The percentages favor the defense not the offense in this situation.

Only-pass or Only-run Effects on Their Own Defense   Another problem in both of the previously mentioned offenses would be found in the effect on their own teams' defenses. It has been estimated that 95 percent of the actual scrimmage time occurs in intrasquad scrimmage. If your offense is run oriented, you have a chance to teach defense. However, if it is pass oriented, it is difficult to establish the jaw-to-jaw situations that are essential in teaching good defense. Conversely, in general run oriented teams are somewhat weaker against the pass, whereas pass oriented teams will suffer in defensing the strong running game.

Flexibility (Multiple Sets)

Consideration must be given to presenting the opponents' defense with as many problems as possible. The opponents are confronted by the same time constraints as you are. They have only a specified amount of time to prepare to defense your offensive attack. A primary goal of any offensive system is ease of learning so that the system can be optimized. This forces the opposition either to spend more time, which they may not have, preparing to defense your offense, or to enter the contest not fully prepared to defense your offense. You can accomplish this by forcing your opponent to make adjustments in order to determine whether his defensive game plan is sound. You might choose to multiply the set theory by using the same basic plays from multiple offensive sets, while forcing the opposing coach to spend time in defending against the *"what if"* principle we discussed previously. Or you utilize multiple series or plays from each set. Or you may use certain basic plays from each set adding *one* or *two* plays to take advantage of the anticipated defensive adjustments to the strengths of your offense.

Illustrations   If you employ the pro-I-set offense with extended motion versus a team that prefers to play *zone* coverage, as an illustration, by sending your "I" back in motion to the side of the split end (X) you now have created a double-wing set, two eligible receivers to each side. Basically, most teams will check to *man* coverage versus the double-wing set since their zone coverage is extended too far and they cannot cover void areas in the defensive secondary. Conversely, if they prefer playing *man* coverage and you send your "I" back strongside toward your tight end (Y) and flanker back (Z), you have created a "trips" situation, which leaves a single defender to cover your split end (X) one-on-one.

While your running attack is limited to a single back (F) off the pro-I-set, when you utilize extended motion you create additional problems by forcing the defense to adjust *after* the play has commenced. If you line up initially in double wing or trips, the defensive team has a chance to adjust immediately. In addition if you also utilize short motion, and your team runs and passes off the pro-I-set, with and without short notice, you create even more problems. The point is you are optimizing your offensive attack with very little more time expended teaching-learning, but the opposition must either devote time in practice learning to adjust to these variations or be taught how to make these adjustments during the game. The latter can result in costly errors and mistakes. The assumption is that you have a passing attack and receivers who are capable of beating defenders one-on-one, your quarterback is capable of getting the football to his receivers, and your receivers are proficient in catching the football. However, if these assumptions are erroneous, then merely putting a back in extended motion limits your offense more than your opponents' defense because the latter need not worry about making pass defense adjustments, and you have limited running attack and blocking power considerably.

Sequence Offense   Regardless of your mode of attack, it must be coordinated completely. A collection of disjointed plays, sometimes referred to as "everyone's favorite eight," should be avoided. The utilization of sequence plays, where one play forces a reaction which in turn sets up a second and possibly third play, should be considered rather than the "grab bag" or "slot machine" approach to devising an offensive theory and system.

Passing Game Mistakes and Errors

The critical mistakes in the passing game are usually centered in protecting the quarterback or receiving errors. However, the passing game like the running game must be designed on the basis of the personnel available to perform the necessary skills. It is also necessary to understand the defensive philosophies of your opponents, which will help you to select the right plays to attack the defense. Therefore, it is important that you recognize defensive alignments and know their strengths and weaknesses. You must also have a knowledge of the personnel necessary to make an offensive system function.

Protection Mistakes and Errors   The method of protection selected must be simple to execute and the team must understand its strengths and weaknesses in terms of what it can and cannot do.

Also, despite the fact you may be fortunate enough to have a quarterback who can handle all types of pass actions and possibly run with the football, too, you must always be cognizant of the teaching-coaching-practicing *time* factor. Otherwise if you attempt to do too much you may end up with a capable quarterback whose skills are not being utilized most effectively. As an illustration, with a running-passing quarterback your passing attack should probably consist of semi-rollouts and rollouts or sprintouts where your quarterback challenges the corner of the defense on the run-pass option, rather than utilizing a straight drop-back passing attack. While your quarterback may be capable of doing the latter, too, you have to allot time to teaching-coaching-practicing all of these skills. It is better to master several and do them well, rather than attempt to do too many and not master any. Also, the protection offered the quarterback is different in these two types of passing attack, as well as in play action passes, so that all of this amounts to a great deal of teaching-coaching and time to perfect.

Quarterback Passing Mistakes and Errors   Most quarterback passing mistakes and errors may be found on the following checklist:

1. *Center-quarterback exchange fumble.* Usually caused by the quarterback pulling away from the center too quickly while getting back to set up. While a quick drop to set up is important, it cannot be at the expense of leaving the football on the ground.
2. *Not setting up at proper depth.* The correct depth is essential as pass protection is predicated on a specific depth.
3. *Forcing the throw.* Trying to throw the football through the defense, rather than in the seams or over the defense, is a common error.
4. *Throwing behind the receiver.* Releasing the ball too late as the result of waiting for a receiver to get open, rather than anticipating the receiver's break on his route. When the receiver breaks, the ball should already be in flight ahead of the receiver's breaking point.
5. *Failing to look off the defense.* Eyeballing the intended receiver all the way leads the defense directly to the football when it is released.

6. *Hanging the ball.* Arching or putting too much air under the ball on the short and intermediate routes in particular allows the defense to cover more ground and intercept it. A good passer must be able to clothesline the short and intermediate passes, and hang the ball for the long pass leading his receiver so that the latter can run under it.

7. *Not certain where he is throwing.* The failure of the quarterback to throw the proper type of pass, which should force the defender to go through the offensive receiver to knock down or intercept the ball. As an illustration, in the sideline pattern the ball should be thrown low and outside, and in the hook or curl pattern the ball should be thrown at the numbers.

8. *Improper ball position.* Not carrying the ball in the proper position for a quick release.

9. *Scrambling.* On dropback protection, your quarterback must stay in the pocket. He should be protected from inside-out and he must be taught to step up and throw rather than scramble and attempt to pass from outside of his pocket protection. When he gets outside of his protection there is the possibility of being tackled from the blind side, being injured, and/or throwing an interception.

10. *Panic.* Some quarterbacks cannot handle the tough defensive rush and they panic by unloading the football throwing it up for grabs. Your quarterback must be disciplined to go up into the pocket, to protect himself, to get whatever yardage he can, and not to unload the football in a tough rough situation when his protection breaks down.

11. *Pass the football, release the string.* While the roll or sprintout pass in particular is easy to execute since the passing motion is like throwing a dart, some quarterbacks complicate the pass by literally trying to hand the football forward to the receiver. They don't release the string, so to speak. The quarterback must have the ball up in position ready to pass or run, depending on the reaction of the corner defender. Basically, "the defender comes, I pass; he covers, I run," is the rule the quarterback applies.

12. *On sprintouts to the left side,* a right-handed quarterback must get deeper and square up his shoulders in order to throw more accurately.

13. *On bootleg plays toward the split end,* your passer must pull up quickly and be set to throw immediately in the event of a tough rush from the split end's (X) side, since your interior lineman (usually a guard) may not be quick enough to block the corner defender and protect your quarterback on a tough rush.

Each of the above mistakes is correctable but requires concentrated attention to detail by both quarterback and his coach.

The rationale for pass offense is not found merely in the number of passes your team completed and the total yards gained by passing, but in the passes completed when your team needed yardage to keep a drive alive or to maintain momentum, and in the passes that resulted in touchdowns or field goals.

Receiver Mistakes and Errors   Errors that lead to incomplete passes and interceptions are numerous. In almost every case, however, the mistakes and errors receivers make are correctable. An effective coach's job is to recognize these errors and mistakes and to correct them. Some of the mistakes are independent in that the receiver causes them; in others he may be just a contributing factor. The following are common mistakes and errors made by receivers in running pass routes and in attempting to catch the football.

1. *Improper alignment.* A receiver must align himself correctly for the formation type of route called and the secondary coverage anticipated. Generally he would oversplit the inside route and undersplit the outside route. Blocking assignments would also dictate his split. Consequently he must constantly vary his alignment to disguise his intent. He must be coached diligently in the latter so as not to tip off his intent.

2. *Improper stance.* Several different stances are acceptable, but vision in to the ball is necessary to prevent both lining up offside or jumping offside before the snap when crowd noise prohibits hearing the snap count. He should step out immediately on his first step, not false step and then release.

3. *Not getting off.* Not getting off on the count is inexcusable for a wide receiver. As he is looking in to the ball, he must practice some fakes to get off versus bump-and-run and other hold upon delaying tactics.

    A tight end must not be held up. He can move out and/or false block, head fake inside and go outside or vice versa in order to release quickly. A coach must give his receiver these techniques and allow practice time under game-like conditions.

4. *Not shortening pass routes when held up.* Since timing is all important in a passing attack, the receiver being held up must often compensate by shortening his route.

5. *Not varying the approach.* Recognizing the pass coverage and changing the initial leg of the route without affecting timing is essential. The receiver must make something happen in terms of the defense's reaction.

6. *Not making sharp cuts.* Not being able to make sharp cuts

and get to the football usually is a result of not running under control. The latter means running as fast as you can and still be able to make your cut. A receiver should run from the waist down not overstriding, to keep his head from bouncing, which affects one's vision in catching the football.

7. *Rounding off and drifting.* Rounding off routes or drifting will cause interceptions. Cuts coming back to the ball should be sharp, for example, into the sideline on the sideline route. If the quarterback starts to scramble, the receiver should come back toward his quarterback and run in a parallel plane with him.

8. *Lack of concentration.* More passes are dropped because of the lack of concentration than are poorly thrown. Good passing teams do not drop simple catches and will make some great catches during the course of a football season. The primary reason for dropped passes is the lack of *total* concentration on the football. The forward point of a football gives the receiver a focus point to eyeball in on that is not found in other balls. The point of the ball will tell the receiver about the ball's flight up, down, up or down right, or up or down left. If the ball is tipped the receiver must make an adjustment with his body and hands to catch it. If he is not concentrating on the point of the football, he must first locate the new flight of the ball then move to catch it.

9. *Failure to catch with hands.* There have been some great cradle or body receivers in football, but the leaping body adjustment is not as easy to make as simply moving one's hands to catch the football. The hands can react quicker and will cushion the ball more readily than the body. It is also impossible to run and gain yardage with both feet in the air. Hand position is important.

General rules are: When coming back to or facing the passer and the ball is thrown below the waist, the receiver's thumbs should be pointed *outward* when catching the football, *inward* when the ball is to be caught above the waist. When running away from the pass, the ball should be caught with the hands cradled, little fingers in and thumbs pointed outward.

10. *Failure to find ball.* The ability to turn one's head and pick up the flight of the ball, looking over the opposite shoulder from where one expected the ball to be thrown, is essential. Most receivers favor a particular shoulder, but the ability to adjust can be made with daily practice.

11. *Running before you catch.*   Catch the ball first and then put

it away and run with it. Some receivers try to run before catching the ball first. Others hear "feet" (defenders) closing on them and do not concentrate on catching the football because they are more concerned about being tackled. As a result, the pass may be on target but the receiver fails to catch it.

12. *Failure to fight for the ball.* Pride is the key here. A receiver must want the football more than the defenders do.

13. *Failure to put ball away.* A receiver may make an outstanding reception but fumble the football after running with it. Proper ball carrying technique must be coached to avoid fumbles.

14. *Failure to get the necessary yardage.* Once a receiver has caught the ball first, he becomes a ball carrier driving for all the extra yardage he can obtain. He must make every effort to get the necessary yardage for first down to maintain offensive possession. It is important that before the receivers release from the line of scrimmage they all know the yardage necessary for a first down.

Training and Coaching Your Quarterbacks

Each coach must decide whether he or his quarterback is going to call the plays. If the coach does it, then he merely sends in plays with messengers or flashes them from the sideline. While there are advantages and disadvantages to both methods, it is suggested one or the other be adopted; a combination of the two methods with both quarterback and coach calling the plays may eventually lead to problems, especially in critical third down situations and/or when the team is coming out of the danger zone or going in from the scoring zone. During the course of a game a coach may make several of these situational calls from the sideline. It is very likely your quarterback will expect to receive help on such calls each time a similar situation arises. The problem then is who is going to call the play. The quarterback may be expecting the coach to make it, and the coach may be expecting his quarterback to go ahead and call the play. The more aid you give your quarterback from the sideline, the less competent he is likely to be in selecting plays during the game. Regardless of the method you utilize, your quarterbacks should understand why you have chosen it. If your method is to have your quarterback call the plays, you cannot assume he will call a good game. Although the entire procedure may appear relatively clear and simple to you, an inexperienced quarterback in particular does not grasp the picture as readily and as clearly. It takes much time and patience to train the quarterbacks, but patience is one of the attributes of a good teacher and a good coach.

Three Types of Quarterbacks   Basically, there are three types of quarterbacks: the quarterback who makes positive mistakes; the quarterback who works to avoid mistakes; and the quarterback leader who directs his team to maximum results.

The quarterback who makes positive mistakes is not a student of the game. He makes frequent critical errors because of his disregard for basic principles of generalship. As a result his team loses frequently because the opposition generally capitalizes on his mistakes. He destroys the morale and spirit of his own teammates. His philosophy is not dissimilar to that of the typical "armchair quarterback," the football fan. If you are his coach, you have done a poor teaching job.

The "common sense" quarterback works to avoid mistakes. Since he sticks to the rules and principles that you have taught, he tends to be conservative in his quarterbacking. Although he is not brilliant in his offensive quarterbacking, he is dependable and does not make glaring errors. Such sound generalship is bound to win in the long run. As his coach you have done an average or possibly a better than average job in training this type of quarterback.

The quarterback who directs his team to maximum results is an outstanding leader and student of the game. His thinking is logical and he studies the game all ways and always. He possesses the necessary and desirable attributes to be an outstanding leader and quarterback. As his coach you have done an outstanding job in selecting and training this type of quarterback.

Horizontal Zones of Play   A more detailed discussion of quarterback play is beyond the scope of this book as this subject itself merits full book treatment. One tool for quarterback training is shown in Diagram 8–1, which simulates a football field showing the horizontal zones of play. Since our book does not include specific offensive systems, a coach may wish to pencil in on Diagram 8–1 the specific running plays and passes in his offense that would be utilized in the three- and four-down zones of play, especially those in his danger zone and scoring zone, where there should be no mistakes in play selection and player execution.

The importance of acquiring and maintaining field position must be stressed constantly to all of your players. An inexperienced player in particular is likely to feel that every play should be designed to score a touchdown, and when this does not occur he and others may feel his offense is not a good one. Where you obtain possession of the football is the key. The closer you are to your own goal line, the more restricted is your offense. You do not want to set up any "cheap" touchdowns for your opponents. Your objective is to make at least several successive first downs before being forced to turn over possession of the football by punting. If you gain possession on your 25-yard line and your opponent regains possession on your 45-yard line, one first down puts your opposi-

DIAGRAM 8–1
A Quarterback's Map of Horizontal Zones of Play·

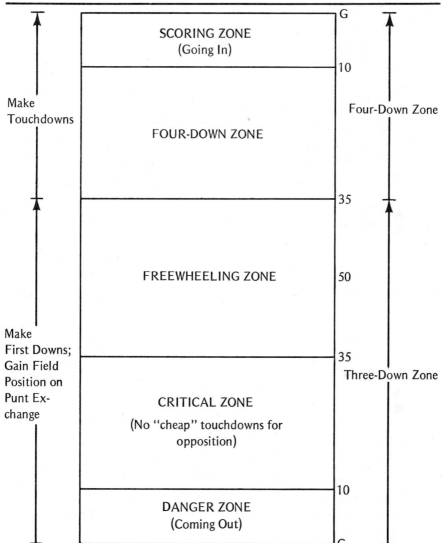

Make
Touchdowns

Make
First Downs;
Gain Field
Position on
Punt Ex-
change

SCORING ZONE
(Going In)

G

10

Four-Down Zone

FOUR-DOWN ZONE

35

FREEWHEELING ZONE

50

35

Three-Down Zone

CRITICAL ZONE

(No "cheap" touchdowns for
opposition)

10

DANGER ZONE
(Coming Out)

G

tion in *his* four-down zone and his chances of scoring have increased by 25 percent. The probability of a team driving seventy-five to eighty yards for a touchdown without stopping themselves is slim, but you want to make at least several first downs before punting the football to the opposition in his part of the field. You must gain field position each time possession of the football is exchanged through playing touch defensive football and having a strong kicking game (see Chapters 9–10).

Give Your Reserve Quarterbacks Experience Every year coaches are faced with the critical situation where, because of injury, the backup quarterback must enter the game. Your second quarterback should be well trained in running the offense, even though he may not be as proficient as your first stringer in the overall picture. He may not have the same skills as your regular quarterback and, therefore, may not be able to run the same offense. As an illustration, your first quarterback passes well but your second does not. It would be a mistake to try to continue your passing game attack with your backup quarterback since he is not skilled in passing.

If the situation arises where a third quarterback must enter the game, it could be disastrous. Operating the total plan becomes impossible as he probably has not practiced with the first team to any appreciable extent, and as a result he probably has not paid too much attention to the game plan. To ensure a greater chance for his and the team's success, provide a period each week in practice to polish a four-play series that the third quarterback handles best.

OFFENSIVE COMMUNICATIONS

The first step after establishing the basic offensive plan is to define the communication patterns that are essential to facilitate the learning and execution process.

Terminology

One of the basic premises for total effectiveness is the establishment of basic terminology. It is important that coaches and players are on the same wave length with regard to the meanings of football terms. Understandable terminology will facilitate learning, ensure comprehension, and minimize communication chaos. Terminology must not be long or wordy but should be short and concise giving clear mental pictures.

Whenever possible the *same* terminology and meanings should be utilized in the offensive, defensive, and kicking games, although the terms "right" and "left" generally are used to indicate direction or the strength of the formation *as seen from the offensive and defensive viewpoints.*

Illustrations An offensive set may be identified as "I"-*right*, which is an "I" backfield with the tailback or running back (R) directly behind his fullback (F), the strength of the offensive line right with the tight end (Y) on the right side, and the flanker back (Z) split out to the formation's right offensively. From a defensive viewpoint, the call would be

"I"-*left* since the strength of the offensive set which they are defensing is to the *defense's* left. Not all verbal transitions are this simple, however.

Terminology should be recorded in the coaches' and players' notebook, and everyone should learn and utilize the proper terminology in meetings and on the field. This principle is applicable to drills, pass routes, and all other football nomenclature. While offensive and defensive coaches may differ to a limited extent in their terminology, since terms depend on how the offensive or defensive players view a situation, but when one offensive coach identifies a pass route pattern as an "up" and another defensive coach describes the *same* route as a "fly" pattern, or one calls a drill "challenge" and another calls the *same* drill "hamburger," confusion ensues. It also implies to the players that the coaches are not well organized. In these particular illustrations *all* offensive and defensive coaches should identify the pass route and the drill using the *same* agreed upon terminology.

Signal System

The offensive signal system should be designed as easy for the players involved to learn. Some coaches devise complicated systems that are not easily comprehended or mastered by their players. While their offensive system may seem logical to the coaches, inexperienced players in particular do not perceive the signal system in this manner. The result is hesitancy, broken plays, ineffective performance, errors, mistakes, and turnovers, since a confused player cannot perform aggressively when uncertain and confused as to his assignment.

Numbers and/or Terms   Some coaches prefer to number their backs and the holes or gaps in the offensive line, so that play 26, as an illustration, indicates the ball carrier at the critical point of attack. To this may be added terms such as "power" and "pass," as illustrations, so that 26 Power indicates power blocking at the point of attack, and 26 Power Pass indicates a play action pass off of the 26 Power backfield faking action. Other coaches may not identify the ball carrier by number and merely identify the plays above as Power Right or Power Right at 6, and Power Pass Right.

Some coaches categorize their plays in series so that plays 10 through 19 may be the split T series; 20 through 29 equate with their tailback offense; their 30 through 39 plays may be off their belly or ride series, and on and on. Their 80 series may be their rollout and semi-roll series, and their 90 series may be their pocket passes.

No matter what method is used it should be built around player understanding. Simplicity plus the ability to teach it are the keys.

Flip-flopping the Linemen   Hole numbering should also be simple and must be coordinated with your back or series numbering. Some coaches prefer even numbers to the right, odd to the left, or vice versa. Some coaches who flip-flop their lines prefer even numbering *always* to the tight end's (Y) side regardless of whether he lines up right or left, and odd numbering is *always away from* the tight end (Y). As an illustration, in the even right-odd left numbering system, the opposite of 26 Power would be 25 Power. When the line is flip-flopped, 26 Power is always 26 Power right *or* left formation, and the same is true of 25 Power which is always run away from the tight end (Y) toward the split end's (X) side. The latter play can only be run off certain backfield sets where a close slot (Z) back to weakside, which is away from the tight end (Y), now replaces the split end (X) to assist the offside or weakside tackle in the double-team power block. The latter is true regardless of whether or not the line is flip-flopped, but it is included to illustrate the type of exception that is likely to occur in most offensive systems. Also, it entails additional teaching; the more plays that are added to an offense the greater are the chances of compounding the teaching since more exceptions are likely to arise. A simple resolution is to run only 26 Power toward the tight end's (Y) side regardless if he is right or left and you are flip-flopping, and do not run the weakside power play to the offside of the formation off of the pro-I offensive set since you really do not have a play unless X lines up in close like his counterpart tight end (Y). This then amounts to a two tight end offense with an I-pro set backfield when you want to run an effective 26 Power weakside.

Regardless of preference, the numbering system should be simple and coordinated to the total package, and the entire offensive system must be thought through in advance to facilitate teaching and learning and to alleviate the number of exceptions that are likely to arise. Otherwise a coaching staff may end up with a hybrid system with so many exceptions that the desired learning objectives cannot possibly be accomplished.

Huddle

Every play commences in the offensive huddle. If communication is not established here the chances of getting off a productive play are negligible. The lack of huddle discipline, in which players other than the quarterback talk, leads to confusion, miscommunication, and noncommunication.

The huddle where players look at the ground and not at the quarterback's face leads to mistakes in alignment, getting off the ball ahead or late on the snap count, possibly running the wrong play, or going in the wrong direction. If a coach is using a messenger or calling plays from the sideline, the quarterback must have a pre-huddle position with vision to the bench.

Huddle breaks should be designed to get players to their positions with a minimum of confusion. Coaches employing the flip-flop should spend extra time in designing the huddle with this factor in mind. In the case of flip-flopping it is well to consider the difficulty involved in defensive keying a well-designed huddle.

The forming of the huddle is the responsibility of the offensive center, who must be coached and encouraged to take pride in doing this job. The center should take his position opposite the football. He must get back five yards from the line of scrimmage and give the players a point of reference in forming the huddle. If he gets too deep, he walks his teammates too much; too close and the opposition can hear the play and the snap count.

Snap Signal

A snap signal must be simple and meet the needs of the coach's offensive philosophy. The coach might do well to consider the advantages and disadvantages of both the rhythmic and non-rhythmic systems. Proponents of the rhythmic cadence maintain their linemen will fire out quicker than users of the non-rhythmic systems. The non-rhythmic believers maintain that players get off better as a unit.

Regardless of the arguments pro and con, the method used must be developed and practiced under all conditions to be perfected. The non-rhythmic snap signal is easily set to quick calisthenics and drills to get maximum practice in all practice periods.

Automatics

If a coach is employing automatics they, too, should be kept simple. There are many types of audibles in which the quarterback may change the play from one side of the line to another, pass or run, change the blocking, change the play from run to pass.

The difficulty lies in that the players must recognize the new play that has been audibilized and make the required assignment changes. Confusion must be eliminated or an audibilized system can cause more problems for the offense than it does for the opposition's defense. Breaking an assignment or being late in coming off the ball can destroy the timing of the play or result in inconsistency in the offensive attack. It may also result in a turnover of the football to the opposition.

Check with Me   The use of "check with me" tends to help players focus in on the call as the point of attack is designated. The how-to-attack is determined by the quarterback at the line of scrimmage. In the huddle the quarterback says:

> *The formation* (Divide right)
> *"Check with me"* (*Middle trap*, as an illustration)
> *The snap signal*

At the line of scrimmage the quarterback simply reads the guard-linebacker alignment and calls the appropriate trap play to the right or left to take advantage of the defensive alignment or personnel. In this system he might call "check with me six hole"—checking to the power, blast, or straight attack at the six hole, which is the point of attack. Calls may include run or pass calls or any combination of calls, allowing the offensive man to focus on a specific area to attack offensively.

"Hot" Receiver Calls   Some teams incorporate simple "hot" calls to the flankers (X and Z) and to the tight end (Y). As an illustration, the quarterback reads the strong side linebacker on the dog and blitz. If he comes on either in a tough rush, the quarterback yells "hot, hot," alerting his tight end (Y) to the dump pass to him.

OFFENSIVE MISTAKES AND ERRORS

Gadgets

Gadget or trick plays must be minimized and used judiciously. This principle is especially true when tricks are utilized at the expense of the basic attack. The perfection of the gadget play requires the use of valuable practice time. Since a gadget or trick play is usually situational specific in that it is based on a particular team's weakness, there is not much to be gained by repeating it over the length of the entire season. Therefore gadgets should not be used at the expense of the overall plan.

Alignment, Stance, and Splits

Upon breaking the huddle the next possibility for critical errors will be those made by the offensive linebacker.

Improper Alignment   Improper alignment will result from poor huddle communication on the part of the quarterback or from the lack of knowledge or discipline on the part of the individual player. These errors can result in illegal formation penalties, aligning offside, and illegal motion penalties where the offender tries to move back to where he should have lined up initially.

A delay of the game penalty is also a possibility and may even force taking an ill-advised time-out. Constant attention to detail in the practice session will help to avoid these errors. Always having a manager on the line of scrimmage checking offsides will also help. Teaching wide receivers to align with the head lineman's foot will also aid them in their proper alignment so that they should never be offsides.

Improper stance   The offensive lineman's stance is his basic foundation for getting his job done. Usually a sloppy stance occurs because of a lack of discipline or fatigue, but it may be from lack of coaching or from over-coaching. If the player has been taught a basic stance and he is inconsistent in getting in it, you should check your coaching, your player's attitude, and possibly his body build and what you are asking him to do. Some body builds just do not fit into standard stances as regimented by a coach. Fatigue also can be a factor; therefore, the lack of conditioning of the entire squad is something you should consider.

Overcoaching sometimes occurs when you flip-flop the line and demand a stance that requires a player to have his inside foot back in order to better block gap situations. Permit your players to take their most natural stance.

Undercoaching occurs when you become so used to looking at mistakes that you fail to correct them. If you have a reason for what you are doing, coach it and discipline it. Do *not* ignore errors and mistakes.

Failure to Split   Teams using varying splits must constantly be coached to vary their splits in practice sessions. Most young players tend to break the huddle and line up on the defensive man rather than forcing him to adjust to the offensive lineman's split.

Your offensive linemen must know why their splits are important, and often a field demonstration is more valuable than chalk talks or notebook diagrams in conveying that knowledge. Frequently this coaching point is overlooked and many coaches talk about line splits but fail to practice coaching line splits.

Failure of Line Blocking

Blocking by the offensive line is essential for a football offense to succeed. It has been estimated that 90 percent of *all* offensive action is blocking. Proficient blocking fundamentals must be taught. Techniques must be perfected and proper execution mastered if a team is to succeed.

One of the primary failures in offensive line play will be evidenced in *not* evaluating what type of blocks your personnel are capable of performing. A big strong offensive lineman may handle the one-on-one block, as an illustration, while a smaller quicker lineman may have to rely on the scramble block. Personnel of small stature and limited strength may be unable to handle the one-on-one block. They may need assistance with double-team blades. It is foolhardy and wishful thinking to design plays with one-on-one blocking if your personnel is incapable of performing these tasks at the point of attack.

The failure of selecting a proper stance has been discussed previously. However, stance must be based on getting a player in a good fundamental position to explode off the ball, pass block or to pull and trap, and/or to lead interference downfield. The point is that you must analyze *minutely* what you are asking your personnel to perform. Some personnel may not be able to perform to your expectations.

Getting off on the ball is important, and a simple snap count aids greatly in accomplishing this objective. The two advantages that the offense has over the defense are knowing the snap count and knowing the critical point of attack. Since the defense must react after the ball is snapped, the offensive team must get off with the ball in order to optimize fully these advantages.

The maintaining of a master plan checklist is essential to ensuring that all blocks are allocated the time needed for mastery. Offensive line penalties usually occur from a lineman being over eager, undisciplined, using faulty or improper techniques, or from a lack of coaching time. If the offensive line coach pinpoints the reason and takes the proper corrective action, the failure of the offensive linemen to get off together in the snap count can be eliminated.

Explosion off the ball is critical and the failure to do so may come as a result of the center snapping the ball too soon, confusion in blocking assignment, or the lack of work using the actual snap count. Since a snap count alone starts all offensive plays, and a whistle stops all action in football, both should be utilized at all times in practice sessions.

The failure of the feet to follow the blocker is also a common error, as is getting the feet too close together in a narrow base. The inability of a blocker to make contact quickly with his opponent and then to drive through him with power generated by moving his feet and legs are common errors that must be corrected for effective blocking to occur.

Center-Quarterback Exchange

The center-quarterback exchange is the focal point of offensive play. Without a successful exchange there is no play. Therefore it is essential that fumbles in the center-quarterback exchange be eliminated. The ball exchange from the center to the quarterback *must become automatic*. In order for this to occur the center-quarterback exchange must be practiced daily, and the quarterback should not be involved in drills without a center exchanging the football first. A checklist for analyzing possible exchange problems would include *for the center:*

1. Not delivering the football hard and fast to the quarterback's hands.
2. Anticipating the count, snapping the ball before the actual count, which makes the line appear late in getting to their blocks and which allows the defense to react sooner and defeat the offense.
3. Firing the snap late and behind the count, which disrupts the quarterback's mechanics and throws off the timing of the play.
4. Overstriding on the first step causing the ball to miss its usual point of impact, although the quarterback's hands should be riding forward on the snap until he receives the ball.
5. The failure of the coach to work centers practicing with a man on his nose or in the gaps. While your opponents may play an even front, at some point they will be in odd and/or gap alignment(s).

For the quarterback exchange problems include the following:

1. The failure to apply firm upper hand pressure in center's crotch.
2. Poor position of quarterback's bottom hand with thumb or fingers inhibiting the exchange of the football. Also lack of pressure on heels of quarterback's hands allows center snap to split receiving pocket.
3. The quarterback's hands must ride forward with the center's movement on the snap, and his arms must be slightly flexed to allow for the ride forward.

When fumbles occur the coach should check the center first, as quite often the center is carrying the football with him on his first step.

Another consideration when substituting at either of these positions: Have your new center and quarterback exchange several snaps on the sideline before entering the game. As each center and quarterback is different in his technique, it is good practice to rotate them in practice situations so that all your quarterbacks work with all of your centers.

Ball Handling Fumbles

A fumble in the offensive backfield usually is a result of an individual player's action or a combination of two players' actions. Fumbles involving the *quarterback* usually occur because of the following mistakes:

1. Bobbling the snap from his center on the exchange and not having the ball under control at the hand-off point.
2. On an exchange with an offensive back, quarterback hurries and does not place the football in the pocket. He may throw it or place it too high or too low for the receiving back, all of which causes fumbles on the attempted exchange.
3. Not using a soft touch on pitchouts. Pitching the ball erratically to the trail back.
4. Carrying the ball improperly. Not protecting it on running plays.

Ball carrying backs make the following mistakes and errors that cause fumbles:

1. Hitting in too quickly or too slowly to get the proper mesh with the quarterback. This usually occurs as the result of improper depth alignment.
2. Not making the pocket for the quarterback to place the football in by dropping the inside elbow or having poor position of the bottom hand.
3. Taking an improper path to receive the football in the exchange, especially in quick hitting plays up the middle.
4. Failure to concentrate on the ball on pitchouts. Like a receiver catching the ball, a halfback must look the ball all the way into his hands, first catching it before trying to evade tackles and run with it.
5. The depth of the tailback in the "I" is critical. It is important that he be deep enough to be on course when taking the ball from the quarterback.
6. Failure to protect the ball and put it away when running with it.

Also, the failure of the offensive line to control the line of scrimmage allowing penetration destroys backfield timing and execution, which frequently results in fumbles.

Failure to Train the Offensive Captain

The wrong decision in accepting or refusing a penalty can be a critical mistake. An offensive captain should always be aware of the tactical implications involved in deciding to reject or accept a penalty. While one should seldom decline a 15-yard penalty, there are exceptions to almost every rule including this one.

The offensive quarterback is the one player who should be on top of these situations and many coaches prefer to use him to make the decision. The coach who is making all the play calls from the sideline should be aware his quarterback may have turned robot and is not concentrating on the tactical situation but is simply relying on his coach for everything and just waiting for his coach's next call. If this is the case at least one offensive starter should be trained to make penalty decisions. If he has any doubt he should ask the official to go over the options again. He should position himself to see the sideline, and his vision should be directed to his head coach for help.

Make the First Down

The philosophy of making the first down first will take care of scoring touchdowns, field goals, and maintaining good field position. The danger in stressing scoring lies in the team's overlooking the fact that there is no easy way over the long haul. They must recognize that the first down comes first. There is usually a time in every game when a first down is critical to maintain possession or to get the opportunity to score. At such times it is essential to concentrate on getting the primary job done first.

Third Down Success

The ability to capitalize in the majority of third down situations is critical in maintaining ball control and attaining good field position. The team that can top 75 percent in this category enhances considerably its chances of winning. Therefore a coach must study carefully the defenses used by his opponent in all third down situations and design his third down attack accordingly.

Danger Zone (Coming Out)

A consistent offense is a must in the danger zone. Consistency is a play that will yield three yards plus. It is not likely that a team will move the length of the field and score on three-yard plays. However, you can probably move the ball for several first downs and get good position for punting the football. You have traded possession for good field position. Now your opponents must start their offense back in their part of the field where a mistake on their part could be costly.

Two-minute Offense—Basic Philosophy

You must believe in your ability to catch up quickly. There is no more frustrating situation than in being behind with the clock running down and not being able to move the ball. You must conserve time. Therefore it would be well to include your two-minute offense in your basic attack and to practice it more than just five minutes a week. Regardless of the formation you employ, your players must be aware of the how to use the clock and how to bleed it.

The following are ways of *saving the clock:*

All out hustle.
Use your game plan.
Down rolling punts quickly.
Punt out of bounds.
Request measurement when close.
Use time-outs wisely.
Hustle to huddle.
Go on the first count or sound in putting the ball in play.
Quick count.
Throw outside pass patterns giving the receiver a chance to get out of bounds.

The following are ways of *bleeding the clock:*

Breaking the huddle slowly.
Go on a long count.
Unpile slowly.
Get back to the offensive.
Huddle slowly.
Run wide plays staying in bounds.
Eliminate the pass.   .
Do not call time-out.
Take the full time allowed to put the ball in play.
Eliminate penalties, which stop the clock.
Keep the ball in bounds.

Penalties

Many games are lost not because of a lack of yardage gained but because of penalties in critical situations that alter the outcome of the game from that point onward. The vast majority of penalties occur on procedural calls: illegal motion, illegal shift, illegal procedure, and offside. It is not the five yards of the penalty that are so costly but rather the yards gained or maintenance of possession nullified by the penalty. Momentum, consistency, and morale are adversely affected when a team is assessed frequent penalties.

Stronger snap and assignment discipline will do much to alleviate these costly procedural penalties. If your players can be made to understand the adverse results of penalties—nullifying team effort and accomplishment—they are less likely to incur them.

Two-point Conversions

The two-point conversion has had great effect on strategy in the game of football. Being able to execute the two-point play can be the winning edge.

Decision   The decision to go for two points must be made well in advance of the actual opportunity presenting itself. It is more difficult to make rational objective decisions considering all of the variable factors in an emotionally charged situation.

In order for a two-point play to be successful you, your staff, and your players must be sold on the choice. The chances of a two-point play succeeding are also greater if it is selected from what your team does best rather than an "off-the-wall" or gadget play.

Selection should be based on the following:

1. *Your personnel.* What your team does best.
2. *Your opponent's personnel.* Do they have an excellent extra point and field goal kicker? Is yours as competent or below average? You must think ahead not only to how one or two points will effect the game, but also, if your team *fails* to make the one- or two-point attempt, how it may affect your strategy and tactics for the remainder of the contest.
3. *Your opponent's defense.* Defensive teams generally have definite tendencies on their goal line moves more than anywhere else on the field. Therefore, you should know basically what alignment you will see, and you probably will also know whether you will face man or zone coverage.

In establishing a two-point play a coach wants to have as many options as possible available to him.

Failure to Score When in Scoring Zone

Some teams are capable of pushing their opponent literally all over the field, but when they get near their scoring zone they bog down. The number of times that you have the ball is important, but the number of times that you score when you have the ball is far more important. Therefore, a coach should review his scoring zone offense live every week and make necessary adjustments for all opponents. It is vital in this area that the offensive team does not break assignments or get penalties.

Your offense should be broken down to high consistency plays by down and distance. The selection of offense in this area should be based on the strengths and weaknesses of the defense and of the opponent's personnel. Play selection in the scoring zone should include your safe ball handling plays.

Practice Periods

Many a team has failed offensively because the situations that come up in the game have been neglected in practice periods. Offensive aspects that often are not practiced to mastery are:

1. Danger zone offense, goal to-10-yard line.
   In this area you must get out to at least the 3-yard line in order to kick from spread punt formation.
2. Scoring zone offense, +10 to goal line.
   Perspective changes here as pass routes become shorter and defenders have less territory to protect.
3. Two-minute offense.
4. Moving the ball from hash mark to hash mark in practice sessions so players experience the effect of lateral field position.
5. Moving the ball so players experience the measured down-and-distance sequence.

For a team to gain a true perspective for tactical as well as emotional involvement in a game the ball should be positioned in drill and scrimmage situations as it will be in a game.

Practice Effects Execution and Morale   A team cannot be successful without good execution and the desire to excel. High morale results from good practices. Good practices produce good execution. When you have poor execution you have low morale. You must have confidence in your offense to execute well. The old axiom, "You play like you practice" usually holds true, although you should "Practice like you want to play" in a game.

Goal Setting

In setting goals, remember that the goals should be challenging yet attainable. Goals may be individual or team goals. A player who sets goals for the team and himself will not only be motivated to do what is neces-

DIAGRAM 8–2
An Offensive Winning Edge Board

SUCCESS – THE WINNING EDGE										
19__ OFFENSE	HAWKS	VANDALS	GOPHERS	HOOSIERS	DUCKS	BEAVERS	COWBOYS	INDIANS	SUN DEVILS	HUSKIES
NO FUMBLE LOST	(W)	1	(W)	2	(W)	(W)	2	(W)	1	(W)
NO INTERCEPTIONS	(W)	(W)	(W)	1	2	(W)	(W)	3	(W)	2
NO BLOCKED PUNTS	(W)	(W)	(W)	(W)	(W)	(W)	(W)	(W)	(W)	(W)
NO MENTAL ERRORS INSIDE 10 YARD LINE	1	(W)	1	(W)	(W)	(W)	1	(W)	2	(W)
HOLD OPPONENTS PUNT RETURN TO 5 YARDS			(W)	(W)		(W)		(W)	(W)	
MAKE 5 BIG PLAYS A GAME	2	(W)	1	(W)	(W)	3	(W)	4		(W)
ALWAYS SCORE INSIDE 20 YARD LINE	(W)		(W)	(W)	(W)	(W)		(W)		(W)
OUT FIRST DOWN YOUR OPPONENTS	(W)		(W)	(W)	(W)		(W)	(W)	(W)	
OUT RUSH YOUR OPPONENT		(W)		(W)	(W)	(W)	(W)		(W)	(W)
BETTER COMPLETION % THAN OPPONENT	(W)	(W)	(W)		(W)		(W)		(W)	
OUT SCORE OPPONENT	(W)		(W)	(W)	(W)	(W)	(W)	(W)		(W)

sary to accomplish the goals but will also increase his confidence as he reaches them. The improvement of his self-image will increase his mental toughness in terms of poise, confidence, and determination. This carries over in terms of building team morale.

An offensive "winning edge board," on which goals are set and recorded after each game, can be hung in the locker room or training room to help promote team morale. Diagram 8–2 is an example of one board used at both high school and university levels.

9 DEFENSIVE FOOTBALL MISTAKES AND ERRORS, AND HOW TO AVOID THEM

The selection of your basic defense and the extent to which you utilize stunting and pass coverages depend on the following criteria: your personnel, your opposition's offense, and what you know best.

Each of these criteria has a relationship to the others and plays an important role in determining what your defensive plan will be. To ignore any of these criteria would be the first of numerous errors which tend to compound themselves.

The first basic precept in placing defensive personnel is to examine your basic beliefs and philosophy as to the value you place on defense as opposed to offense. The kicking game is also a factor, but personnel may be taken from both the defense and offense to make the overall kicking game strong. A game-tested coaching cliche is, "If you can't play defense you can't win," and most successful football coaches seem to adhere to this theory. Coach Bud Wilkinson commented, "If you have your best players on offense and you can't stop anyone, it is usually because 70 percent of the time they are with you on the sidelines. When they do get in they usually press and you can't muster offensive consistency when pressing" (Coach Year Clinic, San Francisco, 1977). Offensive football wins fans, but defensive football wins championships.

You also have to try to determine the football philosophy of your oppositions' coaching staff. Do they put their most outstanding players on offense or defense? Does your opponent favor "ready" defenses or gaming and stunting defensive play? Offensively, does your opposition play conservatively, seldom gambling, or does the opposition try for the big play frequently? Is it a run-, or pass-oriented offense?

By answering the previous questions you come to another facet that has an important bearing on your defensive planning and teaching. What do you know best and how can you adjust it to your personnel and to your opponents' plans? Doing what a coach knows best will always ensure a strong foundation for the defense. Defensive football is a matter of believing. The coach must sell his staff and his players on the overall plan to be successful.

Another key factor in successful defense is your ability to adjust your basic beliefs or design to the abilities of your *present* personnel. The fact that your team led your conference in defense the past year with a straight read defense, as an illustration, will not hold up this year if all the big strong kids are gone and all you have coming back are small, quick, scrappy players.

Alexander Pope wrote, "A little knowledge is a dangerous thing," and this sage comment is especially applicable to defensive football. Adopting another coaching staff's total defensive system has the same pitfalls as adopting someone else's offensive package (see Chapter 8). A coach must know more than where the players line up to teach proper defense. The techniques of playing the 4–4 defense are vastly different from playing the 5–2 alignment. The pass coverages are different, too, as the theory of three deep secondary play is not the same as four deep play. Yet some coaches try to mix the two.

DEFENSIVE FOOTBALL PHILOSOPHY AND OBJECTIVES

Once you have decided what you want to do defensively, then you must decide how you can best do it formulating a master plan. Even though philosophies concerned with how to do it will differ, most staffs agree as to the primary objectives of defensive football.

Defense plays a greater role today in the game of football than it ever has before. Whereas adverse weather and other physical conditions tend to impede a team's offense, these same factors tend to have little effect on a well-prepared defensive unit. A team built around the single thought of being good only offensively is not going to defeat a team balanced with both a good offense and good defense.

The strong defense will not only have a demoralizing effect on its opponents by its unyielding tactics, but it will also give a psychological lift to its own offense by gaining and maintaining outstanding field positions. There have been many teams whose offenses have been stopped but who have won the games with points scored by the defense.

Failure to Set Goals

Goal setting is as important for the defensive team as for the offensive team. Setting realistic, challenging goals aids in achieving good morale.

The scoring odds favor the defense; therefore, it is advisable to remind the players about the offensive defense and scoring while on defense. How many points did the defense score? How many fumbles were recovered by the defensive team? How many passes did the defense intercept? How many *big* plays did the defense make?

In building morale two points of view should be cultivated toward the opposition's passing game. A pass is an opportunity and an invitation for the defense to intercept and gain possession of the football. Secondly, conceding the facts that there is no defense against the perfectly thrown forward pass and that the opposition will probably complete a number of passes inside the rubber band perimeter, still one interception will nullify a number of completions, providing the offense does not score on one of those completions.

Defensive morale means maintaining confidence and not panicking when the opposition completes several passes. The next pass will be the interception. Positive morale is built by cultivating the idea that the closer the opposition gets to the goal line, the more difficult it becomes for them to score. Morale is also built by cultivating the idea that you give away nothing to the opposition. They must earn everything they get.

Goals that you might set are as follows:

1. No eight-play drives.
2. Force three fumbles per game.
3. Intercept two out of every thirteen passes thrown.
4. No long passes completed.
5. No long runs.
6. Limit third down success.
7. Five big plays per game.
8. Do not permit your opposition to score (shut out).
9. Score on defense.

An example of a "winning edge" board, which we have used to build morale and to measure and record accomplishment of defensive goals, is illustrated in Diagram 9–1.

Failure to Meet Objectives

The main objectives of defensive football are to prevent an easy touchdown, to obtain possession of the football, and to score. The failure of

DIAGRAM 9–1
A Winning Edge Board for Defense

SUCCESS – THE WINNING EDGE										
19__ OFFENSE	HAWKS	VANDALS	GOPHERS	HOOSIERS	DUCKS	BEAVERS	COWBOYS	INDIANS	SUN DEVILS	HUSKIES
LESS THAN 20 YARDS PER KO RETURN		W	W	W	W				W	W
1.5 INTERCEPTIONS	W 3	1	W 2		W 3	2	W 2	1		W 4
NO THIRD DOWN SUCCESS	W	3/6	4/8	W	7/15	3/11	6/12	W	4/9	W
CAUSE 3 FUMBLES RECOVER 2	W	1	2	W	1	0	W	0	1	2
BLOCK 1 PUNT, X-POINT OR FIELD GOAL			W			W			W	
NO LONG RUNS 20 YARDS	W	1	1	W		W	W	W	W	2
NO LONG PASSES 25 YARDS	W	W			W	W	W	W	W	
SHUTOUT	W				W			W		W

a team to meet the first two objectives usually implies disaster, while accomplishing the first two almost guarantees team success. Frequently the teams that play tenacious defense also score points.

To be successful a defensive football team must master the following:

Prevent an Easy Touchdown   While the obvious basic objective of defensive football is to keep the opposition from scoring, a more functional objective of defensive play is to prevent the opposition from scoring an "easy" touchdown via a long pass or a long run. Defensive teams that are able to prevent the easy touchdown generally are difficult to score against, and they are seldom defeated.

Obtain Possession of the Football   A second objective of defensive play, which is often overlooked, is to obtain possession of the football. A defensive team may gain possession of the ball by holding the opponent for downs, forcing a punt, intercepting a pass, recovering a fumble, or recovering a blocked punt. The latter may be considered separately or as a facet of forcing a punt.

Score   The third objective of defensive play is to score. The defense can score on a punt return, on an intercepted pass, by advancing a blocked punt, by recovering a fumble in the end zone (or by advancing any fumbled ball for a score under high school rules), and by forcing the offense to give up a safety. The offense can score, of course, only by running, passing, kicking a field goal, or extra point.

Need for Flexibility

The ease of adjustment to the various offensive sets of your opponents is also a major consideration in defensive planning; when you use two or more defensive fronts the problem often is compounded. If defensive personnel switches are involved, the problem becomes even more complicated.

The practice of set recognition by breaking the huddle in a drill and aligning against numerous types of offensive sets will create confidence in these basic situations. As an illustration, the use of motion and flanker sets is designed with several objectives in mind: to stretch the defensive perimeter, to get a mismatch in personnel, to force the defensive to adjust, to gain an advantage if the defense fails to adjust, to limit defensive stunts, especially dogs and blitzes. Therefore, defensive personnel in particular must be taught and drilled when to check out of defensive stunts and coverages so that the defensive alignment is not unsound. There must be no void areas in the coverage or mismatches in personnel where the offense has an advantage over the defense.

Defense Consists of Two Coordinated Units

In attempting to realize the objectives of defensive football, as cited above, several factors must be considered further. In order for any defensive alignment to be sound, the personnel must be deployed in such a manner that the defense is one of *depth* as well as *width*, and you must be able to defend against both the run and pass at the same time. No defense is perfect as the field is too large to cover adequately. While there are numerous different defensive alignments, a sound defense consists of both a *forcing unit* of players on or near the line of scrimmage, and a *containing unit* of players. The number of players in each unit will fluctuate, depending upon the deployment of the defensive personnel and their duties and responsibilities. This will be governed by the tactical situations on each play.

The Forcing Unit   In addition to the general objectives of defensive play mentioned already, the methods of obtaining possession of the ball are for the forcing unit to block a punt (and score), force a fumble, or force the opposition to surrender the ball on downs. The forcing unit can also cause interceptions by forcing a passer to throw the ball quickly or to release it at a higher arc so that its trajectory is higher and longer, giving players in the containing unit a better opportunity to intercept the pass. The forcing unit cannot permit the opposition to retain possession of the football for an extended series of first downs, especially in the four-down zone, since the opposition increases its chances of scoring by 25 percent after it reaches this zone of play.

On the other hand, excluding factors in the tactical situation other than down, distance, and position on the field, when the opposition has the ball back in its own territory in the three-down zone in a first-and-ten situation, it is not faulty thinking or poor defensive play to hold the offensive gain to three yards. If the opposition runs the ball two more times and comes up with a fourth-and-one situation, in the three-down zone they will, in all probability, still punt the football on fourth down. Any yardage a team makes in defensive territory that does not get it out past its own 40-yard line is of limited value. Even if the offensive team should make a first down or several consecutive first downs from deep in its own territory, it is difficult to keep a sustained drive going on the ground by grinding out the necessary yardage. The odds favor the defenders that the offensive team will make a mechanical error, such as fumble the ball, miss a block, hit the wrong hole, or be penalized, which causes the drive to falter and forces them to give up the football to the defense. The forcing unit must maintain pressure on the opposition, however, and *both* units must eliminate the long pass and the run for the easy touchdown in order to be sound defensively.

The Containing Unit   The objectives of the containing unit are the same as the three objectives of defensive football mentioned previously, but in addition they must contain the offensive play. The defensive perimeter may be thought of, and has been referred to, as a *rubber band defense*. This is one that will bend but will not permit the ball carrier to break through for the easy touchdown, and one that will snap back, affording the defense proper angles for team pursuit and opportunities for gang tackling. In a diamond secondary, the three deep men and normally the ends are the rim men in the defensive perimeter, with the ball as the hub of the wheel. In a box-wing secondary, the twin safeties and the corner or wing men are the rim of the defensive perimeter. As the football moves, the rim or defensive perimeter should stay intact and revolve with the football. The objective of the containing unit is to keep all of the offensive operations within the rim of the rubber band perimeter, which will enable the interior men to assist in all situations. The secondary men in the containing unit assume that every play is a pass until they are positive it is a run. Consequently these players should make fewer errors, having only one pattern of play, and should be able to prevent the easy touchdown—which is a primary objective of defensive football.

Eliminating the Bomb

A team that plays good pass defense and eliminates the bomb will be difficult to defeat. They may get beaten, but they are not giving up the easiest of all touchdowns. They are making the opposition work for its score if they eliminate the bomb.

All secondary defenders must know their coordinated pass coverages and their individual responsibilities for each type of coverage a team employs. The defensive linemen must realize they are not blameless when a long pass is completed in their defensive secondary. They must be relentless in their pass rush. If the opposing passer is allowed more than three seconds' time to pick out his receiver, that receiver will generally beat the secondary defender.

Prevent the Long Run

To be sound defensively, a team must first eliminate the long pass, and then eliminate the long run. In playing pattern or team defenses, each player must do his own job first and help second. He cannot play his own game; he must be a team player and carry out his specific team assignment. If a defender "freelances" on his own, and the critical point of attack is in his immediate area, there is likely to be a long run and/or six points for the opposition.

A coach cannot permit a defensive player to freelance on his own any more than he can permit an offensive player to run his own plays. You have to make your opposition grind it out in order to defeat your team. The opposition must work for its touchdowns rather than get them easily via the long pass or run.

Proper Angle of Pursuit Is Imperative

A proper angle of pursuit is nothing more than getting to the spot where you are going to make a tackle. This is probably the most important factor in defensive football today. What good are good tacklers if they lack team speed and cannot or will not get to the spot where they need to be in order to make a tackle? A defensive man may be blocked, but a good defensive player never stays blocked. He should recover as quickly as possible, react to the ball, and begin his proper angle of pursuit. Every man on the defensive team can take some angle on the ball carrier. If a defensive player starts his pursuit at the wrong angle, he immediately eliminates himself, as he is running an inside arc and chasing the ball carrier from behind with no chance of heading him off.

Angle and Pursue, Do Not Arc and Chase   Players must be coached in the proper angle of pursuit because this principle of defensive play is violated more often than any other. Coaching the correct angle on every defensive play in practice is the only way to get satisfactory execution during a game. It must be infused into the overall defense or you will be unable to defend against all of the different offensive sets and plays your team is likely to encounter. Briefly, the further the defensive man is from the critical point of attack where the ball crosses the line of scrimmage, the greater is his angle of departure from the line of scrimmage. One defender on the side removed or away from the flow of the play generally is designated as a container or chase man to take care of the reverse, the bootleg to the offside, or the cut back behind the line of scrimmage. The contain man may be an end or tackle.

Such errors as penetrating too deeply, running around blocks, and taking an inside arc places a defender in the position of being a chaser instead of a pursuer, with no chance of heading off the ball carrier downfield. This is individual defensive play, not coordinated team play, and it contributes toward the success of the easy touchdown for the opposition.

Factors Governing Pursuit   It is a natural tendency for a defensive player to penetrate too deeply on his initial charge. When playing a stunting defense, a player must go to his point of responsibility, then either accelerate his charge if the play is toward him or reduce his charge and change direction, taking the proper pursuit angle immediately, if the play is away from him. When playing a hitting and reacting road type of defense where little penetration is desired, moving your linemen back off the line of scrimmage so their initial charge will not carry them beyond the line of scrimmage until they have had a chance to analyze the play will overcome this tendency of penetrating too deeply. Or employing the hand or forearm shiver, instead of the forearm or shoulder lift, will achieve similar results.

A defensive player can make maximum use of the one advantage he holds over the offensive player, that is, he is permitted to use his hands when he employs a hand shiver. Also, a defensive lineman can pursue faster by using a shiver rather than a lift on his initial charge. It is difficult to get penetration with a hand shiver. A forearm lift is generally used when penetration is desired, such as in a short yardage situation when the defense must meet force with force. The following axioms govern penetration and team pursuit: "The farther one penetrates, the farther one must pursue" (assuming the critical point of attack is not where the defender gets his penetration); "Minimum penetration, maximum pursuit and maximum penetration, minimum pursuit." These axioms cannot of course be considered out of context, as tactical situations will dictate the necessary type of coordinated team defense, which might be a gap charge demanding defensive penetration.

Gang Tackling Is Essential

Rapid play recognition contributes to the proper angles of team pursuit and gang tackling. Proper and comprehensive scouting techniques in order to secure pertinent information will reveal offensive tendencies. This is especially true in high school football where a quarterback and/or his coach will invariably follow a particular pattern or sequence in long and short yardage situations, in the scoring zone, and when trying to get the football out of the danger zone. Factors that contribute to rapid play recognition, also build defensive morale and aid in team pursuit for gang tackling. If the opposition counters by changing its offensive attack, the advantage still lies with the defense as the offense has been forced to run other than its favorite plays and passes. If the opposition reverts to the obvious, such as the use of the long pass in an obvious passing situation, or gambles, such as the failure to punt on fourth down or waiting until fourth down to punt from deep in its own territory, the defensive team gains the advantage.

Good Pass Defense Is Imperative

Pass defense is undoubtedly the most important phase of defensive football, particularly at the college level. It is difficult to teach and requires a great deal of time and practice. Pass defense has four important phases:

Rushing the passer aggressively.
Delaying eligible receivers at or near the line of scrimmage.
Secondary pass coverage.
Intercepting the pass or tackling the receiver.

Rushing the Passer Aggressively   In order for the defensive men to reach the passer, they must rid themselves of offensive blockers. Many times defensive players try to rush through offensive blockers. Unless the defensive men are physically stronger than their opponents, they will not be able to rush through them. The defensive men should use their hands to rid themselves of blockers, after executing a fake inside and going outside or vice versa, depending upon whether or not they have outside containment responsibility. In applying pressure on the passer, it is essential that the defensive players rush aggressively, proceeding through their assigned areas of responsibility. The number of men rushing the passer will vary, depending upon the tactical situation and your philosophy, in that you decide to rush or to cover. Someone should always be assigned draw and middle screen responsibilities, and others should handle containment and side screen responsibilities. The best drill for rushing the passer is having the players do just that. The passer learns to pass under pressure, and the defensive players learn to react to his movements.

Delaying Eligible Receivers   It is not possible for the same men to hold up the receiver *and* still rush the passer aggressively. It is almost impossible for one man to hold up a receiver and do an effective job, taking into consideration the techniques a proficient receiver can use in releasing from the line when defenders try to hold him up. One defender can throw off the timing of a pass, especially a quick pass, by pushing and shoving the intended receiver or forcing him to alter his course as he releases downfield. Two defenders are needed to hold up a receiver, and this is not always successful. All defenders must exercise care in holding up intended receivers so they are not guilty of defensive holding.

Secondary Pass Coverage, Intercepting the Pass, or Tackling the Receiver In the third phase of pass defense, secondary pass coverage, and parts of the fourth, intercepting the pass or tackling the receiver, the linemen must react toward the ball as they rush the passer and the ball is thrown, in order to obtain the maximum return on the interception or to assist with gang tackling in the event of a completed pass. A coaching mistake is the failure to drill these techniques in practice. Most often, intercepted passes and punt and kick-off returns are not practiced live due to the possibility of injuries. As a result, it is difficult to perfect the time of these returns for maximum yardage. While this is understandable in that you do not want to play your game on the practice field, a greater coaching error is the failure to practice and emphasize the necessity of linemen reacting toward the football after it is thrown.

DEFENSIVE FOOTBALL IS REACTION FOOTBALL— FUNDAMENTAL PRINCIPLES

Offensive football is *assignment* football because the offense has the advantage of knowing *when* the play will start and *where* it is directed.

The failure of the offensive team to exploit fully this advantage and to get off with the count, is to sacrifice its edge over the defensive team. The offensive team is restricted in accomplishing its objectives only to the extent that blockers are not permitted to use their hands in carrying out their offensive blocking assignments. Whether an offensive player is proficient in his blocking, largely depends on his response to the defender's initial reaction and his being able to execute his blocking techniques successfully in sustaining his block.

The defensive team's advantage is that the players *are* permitted to use their hands to dispose of blockers, but defensive play is *reaction* football because the defenders must react *after* the ball has been snapped. Failure by the offense generally means loss of yardage, loss of a down, and perhaps loss of the football. Failure on the part of only one man on the defensive team to react properly may result in a touchdown for the opposition. Such a pertinent fact cannot be minimized and must be stressed frequently, if the objectives of defensive football are to be realized.

Regardless of defensive alignment, the principles of defensive line play are proper block protection, playing through resistance, second reaction, pursuit, tackling, and maintaining good football position at all times. The basic defensive fundamentals, which must be taught to all linemen, are as follows:

Stance: three- or four-point stance.
Alignments: head-on, offset to either side, and off the line.
Charges: control the opponent, control one side of him or the other, penetrate, gap charge, loop, slant, veer, stunts.
Responsibilities: own territory, angle of pursuit, leverage, pass rush, reaction to traps, and reaction to keys.
Tackling: head-on, angle (side), and gang tackling.

These basic fundamentals will be presented here as the principles of defensive line play. We will not go into a detailed discussion on *teaching* tackling fundamentals and techniques.

Stance

Excluding the stance of the defensive ends, who may or may not be in a semi-upright two-point stance depending on their duties and responsibilities in a particular defensive alignment, the interior linemen will employ either a three- or four-point stance. The weight will be evenly distributed on feet and hand(s), since the defender must be able to step with either foot first. His center of gravity is likely to be lower than when he is in his offensive stance, since a defensive lineman's base will be wider, that is, his feet are wider apart than his shoulders. His feet will be staggered more so than when he is in his offensive stance, although his rear foot cannot extend much farther than beyond the heel of his forward foot or he will have difficulty stepping quickly with either foot, especially if slanting, veering, or looping. His down hand, if he is employing a three-point stance, will correspond to his rear foot. Some coaches, however, specify a left- or right-handed stance for defensive linemen on the right and left side of the line, respectively, as they prefer having the outside foot forward. Other coaches prefer a natural stance and permit their defensive linemen to stagger either foot.

The weight on the down hand depends on whether the defensive lineman is always charging straight forward or varying his charge by looping, slanting, or veering. He should not noticeably vary the amount of weight on his hand, tipping off the type of charge he is going to employ. Except when he will take a gap charge and wants penetration, if he has too much weight forward he will encounter difficulty when stunting. He must be able to move quickly on the movement of the blocker opposite him or on the snap of the ball, or else the blocker will outcharge him.

Some players are able to view both the movement of the ball and the opposition across the line of scrimmage simultaneously, which is known as split vision. Your players should watch their opponents, move when the ball moves, and still be able to react to the movements of the opponent. There is a difference of opinion among coaches as to whether a defensive player should watch his opponent or the ball, and move on his opponent's movement or the snap of the ball, if he does not have split vision. Some coaches maintain the defender should watch only for the movement of his offensive opponent, while others stress watching the ball. The latter case is especially true where the defensive linemen are looping, slanting, veering, and not playing a straight hit-and-reaction type of defensive play. Under *no* circumstances however, should the defender wait and catch on defense; he should meet the blocker in the neutral zone and control him.

Alignments and Charges

Deliver a Blow or Block Protection Techniques   Football is a game of contact, and it is either hit or be hit, especially in line play. Where the emphasis is on the nonpenetrating type of reacting defensive play, an inexperienced player is likely to forge the necessity of first delivering a blow to his opponent, then reacting, in order to neutralize his charge, control him, and maintain freedom to carry out the other fundamentals of defensive play. The type of blow he delivers or his block protection technique depends on the defensive philosophy of his coach. The most common types of block protection are the forearm or hand shiver and the forearm or shoulder lift.

Forearm or Hand Shiver Techniques   The forearm shiver consists of stepping with the rear foot and hitting with the heels of the hands simultaneously under the shoulders of the opponent, in order to straighten him up and break and neutralize his charge. The feet should be even when the hands are extended forward. The wrists and elbows must be locked in order to deliver the blow with strength and authority. Otherwise the offensive player's charge will collapse the arms of the defender, and he can get at his legs with a shoulder block. The blow must be delivered from up under the blocker, and the defensive lineman must follow through with short driving steps until the ball is located or until the defender determines where pressure is being exerted.

Forearm or Shoulder Lift Techniques   The shoulder and forearm should be coordinated with the same foot, giving the defender the strongest possible position. The defensive lineman takes a short step forward with either foot and uncoils with the same shoulder and forearm, delivering a blow to the chest of the blocker, striking his numerals with his forearm. The opposite hand is used for leverage on the blocker, keeping him away from the defender and destroying his balance.

The shoulder or forearm lift is generally used in a short yardage situation, especially when the defense wants to meet force with force, as when near the goal line. The defensive maneuver should be executed from as low a position as possible. The defender must retain balance quickly, and be able to pursue laterally if the play is away from his area.

It is a well-known fact that football games are won and lost in the line, and the player who establishes physical toughness or supremacy immediately will generally control that particular piece of territory. Thus it is essential that striking or delivering a blow be one of the basics of your defensive line play.

Neutralize the Offensive Charge of the Blocker   The charge of the defensive linemen must be low and hard, and each player must be on balance and in good football position to move laterally if necessary. The defender must neutralize the offensive charge of the blocker so that he can control his assigned territory. The offensive team cannot gain yardage through any area of the line if every defensive lineman plays his position properly and is not whipped by his offensive blocker. Further, when defenders deliver blows to the offensive linemen all the way down the line, the offside blockers cannot get in front of the ball carrier and align themselves with the running lane in order to lead interference or block downfield in the secondary.

Charge to a Spot on Defense   In order for a defense to be successful, each player must reach his designated spot on his charge. The spots or areas of responsibility will differ depending upon each player's individual alignment and assigned area of responsibility. He may be head-on or shaded to one side or the other of the opponent, offsetting to various degrees, including in either gap or off the line of scrimmage. His alignment to his opponent may be nose-to-nose, nose-to-ear, foot-to-crotch, foot-to-foot, or in the gap. His defensive charge may be to control the opponent opposite, control one side or the other of the opponent, penetrate the gap, loop, slant, or veer into the offensive lineman or into the area to either side of the blocker opposite his initial alignment. His reaction after his charge, depending upon whether the ball is coming to or going away from him, has been discussed already.

Responsibilities

Protect Your Territory   Each player should be made to feel that his particular territory or area of responsibility is the most important area in the team's coordinated defense. Since the combination of all defenses becomes the coordinated team defense, it is necessary for each player to protect his position. Players know they will be blocked at times, but a good player does not stay blocked. He reacts and still protects his territory. Two cardinal principles of defense are: never make a mental mistake; and play your position first, help second. As we have pointed out, a single mistake by only one defender can penalize his entire team six points if the ball carrier hits in the particular area where the mistake has occurred.

Locate the Football or the Ball Carrier   Each defender must locate the football or the ball carrier quickly before reacting. If a defender fights pressure and plays through resistance, instead of looking into the backfield watching the action there, he will not be fooled by the faking techniques. He must move first, deliver a blow, then locate the football before reacting. A common error for an inexperienced player is to attempt to locate the football without first delivering a blow. He takes a fake and leaves his territory unprotected. The defensive lineman's key is in the immediate area of the blocker opposite him and those offensive linemen to either side. Although he may be fooled by influence blocking at times, if he reacts to his key and locates the ball carrier or the football, his defensive play will be sound. If he ignores his key and watches the play of the offensive backs, he probably will be fooled again and again.

Fight Pressure or Play Through Resistance   Although some coaches now take a contrary point of view, most coaches advocate that a defensive lineman should not run around a blocker. They feel when this occurs the defender becomes a chase man instead of a pursuer and he does not have the opportunity of heading off the ball carrier downfield. Secondly, he also opens a running lane for the ball carrier. There are several ways of getting through a blocker to the ball carrier after contact is made. If the defender is more powerful than the blocker, he merely overpowers him and goes through the blocker. He can submarine through his man and plug a hole, or he can go over the blocker and attempt to make a tackle. Or he can neutralize the blocker, control him, then break laterally in the direction of the ball carrier as the latter attempts to break off of his blocker. Another technique is to roll out, using leverage on the blocker.

Rollout Techniques The defensive player should collapse the knee inward that is receiving the pressure, drop step quickly with the foot away from the pressure, and swing the same (far) arm and shoulder to assist in a quick roll around the offensive blocker, toward the direction where the pressure is being exerted. He should maintain a low center of gravity and use the offensive blocker as leverage, which should put the defensive lineman in the middle of the offensive hole when he recovers from the quick roll. If the defensive player whirls quickly and lands on all fours in the next hole, he should be prepared to make a tackle or get up quickly and pursue the ball carrier.

Tackling

The importance and necessity of the proper angle of pursuit and gang tackling have been discussed already. It has not been pointed out previously that the best way to teach gang tackling is to use a *slow* whistle in practice. If a coach permits the use of a quick whistle all of the time, the players will become accustomed to it and will not hustle to assist with a tackle. In a game this permits the opposing backs to drive for extra yardage or even break loose for long gains and touchdowns.

DEFENSE COMMUNICATIONS

With the exception of the defensive signal caller, the defensive team should not be overly concerned with total defensive strategy. Each individual player should concentrate totally on his own assignments and responsibilities. As we pointed out in the previous chapter, you should decide in advance whether the defensive alignment, stunts, and coverages are going to be called by the coach by messenger, substitutes, or hand signals, or whether the defensive signal caller is going to be trained to make the defensive calls. Obviously, if you choose the latter, more time will be needed to train your defensive signal caller. Regardless of the method utilized, however, he must be taught and drilled to check out of alignments and stunts, and the defensive backs must be taught and drilled to change coverages in certain situations so as not to be caught in a vulnerable alignment or coverage as the result of offensive strategy.

Failure to Establish Meaningful Terminology

As in offense and the kicking game, descriptive terminology that is both clear and concise is essential for defensive communications. Whenever possible there should be as much carryover as possible in the terms used, especially when players are used on both the offensive and defensive teams and/or are involved with special teams.

Keeping terminology the same is easy to do in terms of offensive and defensive sets and pass routes, where frequently only the direction of strength needs to be reversed in the sets called; this is easy to learn once exposed to the theory.

Also for uniformity and consistency, *offensive* football is almost always explained by a coach at a chalkboard with the defensive alignment placed *above* the offensive set so that the offensive team is going *up* the board, south to north; conversely, *defensive* football is explained with the teams' positions reversed so that the offensive unit is *above* and coming *down* the board, north to south, and the defensive alignment and coverage are illustrated below. Obviously both offense and defense are practiced in both directions on the field.

Terminology should be grouped under the following categories:

Alignment and techniques
Movement
Responsibilities
Pass coverages
Field position
Offensive alignment
Offensive pass patterns
Offensive blocks and plays
Defensive stunts and calls

Meaningful Numbers, Names, Phrases   It is suggested that you draw up all of the offensive blocks that your defensive linemen will encounter and then identify them as your offense identifies them, such as trap, power, blast, one-on-one, scramble, cutoff, and so on. The backfield actions and pass patterns should be identified as viewed from the defensive standpoint. Where you do not employ your opponents' offensive sets and have none of your own terminology to identify a particular segment of offense, you might do well to name them after your specific opponent who employs them, such as bear, trojan, cougar, or husky; they will have meaning since they are identified with a specific opponent.

General terms should be clear and concise and to the point. Verbosity should be avoided so that calls can be made quickly and recognized instantly. Directional calls for the secondary and stunts should give a picture or have a definite meaning of what your team is doing. For example, the words slant and loop typically refer to down linemen techniques, blitz refers to a safetyman, dog refers to a linebacker, and so on. In your terminology, 53 Blitz might mean a stunt off of a 5-2 defensive alignment with both linebackers and the strong safety rush with a three dog zone secondary. The latter could be changed from zone to man coverage by calling 53 Blitz Red. However, the second digit could mean a line slant or stunt; that is, 51 would be a slant-loop to the left, 52 a slant-loop to the right, and 53 a tight pinching movement.

Another method is to "name" the defensive linebackers and secondary defenders, as illustrated:

SAM—Strong Linebacker
MIKE—Middle Linebacker
WILL—Weakside Linebacker
SID—Strong Safety
FRED—Free Safety
ROB—Right Corner
LEN—Left Corner

Therefore, 50 zone would be a straight reading defense with the zone rotation called in the same manner as the strength of the offensive defense, left or right. To include a linebacker in on a stunt you might call 51 Sam, Zone, which indicates the defensive line is looping left and the strong linebacker will fire (dog) backside *if* the flow of the play is away from the strength of the offensive set or the quarterback goes back into the pocket to pass. A 58 Sid Blitz, Red, would send both linebackers and the strong safety on to rush, and a 51 Rob Fire, Red, would have the defensive line looping-slanting left with the right cornerback coming on a tough rush off the corner and the linebackers and secondary in man coverage. The words can have any significance or meaning that you wish, but they should be thought out well in advance and your entire defensive system should be highly correlated so the intent of the terms is always clear. Pass coverages must be coordinated with defensive stunts in particular since the more defenders you rush the greater is the gamble that you are going to get to the ball carrier or passer, and the weaker is the defensive secondary against the pass. From a philosophical standpoint you must either rush or defend, as it is impossible to do both.

Do Not Confuse Your Players   Since coaches do not want to tip off their intent either offensively or defensively, at times they utilize their own terminology instead of adopting commonly accepted terminology. They theorize that they will fool the opposition with different terms and calls, and they want to hide the fact their defense (and/or offense) is the same or similar to many other coaches'. A defensive front is either odd or even and it is a seven or a six man front. The opposition is not concerned with how you identify your defenses. Do not confuse your players in an effort to try to fool your opposition by identifying your defensive alignments, stunts, and coverages with unusual names and numbers, unless they have meaning and are understood by your players.

The purpose of adopting terminology is to communicate. Therefore, whatever terminology is adopted should be utilized by your entire staff and players. If a staff member utilizes his own particular terminology, the result is likely to be ineffective communication. As unlikely as this may appear to be, there are coaching staffs who have not adopted a common terminology; a scout coach, for example, may give the scouting report in language no one else on staff recognizes, or a freshman football coach uses his own football terminology and not that of the varsity staff members. These are coaching mistakes.

Whatever you adopt must be taught, and subsequent performance must be evaluated for effectiveness. Probably most coaches try to teach too much defensively as well as offensively, but err in failing to evaluate what they have attempted to coach to determine the learning effectiveness.

TRAINING THE DEFENSIVE QUARTERBACK

It is as important to have well-trained defensive quarterbacks to call the correct defenses as it is for the offensive quarterbacks to call the correct offensive plays. For defensive quarterbacks to be effective, they must be trained to do their job properly, which is accomplished through progressive teaching and coaching where they learn through repetition and practical experience.

To accomplish training more easily, the coaching staff and the defensive quarterback's teammates must realize the importance of the signal caller's position and his duties. Yet in many coaching situations this important factor is given little or no attention. This may be due to time constraints that do not allow for proper training or a staff philosophy of "we will handle it from the sideline."

Failure to Allot Time   Recognizing the fact that time is both a situational variable and a constraining factor in coaching, you must set priorities placing emphasis on the activities and details that give you the opportunity to win. The "as is" situation may not permit you to have assistant coaches on the sideline and in the scouting booth, too. A method we have found helpful on a small coaching staff is to put the defensive quarterback on the sideline phone to the defensive coach in the booth. The defensive signal caller either relays the incoming information from the coach in the booth to the head coach, or he flashes the defensive call given to him by the scouting booth coach or the head coach. The defensive quarterback on the sideline phone familiarizes himself with the defensive calls and the strategy, and the coaches on the sideline and in the booth are able to focus on each specific call that has been made observing executions and breakthroughs. The error is the failure to master the elementary rudiments which must be considered in defensive signal calling, that can only lead to a less than satisfactory performance on the field.

The Defensive Quarterback's Responsibilities

A defensive signal caller must master his coach's specific strategy and communicate it to his teammates. To prevent defensive errors it is important that a defensive quarterback be a leader, taking charge, showing poise, backed up with the knowledge of defensive strategy, its strengths and weakness, as outlined by his coaches. Not only must he have this knowledge, he must communicate it to his teammates and motivate them in its execution.

Down and Distance   The defensive quarterback's first consideration should be down and distance. He must recognize normal, long, and short yardage situations. Normal yardage is when an opponent must average over three yards per try in the remaining downs to make a touchdown or first down. A long yardage situation is when an opponent must make more than three yards per try in the remaining downs for the first down or touchdown. Short yardage is when an opponent must average less than three yards in each of his remaining downs.

Third-down Calls   The ability to control an opposition's offense on third down is the key to winning defensive football. The defensive unit must get the ball for the offense in good field position, and it is the defensive signal caller with poise, knowledge, and leadership who is most effective in these situations. The ability to stop a third-down play, especially in the three-down zone of the field, and to force the offensive team to turn over possession of the football are the marks of a good defensive team.

Field Position   The opponent's moves at given field positions, yard lines, hash marks, and in three-down and four-down zones are tendencies that are fairly well established, especially at the high school level. It is for that reason that competent scouting and statistical breakdowns are much more important than the cursory treatment many high school coaches give to this phase of preparation. The more evident the tendencies, the easier to defense the opposition. With proper training, defensive quarterbacks can be taught field tendencies and the appropriate defensive tactics.

Score   The factor that determines whether a team follows normal play or gambles more frequently is the score. While most rules are fast, the most important rule is to break any rule in order to win. However, not infrequently when a defensive team gambles on shutting off a play for no gain or throwing their opposition for a big loss, the result is a long gainer for the offensive team. Breaking rules of defensive and/or offensive play in order to win should be exercised with much discretion. It is for this reason that gamble calls are most frequently sent in from the sideline rather than called by the signal caller. They are great when they accomplish the objective, but when they fail, peer pressure may be too much for a signal caller who has gambled on calls and guessed wrong. While players may be reluctant to second-guess their head coach, they are not reluctant to be critical of a teammate. They are also likely to lose confidence in his ability as a signal caller, which defeats the purpose of playing aggressively and with confidence on defense.

Time Remaining and Weather   The time remaining to play also has a decided effect on game strategy, especially at the close of the half and at the end of the game. A defensive quarterback must realize this and adjust his calls accordingly, being especially aware of the score in relation to the time remaining. Tactical factors seldom should be considered by themselves but rather in relation to each other. Another such factor is weather. Wind, rain, and mud have a decided negative effect on the kicking and passing game, and defensive strategy is likely to be changed almost entirely by these conditions.

Forming the Defensive Huddle

The purpose of the defensive huddle is to establish a place for the defensive team to meet as a unit to call the next defense in a calm, confident manner. Huddle discipline must be taught. Emphasis must be placed on the huddle being formed quickly by the defensive quarterback. He should insist on disciplined quiet. The style of huddle selected will vary, but it must be designed for maximum vision to the signal caller by all players. The caller should insist on heads being up, looking at him, listening intently, and able to see his face. This all aids in communicating the call when crowd noise may make hearing difficult. If signals are coming from a coach on the sideline or by messenger, the huddle should be designed so the player calling the signals has vision to the sideline. Signals should be short, concise, and meaningful, as we explained and illustrated previously. At least one player should have the responsibility of watching out for a quick line-up of the offensive unit in a surprise situation. The huddle should be broken quickly and the defense set.

The formation of the huddle, its mechanics, and its break should be done with pride and class. Defensive plays start in the huddle and if plays begin sloppily, they may continue to disaster. A coach should insist in practice on its perfection. Huddling is one of the little things that count.

DEFENSIVE LINE MISTAKES AND ERRORS

Failure to Align Properly

One of the most common errors found in defensive football is the failure of the defensive unit to take the proper alignment. If a team or individual does not maintain proper alignment, the strength of the defense is diluted, as it makes proper team coverage impossible by creating chinks and gaps in the defensive armor.

Usually improper alignment is the result of faulty communication, or a lack of knowledge and concentration, or poor attitude. When a primary consideration is to get a player into proper position to accomplish his task, it is well for a coach to examine the "why" of misalignment. In most cases it can be easily corrected by better communication and drill involving breaking the defensive huddle and aligning on the various offensive sets employed by your opponents.

Putting a player in the position from which he will function most effectively is also important in placing personnel. You must allow for individual differences as not everyone can perform in the same manner. Every effort should be made to place players in positions that give them the opportunity to perform to the maximum of their ability.

Guess Complex

Critical errors that destroy good defensive football play occur when the players start guessing or freelancing on their own. The following are illustrative:

"*I thought he would or I think he will . . . ,*" which is guessing. Sound defense excludes playing hunches at the expense of the ten other players on the defensive unit who are playing the designed potential defense and following the game plan.

"I must help outside . . . ," if this is *not* a player's assignment but he decides to help out a teammate, it can be disastrous. It reflects an undisciplined approach to the defense and/or a lack of confidence in the defense or his teammate's ability to handle his responsibility.

"I know they are going to . . . and I must . . . ," represents the proper approach to team defense. The player *knows* what the opposition is going to do and he *must* carry out his responsibility as it has been incorporated in a team plan.

The "I know" and "I must" represent the ultimate goal in defensive football, where a plan has been developed by studying an opponent, and where each player has been taught how to stop what is about to be executed.

Failure to Utilize a Proper Stance

Placing the defensive player in the proper stance to accomplish his defensive assignment is of vital importance in defensive execution. A player's body build will in part determine the stance he must take. A poor stance is a restraint to a quick, controlled charge.

Whether a three- or four-point stance is utilized it is not as important as the balance position, with the legs well up under the body, the knees bent not more than 90 degrees, the back parallel to the ground, head up, and eyes open. Weight should be distributed to give an explosive charge. Faults in the defensive stance for linemen are typically that the player is extended too far or bunched up too tightly.

Analyzing each player's build and placing him in a correct stance allows for your line to get off the ball on the snap or on an offensive movement.

Failure to Explode

The defensive lineman who is aligned properly in a good stance must explode on the first movement of either the blocker or the ball. He must explode and read as he attacks. To accomplish this he must master an explosion step with his first move and a balancing step with his second move.

Common faults in the charge are an overextended first step or a lethargic second step. The steps must be both short and straight keeping the feet and the shoulders parallel. Another mistake involves becoming so intent on the read that the charge is soft rather than exploding. The initial charge may be perfected on sled blocking dummies or against live competition.

Failure to Neutralize the Blocker

Neutralization of the blocker can come only after proper alignment, stance, and exploding. There are many methods of neutralizing blockers and no one method is more correct than the others. The best method is of course the one most-suited to the player employing it. Recognized methods are the forearm shiver, hand shiver, and shoulder charge. Each has its merits, but the individual differences of the players must be considered.

In each of these techniques it is essential for the defensive man to attack the blocker and destroy his blocking pattern. He must not fail to keep his feet moving and following through with his legs, as these are critical errors in any technique.

Failure to Pursue Properly

Every defender must be coached on the proper angle of pursuit to ensure defensive success. The common failures found in pursuit patterns are as follows:

1. The failure to hustle and pursue all out on every play.
2. Taking the improper pursuit angle. The farther a defender is from the point of attack, or the slower he is, the sharper is his angle of pursuit to the ball carrier. The closer he is to the point of attack, the flatter his angle of pursuit.
3. Overrunning the play. Not keeping the ball carrier in front of and slightly outside of the previous position on running plays to outside (assuming you are not the contain man); and not keeping the ball carrier in front of and slightly inside of the pursuer's position on inside plays.
4. The failure of a defender to pursue at a slightly deeper angle than the next pursuit man between himself and the ball.
5. The failure of a pursuer to keep his shoulders square to the line of scrimmage in order to change direction quickly or to break down for the tackle.

Chase Man or Spy   Frequently, a ball carrier will be cut off by containment on the side toward the flow but will reverse his field and get outside of containment around the opposite end because the chase man or spy has not pursued properly from the backside of the play. Chase errors are as follows:

1. Not following as deep as the ball and failing to be alert for the reverse, bootleg, waggle, or end around. Coming back against the grain or flow of the play.

2. Failing to keep the ball carrier in front of and slightly inside your position, yet maintaining a containing position from the backside of the play.

3. Leaving the chase lane before the ball carrier crosses the line of scrimmage.

Failure to Tackle

Tackling is the keystone of defense. If a player cannot tackle he cannot play defense. Tackling is 90 percent desire; technique is a far second in getting a ball carrier on the ground.

Failures in tackling are as follows:

1. The failure to keep the head up and eyes open, focused on the football. Sliding the force to the side of the body for a hard shoulder tackle causes fumbles.

2. The failure to get in close and keep the feet moving when driving through the ball carrier.

3. Not breaking down under control in the open field, and getting the body under control.

4. Not clubbing the arms, therefore failing to wrap up the ball carrier.

5. Loafing or watching a teammate tackle when it is usually the third or fourth legal hit that causes a fumble. Only the whistle stops the play.

All critical errors in tackling can be corrected with practice if the innate desire is present. Everyone has some fear of the unknown. Proper teaching of technique and pattern recognition will eliminate most fear, which is usually related to not knowing how, what, or why things happen.

Failures in Pass Rush

Sacks of the offensive quarterback are "frosting on the cake," providing a team is strong in its defense against the run. More important than quarterback sacks, however, is keeping unrelenting pressure on the passer, which forces him to throw high over or around rushes, does not permit him to set up properly and pick out his receivers, and forces him to throw more quickly or scramble to evade the rush. Player containment must be coached so the passer cannot escape from his passing pocket, which destroys not only the rush but also defensive morale.

In man coverage in particular, if the passer has sufficient time to pick out his receiver more frequently than not, the receiver will beat the defender since the former knows the route and where the ball will be thrown, and the defender does not. The defender must react to the moves of the receiver. For effective man coverage, then, the defender must play the receiver close, without a cushion between himself and the receiver as in zone coverage. Consequently, in man coverage the receiver need only gain a step on the defender to beat him. In zone coverage a defender who is beaten may get help from a defender coming from another zone, but in man coverage a defender is unlikely to receive any backup aid in defending deep. If a tough rush does not force the passer to throw the football before the receiver makes his break to get open, and a defender is beaten in man coverage, he will lose confidence in his ability to play the receiver closely. He is likely to start playing his receiver cautiously instead of tenaciously, separating himself from the intended receiver. When this occurs, it is certainly not difficult to complete passes to the intended receiver. Obviously, laying off the receiver is not the way to play man coverage. Also, from a strategical standpoint man coverage should not be utilized unless there is an all out tough rush where the rushers outnumber the blockers and force the passer to unload the football before he is set to do so. Otherwise the strategy is faulty because the defense accomplishes neither the sack nor harassing the passer, and because the advantage is with the receiver not the defender in one-on-one man coverage.

Pass Rush Errors and Mistakes   In the past twenty years, the greatest changes that have occurred in the game of football have been in the passing game and in defensing the pass. While coaches may practice numerous multi-coverages, not infrequently the pass rush receives only cursory treatment. Other pass rushing errors and mistakes are as follows:

1. Sloughing off on a rush through fatigue, whether real or imagined.
2. Not studying an opponent enough to recognize his pass giveaways.
3. Failing to perfect more than one technique in the pass rush. The player must have a change-up to counter the offensive blocker's moves.
4. Not rushing in a path that will put the defender close to the passer if his protection breaks down.
5. Not gaining controlled speed in getting to the blocker who sets up to protect the passer.
6. Not going through the protector on his outside shoulder to prevent rollouts and waggles.

7. Not keeping in the rushing lane to prevent chinks and gaps from developing in the rush.

8. Not keeping his feet moving, driving until he reaches the passer. A rusher should leave his feet and leap at the passer only below the blind side or when he sees he cannot get to the passer before the release of the football otherwise.

9. Not keeping his eyes on the passer as he drives through the protector, so if the quarterback breaks he can level off and break with him.

10. When in line with the throw, not getting his hands up to obstruct the quarterback's line of sight to his receivers.

11. Easing up on the rush when not in the quarterback's line of throw, especially if he is a good rusher.

12. Coming in too high on the rush, making changes in direction difficult in reaction to the quarterback's moves. It also allows the rusher to be cut down more readily.

13. Failing when blocked by two protectors to rush through the outside blocker. He cannot permit himself to be rolled or stacked to the inside, especially if he has contain responsibility.

14. Failing to veer more toward the middle against the protector who likes the cross-body block, which forces the defender to throw his block quickly leaving an easy path to the quarterback.

15. Giving ground to the outside when the blocker sets up inside rather than taking a regular course until even with him then driving for the quarterback. If the rusher attempts to beat the blocker to the inside, he must accelerate quickly in doing so.

16. Giving ground when blocked by an offensive back rather than driving over him shearing off to his outside.

17. Failing after the pass has been thrown to cover to the side the ball is thrown, or where the ball is thrown down the middle to cover to his own side.

18. Not knowing the type of quarterback he is facing. Some quarterbacks seldom if ever scramble out of the pocket as they have been trained only to do so as a last resort. Others like to run with the football when trapped. The former are easier to rush than the latter, since they want to pass not run with the football. Therefore, the defender can rush this type of passer with more reckless abandon than the scrambler. Also, he should be tackled high in an effort to strip him of the football and cause a fumble. If not close enough to strip him of the ball, the rusher should get his hands high clouding the

quarterback's vision and forcing him to throw high over the top or around the rusher.

19. Failing to look for the screen his way after a successful pass rush.

20. Roughing the passer after his release of the football. If the ball has been released, veer away from the passer. Do not sustain a penalty for a late hit.

Playing Screens   Screens must not be played at the expense of rushing the passer. A defensive man cannot be thinking about dropping off to play screens and still be an effective pass rusher. Well-conceived defenses usually assign specific defenders screen and/or draw responsibilities. However, a pass rusher should do the following:

1. Knock off any potential receiver he can reach releasing from the line of scrimmage without going out of his path. If he senses a screen, the defensive man should charge over the receiver attempting to knock him down or off balance, destroying the timing of the play on his way to the passer.

2. If already past the receiver, the defensive man must make every effort to make the passer's throw difficult.

3. Play the screen immediately after the ball is thrown.

4. Never fail to recognize and hold up potential screen receivers to his side.

5. Look especially for a screen to his side after rushing the passer aggressively.

6. Communicate, calling out, "*Screen, screen,*" when it occurs.

Playing Draws   Stopping draw plays is never the primary job of the rusher, except where the defense called may designate a defender to be responsible for a draw. There are two basic types of blocks on draw plays: man-to-man and trap blocking, and both may be tough to recognize in combat situations. The common errors in playing the draw are as follows:

1. Failing to communicate and call out, "Draw," when recognizing it as such.

2. Running around blocks, which aids offensive success in a draw play.

3. Continuing to rush the passer after a draw play is recognized.

4. Failing to throw off the offensive man and react back toward the line of scrimmage and the ball carrier.

5. Failing to stay low when spinning off the block, which creates a large blocking surface for the offensive blocker.

Stunting Failures

Stunting by defensive men can be effective when used intelligently and with discretion. Proper use of stunts will destroy offensive timing and upset blocking patterns causing the offensive blockers to hesitate when coming off the ball. This has a decided effect on controlling the line of scrimmage.

Common errors and mistakes involved in stunting are as follows:

1. Stunting without planning or reason. Stunts must be devised to take something away from the offense—oversplitting the offensive line, for example, or destroying blocking schemes utilized in the running game or obtaining a better pass rush.
2. Failing to communicate or execute the desired stunt. Basically, stunting is exchanging responsibility with a teammate. A defensive player who does not get the word or gets cut off in his execution leaves the defense vulnerable to a long gainer and possible touchdown.
3. Failing to anticipate and quickly recognize a pass. Move directly *toward* the passer not away from him on the stunt.
4. Not making a quick and decisive move to get to one's area of responsibility on patterned defenses. If a defender is cut off, there is a void in the defense.
5. Failing to charge to the area of responsibility initially on looping and slanting stunts. If offensive flow is in the same direction as the stunt, accelerate and tackle; if the loop is away from offensive flow, break at the proper pursuit angle back toward the line of scrimmage to intersect the ball carrier's path to the line of scrimmage. Do not continue following through on the stunt and loop-slant away from the ball carrier when offensive flow is in the opposite direction.
6. Failing to penetrate or neutralize a block when the stunt responsibility indicates doing so.

LINEBACKER ERRORS AND MISTAKES

Linebacker errors like those of the down linemen involve vertical and lateral alignment, stance, not meeting and destroying blocks, improper pursuit, and failing to make tackles. Your linebackers should be your "search and destroy" players. Common errors and mistakes which inhibit linebacker play are as follows:

1.   Aligning too wide creating gaps and blocking angles in the defensive front for the offensive linemen.
2.   Aligning too tightly (up on the ball) in a normal yardage situation, thus getting cut off when attempting to pursue laterally.
3.   Aligning too loosely on short yardage situations, thus giving up valuable yardage and creating a running lane for the ball carrier to break off of a block.
4.   Failing to explode on the snap of the ball or movement of the offensive blocker.
5.   Failing to read keys properly. Offensive line blocks will indicate the type of play being run. Few teams false key, and competent scouting will indicate which of your opponents do so.
6.   Improper fill procedure to meet running plays. Meet the ball carrier in the hole at the line of scrimmage.
7.   Failing to take the proper pursuit angle when running plays are away from the linebacker.
8.   Failing to pick up check-off backs in man-to-man coverage.
9.   Failing to clothesline potential receivers on crossing patterns and to knock off the tight end as he releases downfield.
10. Failing to communicate to teammates the strength of an offensive set and the type of play developing, such as pan, draw, screen, sweep, trap, bootleg, and so on.

Linebackers in Man-to-Man Coverage

Usually linebackers are assigned to cover offensive backs positioned in the offensive backfield when man coverage is utilized. If the back to whom a linebacker is assigned releases out of the backfield, the linebacker should pick him up immediately. Otherwise the linebacker generally moves to zone coverage. There are four areas to be mastered by linebackers: concentration, position, drive, and hang coverage. Mistakes and errors are as follows:

1.   Concentration. Failure of the linebacker to pick up his intended receiver, whether he releases immediately or slow blocks and then releases on a delay.
2.   Position. Failure to get a two-yard cushion in depth and one yard inside or outside the intended receiver when he makes his final cut.
3.   Drive. Failing to close on the receiver when he makes his final cut, allowing the receiver to change direction and evade the linebacker.

4. Hang technique. Failure of the linebacker to drop hang in his area when the offensive back does not release but stops in to block. In order to give maximum support the linebacker should get back to his designated zone coverage area (usually book) and look up other intended receivers. However, the linebacker still has man coverage responsibilities if his man releases on a delay pattern.

Linebacker Errors and Mistakes in Zone Coverage

Errors and mistakes in zone coverage will be found in the following four basic techniques required of linebackers: drop, reaction, ball, and wall techniques.

1. Drop. Aligning too tightly to read pass indicators and failing to get sufficient depth when dropping back in zone coverage.
2. Reaction. Failing to drop at the proper angle. When a linebacker rounds out or drifts, intended receivers usually can get open easily by breaking back inside of the linebacker.
3. Ball. Waiting on the ball rather than taking it at its highest point. Break for the football when it is released. Do not wait to catch it or make the tackle after it has been caught by the receiver.
4. Wall. Failing to prevent possible receivers from running through his area. If he cannot physically wall a receiver off he should stay with him to the border of his zone. A linebacker should get depth and width quickly getting back to his zone responsibility. Then he should not "stand on a dime" but should look up receivers in his zone.

SECONDARY MISTAKES AND ERRORS

There are many physical errors that are made by secondary receivers, but these are easily corrected by constant drill and repetition. The mistakes that are hardest to correct are mental errors—and they are also the most critical. The correction of mental errors requires the constant effort of the coach, and it demands self-discipline on the part of the player.

Failure to Align Properly

One of the most common mistakes in man-to-man secondary play is not taking the proper alignment in depth or width initially with regard to the offensive receiver. Basically the defensive back will be one or two yards on the outside shoulder of the receiver five to eight yards deep with his outside foot forward. He should be in a balanced basketball stance with his weight evenly distributed on the balls of his feet, knees flexed, with good balance. He wants to use the sideline to his advantage when possible. He wants to play his correct alignment but change the look for the offensive receiver. The most common error in secondary alignment is the lack of self-discipline, which makes the defensive back careless or indifferent with regard to taking the proper position.

Failure to Key

Keys will vary from opponent to opponent but a player must be able to recognize the formation's strength. A secondary defender's keys and reactions are different if the strength of the offensive set is to his side and there are two eligible receivers who can release immediately, such as the tight end (Y) and the flanker back (Z), as opposed to a set with a single eligible receiver, such as the split end (X), on the opposite side of the formation. Should the running back (R) cheat or shift up to his split end's (X) side, the defensive secondary must recognize there are now four eligible receivers, two to each side, who can release immediately. The pass coverage is subject to change, too.

Many players fail to key through an offensive tackle or uncovered lineman to the ball for a quick pass and lose the opportunity to intercept it.

The common errors of set recognition can be prevented by using a five-minute drill period for recognizing your opponent's sets for the upcoming game. By using two offensive units to huddle and come out as rapidly as possible, the defense can get a picture quickly. Surprise or review sets may be added to keep quick adjustments in the defensive players' minds.

Lack of Concentration

Perhaps the key error in man-to-man coverage is the lack of total or consistent concentration. This might also include guessing, not reacting to what the receiver is actually doing but trying to guess what he *might* do.

After a defender has his key, he should focus his attention on the receiver immediately, concentrating on the receiver's number until the latter makes his final cut. The defender must ignore everything else but the receiver. He must discipline himself to not let anything distract his concentration on the receiver. Many coaches feel that total concentration makes up 80 percent of man-to-man pass coverage.

Failure to Backpedal Correctly

A defender must backpedal straight back with his shoulders parallel to the line of scrimmage, weight on the balls of the feet, and with good balance. His weight must be distributed evenly so he can drive or move laterally with ease. Common failures in this area involve getting the weight back over the heels and not using the arms correctly to help in the running action, in twisting the hips and body side to side, and in maintaining a low center of gravity.

Failure to Maintain Proper Positioning

A defensive back must gain a position of one yard outside and two yards deeper than the receiver coming downfield. He also must never let the receiver gain a head position with him but must maintain a two-yard gap staying in his original outside shoulder position on the receiver. He should always be strong on one side or the other off the receiver.

When the receiver breaks to beat his defender and get open, the defender must drive quickly with the receiver while still concentrating on him. When driving with a receiver who changes direction, the defender must be in a position so that the offensive receiver must make contact with him in order to make that change. He must gear himself mentally to explode on the receiver's final break.

The main errors in proper execution of the drive technique are in allowing the receiver to be too close and in having poor weight distribution, which prevents the quick change to the drive technique. Once the back has made the drive he should be in stride with the receiver step for step, looking for the ball through the receiver.

Failure to Play Football

When the ball is in the air a defensive back should always be in a position to explode through the receiver or be in a position to step in front of the receiver to intercept the flight of the football at its highest point. As he explodes through the receiver, he should strip the receiver of the football.

On a deep pass when forced between the receiver and the football a defender must be sure he can feel the receiver. When he can only get one hand on the football, he must have his other hand in a position to grasp the receiver. Playing the receiver instead of playing the ball is the worst situation. Here the defensive back must play the ball through the intended receiver, or he must release from the receiver and play the ball.

ZONE DEFENSE ERRORS

The basic technical errors in zone defense are the same as those in man-to-man with the following exceptions:

1. Alignment. Alignment must be the same, but there is a tendency for cornerbacks to deepen and the safety to take the deep middle to cheat over and back in order to get the jump. The players must discipline themselves to keep the physical alignment the same knowing where they must get to in order to cover zone responsibility if a pass shows. In the event of no pass, they must fill properly to shoulder off a run depending on the predetermined call versus a run.
2. Drop. The backs should backpedal to their areas indicated by the defense. Safeties and cornerbacks have a tendency not to get sufficiently deep enough but to come across flat, which sets up crossing patterns for the receivers.
3. Focus. The concentration is now on the ball *and* the receiver not just on the receiver.
4. Position. The deep middle of the zone is now paramount, not the man. The back must be in a position to play the ball perfectly driving to meet it at its highest point or to strip the receiver.

ERRORS AND MISTAKES IN BLITZ COVERAGE

The coverage techniques on the blitz are similar except that the safeties and cornerbacks can take away either the inside or outside position but must have the same relative two yards off when the receiver reaches the four-yard depth. The error lies when a defensive back fails to drive hard on the receiver's first break as usually the passer must dump the ball much sooner than anticipated or sustain a sack and loss if the blitz is effective.

ERRORS IN COMBINATION COVERAGES

In combination coverage all of the basics are the same except the cornerbacks play either man or zone depending on the route of the receiver. If the receiver breaks outside, the defender should play him man-to-man; if he breaks inside, the defender should remain in his designated zone ready to play the football and/or receiver coming into his area. A defensive corner must gain the self-discipline to play man coverage on the outside break and to stay in his zone when the receiver breaks inside. The inside safeties and corners need a lot of recognition work or pass skeleton work if this type of defense is to be successful.

SECONDARY COVERAGES

The failure to teach defenders to recognize the strengths and weaknesses of the various secondary coverages is a serious mistake. Many defensive secondaries while well coached in technique do not recognize the strengths and weaknesses of the pass coverage they are using in a given tactical situation. Complete comprehension of the secondary used in certain situations will help defenders to anticipate the offense's method of attacking it.

Basically there are three types of defensive secondary coverage: man-to-man, zone, and a combination of the two.

Zone Defense

Strengths   The zone defense is relatively easy to teach and does not need the outstanding athlete to perform; the defensive back learns to get to a specified area first and then to cover the receiver in that zone. He will be able to keep his eye on the ball reacting while it is in the air coming up to make the tackle. The main purpose of the zone defense is to stop the long pass.

Weaknesses   If the defense chooses to play several linebackers with their secondary, the defensive seams will be smaller but will allow the offensive line an opportunity to protect the passer more adequately. In order to increase the rush the defense must dog linebackers, thus widening the seams the defenders must protect. The zone defense is also vulnerable on the goal line as quick passes force the defenders a minimum of cushion so that the defensive secondary play is almost man coverage.

In general, when employing the zone defense, a defender should be aware the offense will attack by the following methods: short hooks, sideline, and flat patterns; flooding a given defensive zone; and diagonal patterns across the field.

Against the weak rotation of the zone defense the offense will attack as follows: the deep outside; in the flats; and with throwback pass action.

Against the four deep rotating zone the attack will concentrate on the deep outside and throwing back. Against a zone *invert* the offense will attack the deep middle and the flat areas. Against a *revert* or corner rotation zone, the offense will concentrate on attacking the deep middle and the deep outside.

Man-to-Man Coverage

Man-to-man defense has its own strengths and weaknesses and failure of the defensive team to understand them is considered a coaching error.

Strengths   Man-to-man coverage offers the defense much closer coverage of the offensive receiver than does zone. The use of man-to-man requires the offensive receiver to spend much more time on his release and route technique.

Weaknesses   Knowledge of the weaknesses of man-to-man defenses will indicate the method of attack by the opponent's offense. Basically, man-to-man defenses have the following weaknesses:

1. It places the defenders in a one-on-one situation and a defensive man must discipline himself to his correct alignment, keys, and responsibility. Individual technique must be mastered for man coverage to be effective.
2. Running plays in which the tight end releases, as in the pass situation, disrupts effective keying and forces a secondary defender to fill more slowly and less effectively versus the run.
3. Opponents usually try to release five receivers versus the four deep secondary and four receivers versus three deep situations, forcing linebackers into man-to-man coverage of the offensive backs.
4. The play action pass is strong versus man-to-man coverage.
5. Crossing routes and pick patterns are also favorite ways to free receivers versus man coverage.
6. Delay patterns, comeback routes, and surprises such as an unbalanced line with an eligible receiver on the short side or two backs flanked wide to the shore side (trips), cause problems for man coverage.
7. The use of wideouts and long motion can force the defensive secondary into having three defenders on one side of the field versus a single defender covering almost two-thirds of the width of the field one-on-one.

Linebacker Coverage

The linebacker unit must also be aware of the strengths and weaknesses of the defensive tactics that are being employed. It is essential they understand the weaknesses in order to recognize the methods their opponents will use to attack them.

The offense does the following in attacking linebackers:

1. Uses the play action pass forcing linebackers to play the run from which the quarterback will pass.
2. Against linebackers who overpursue, the offense will run delay patterns to the tight end, and throwback patterns and check patterns to receivers coming out of the offensive backfield.
3. Checks in terms of draws and screens are also favored against linebackers who overcommit themselves.

Failure of Groups to Communicate

One of the common errors of defensive units is the failure to communicate with each other. Communication is essential in unit strength and in the coordination of the force and contain units.

A coach must insist on immediate, loud, and clear calls giving direction of strength, type of rotation, or the stunt or adjustment that must be made. Defensive morale is built upon having players talk and communicate with each other. When the opposition attempts to pass, all defensive players should yell, "Pass," on an interception, "Apache," "Bingo," or some other agreed upon terminology; the same holds true for "Sweep," "Pitch," "Reverse," "Trap," and so on. This not only builds defensive morale and confidence by keeping each player informed and removing uncertainty, it is also good football. These calls must of course be made using the correct terminology.

Failure to Disguise the Secondary Coverage

Regardless of the types of secondary employed, they must be disguised to appear to be the same from vision on the field, the sideline, and the scouting booth. When disguising the alignment it is essential that a defensive man take almost identical alignments each time, being able to concentrate and discipline himself mentally and physically to be where he is supposed to be. False calls are essential when calling defensive coverage; use terms that though meaningless sound authentic.

GOAL LINE AND SHORT YARDAGE DEFENSES

It is best when your goal line and short yardage defenses are not tested too frequently in actual games. It is, however, an error not to test them in practice. In goal line and short yardage defenses there can be no physical or mental mistakes. Each player must master his alignment and defensive assignment. There must be flawless execution. Guessing and not getting penetration are common defensive linemen mistakes, and guessing in reading and reacting to keys are typical faulty play of defensive backs. There can be no easing up or loafing in short yardage or goal line defenses as each defender must make a maximum effort in his play. Each player must have confidence and pride in the defense, which comes from belief in the defense, his teammates, and his own individual ability to accomplish his assignment.

When defending its own goal line, the defense must be cognizant of the following:

Penetration and force on the keys.
Not defending the end line; it's the goal line plane that counts.
No readers. Attack the offense.
No guessers. Attack the offense.

TWO-MINUTE DEFENSE

Not infrequently the most critical part of a football game is the two minutes remaining to go in either half. Many games are won or lost in this short period of time. Therefore, it is essential that the team captain be aware of not only when the time is out, but whether time starts with the snap of the ball or by the referee indicating time has begun again, for each play. The remaining time-outs must not be used indiscriminately; on occasion you will want to work or bleed the clock if ahead in score and save the clock if behind in score.

When Possession Must be Gained

When time must be conserved a team should use its basic defenses, which are strongest against the run. The stunt or blitz should be used only when confusion might cause a fumble. Points to remember would include the following:

1. Unpile quickly and get into the defensive huddle. The next play must commence within twenty-five seconds after the referee

signals the ball is ready to play. The quicker the defense is ready the quicker the referee will indicate time commences.

2. Every effort should be made to force the ball carrier out of bounds on all wide plays or where he is near the sideline. The objective is to stop the clock.

3. It is important to know the clock is stopped on all incomplete passes, when the ball is out of bounds, or when the referee stops the clock to assess a penalty, or for measurement, or for other discretionary reasons.

4. The defensive captain must not waste a time-out when the clock is already stopped. He should use his remaining time-outs strategically, calling time as soon as the whistle terminates a play.

5. If a penalty is refused, the clock will start immediately. Otherwise, time does not commence again until the ball is put in play.

When Time Must Be Expended

The tactical situation is important here: time must be expended but knowing whether your opponent must score a touchdown or a field goal will determine how much field position you can give up. Points to remember in this situation would include the following:

1. Get up slowly from pile ups.
2. Do not permit the ball carrier or receiver to get out of bounds. Their objective is to save the clock; yours is to bleed the clock.
3. Blitz in only crucial situations.
4. Keep pass completions to short passes. Make sure tackles.
5. If a time-out is needed, do not call time while the clock is running.
6. If you are in doubt from a tactical standpoint, refuse penalties so the clock will keep running.

Just as practicing your two-minute offense in attempting to score is important, it is equally important to practice your two-minute defense, from the standpoint of running out the clock when you are ahead and of regaining possession of the football when you are behind.

SUSTAINING DEFENSIVE PENALTIES

Many of the penalties assessed against the defensive unit are judgment calls, others are rule violations. Through exercising self-discipline, utilizing proper techniques, maintaining poise, and being in good physical condition, a defense can eliminate most penalties. To sustain penalties is a player error. Not to correct them is a coaching mistake. The most commonly occurring defensive penalties are:

Offsides By either alignment or movement this penalty is inexcusable as the defenders should be exploding on ball movement not on guessing when the ball will be snapped.

Delay of the Game Easily avoidable when communications function and you have the proper number of players at their correct positions on the field ready to play. Otherwise, such a violation is almost a direct indictment of poor coaching.

Defensive Pass Interference One of the most difficult rules to interpret but can be decreased by proper attention to correct technique and self-discipline. The rules for chucking the receiver and playing the pass must be understood and basic techniques taught.

Illegal Use of Hands Mastery or proper techniques in neutralizing the offensive blocker and rushing the passer will take care of this, along with the player's self-discipline. The use of such terminology as "Hold up the receiver" may not be fully comprehended by an inexperienced defender.

Roughing the Passer Usually the result of frustration ending in a cheap shot. While defenders should go all out in an effort to get to the passer and make a sack, they must be taught and disciplined *not* to tackle or hit the passer after the whistle has blown the play dead.

Face Mask The face mask penalty is inexcusable when done intentionally, but it is not difficult to sustain this penalty as the result of accidentally grabbing a face mask. Great care in tackling technique and not being in the position of having to reach in or grab on will help in avoiding this penalty.

Spearing The objective is to pile up the runner not to pile on the runner, especially on a late hit. Knowledge of the rules and self-discipline will eliminate spearing.

Unsportsmanlike Conduct and Expulsion These are inexcusable penalties, and your players must realize this. Every player must be made to understand that you do not have your best team on the field if a regular is expelled from the game. An individual who sustains such a penalty hardly contributes to his team's victory by sitting on the bench.

Hidden Yardage   Sustaining the above defensive penalties not infrequently allows your opposition to maintain possession of the football, improves their field position, puts your team in poor field position, nullifies great defensive plays, and adversely affects team morale. Effective coaching entails correcting all of these errors to minimize their occurrence.

10 KICKING GAME MISTAKES AND ERRORS, AND HOW TO AVOID THEM

The first prerequisite in eliminating kicking game mistakes and errors is to establish a *positive attitude* as to your kicking game's value and importance. It is a well-established fact that in order to win you must be superior to your opposition in two of these three main categories: kicking game, defense, and/or offense. Yet most coaches probably consider these three phases of football in the reverse order from that just listed; some relegate their kicking game to a minor role of importance, and as a result, their players view it the same way. Frequently the practice of kicking game techniques not only receives the lowest priority in terms of the time allotment and attention by the staff, but usually it is practiced last when the players are tired. While the kicking game does not share equally in importance to offense and defense, the kicking game's importance must be considered in its proper perspective as a transitional phase of the game. Excellence in the kicking game can probably get a team out of trouble more quickly than any other phase of football, and the failure to perform competently in kicking game skills can create innumerable problems, from which a team cannot extricate itself by its offense and defense. Unless you have a superior offense, it is difficult to acquire consistently favorable field position without a competent punting game, including returning punts, because few offensive teams are capable of driving the distance of the field for a score. Statistics reveal that even the outstanding offensive football teams score only one-third of the time they gain possession of the football. To drive the distance of the field and score is rare.

Also, even with a good offense, when your team turns the football over to your opposition your intent is to do so in their three-down zone, and frequently this is accomplished by punting the football down field and then limiting the run back of the punt by good coverage. Conversely, without a good defense, including the ability to return the punt to attempt to attain desirable field position, your outstanding offensive team may spend most of the game on the sideline. Therefore, if the kicking game is thought of in positive terms, it takes on more importance than merely something to be done when the offense bogs down or a team is about to acquire possession after a kicking game task occurs. The kicking game is the transitional phase of football, and not infrequently mistakes and errors in the kicking game result in big plays that change the course of the game completely. There is more hidden yardage in the kicking game than in any other phase of football, and usually a coach does not realize this and put it into its proper perspective until he analyzes his offensive and defensive drive charts and statistics after the game (see Chapter 8).

KICKING GAME STATISTICAL BREAKDOWN

An analysis of statistics of a typical football game is likely to reveal at least 25 percent of each game is spent in some form of the kicking game. In professional football, it has been found that 60 percent of the lost yardage in a game comes as a result of the kicking game, along with 25 percent of the scoring. Probably the most meaningful statistic, however, is where one team turns over to its competition possession of the football as the result of breakdowns in kicking game skills, some of which may result immediately in scores or may set up eventual scoring opportunities. Games have been lost as the result of such mistakes and errors as failing to punt on fourth down when back in the three-down zone of play, slicing or shanking the ball on the punt or kick-off, mishandling the snap from center, partly to cover properly on punts and kick-offs, failure to kick the sure field goal, mishandling the opposition's punt inside the 10-yard line, having punts blocked, roughing the punter, nullifying a good return by clipping, and on and on.

Analyze Your Kicking Game Breakdowns

As former members of several major college football coaching staffs with many years' experience, the authors have had personal involvement in more than two dozen games that were won or lost as a result of kicking game breakdowns. We suggest you analyze your game films carefully, and should you decide to make a training film at the end of the season of kicking game mistakes and errors (see Chapter 12), you will probably be able to assemble hundreds of feet of film illustrating breakdowns in the kicking zone. It is well to keep in mind that probably most coaches spend far less than 25 percent of their available practice time on the kicking game, despite the fact that in the typical game approximately 25 percent of the contest involves the combined phases of the kicking game. From a positive standpoint you can win with your kicking game. However, you must be sold on it, and you must devote sufficient time to practicing its various phases.

Practice

Almost every session should include practicing some phase of the kicking game under various situational conditions, including weather variables. While games are played in adverse weather, many coaches fail to practice particularly their kicking game under less than ideal conditions. You should practice your kicking game under adverse weather conditions, punting with and against the wind, with a wet football, handling bad snaps from center on critical situations, such as when punting from your own end zone, squib kicking, punting out of bounds, the on-side kick, and so on.

Factors to Consider   Knowing how well your defense can play will have a bearing on your kicking game. Knowing how well your offense can move the ball also affects your kicking game philosophy, as does your knowledge of the strength and weaknesses of your opponent's kicking game. All of the foregoing elements should be considered in formulating your individual practice time plan.

SPECIAL TEAMS PHILOSOPHY

Even though your coaching situation may not allow you to use entirely different teams in your kicking game, the special teams philosophy is worth a coach's serious study and consideration. Basically, it involves getting your best players on the field in all areas of the kicking game. They may be a mixed bag of offensive and defensive starters and substitutes, but they must have a burning desire to make something happen in the kicking game.

Proper execution of the kicking game requires a combination of pride, desire, and discipline. Each team has many players who fit this description. They are not always the starters so this gives others an opportunity to perform and contribute to maximum team performance.

No one method of designing special teams is correct: One example might be to use your total defensive team minus one for the punter in order to cover punts. Since field position is of the utmost importance, who should have greater pride than the defensive unit in securing it? The defensive unit is also likely to be more rested and capable of all-out coverage than your offensive unit.

Goal Setting

Each of these units—offense, defense, special teams—should set realistic goals for itself in attaining excellence. These goals may be set based on the previous year's performance of their own team and perhaps compared to the conference leader in their league. Their goals may be general in nature, such as the following:

> To make at least one big play to break open the game.
> To score on special teams.
> To win at least two games by special teams this season.

Giving recognition for accomplishments to special teams members and units not only does much for morale purposes but also aids them to achieve their goals.

COMMUNICATION

The ability to communicate clearly and succinctly is as important for the kicking game as it is for the offensive and defensive phases of football (see Chapters 8 and 9). The huddle system and the importance of adopting simple, concise, meaningful terminology were explained previously.

In the huddle, the signal caller need only say:

> "Spread punt on the ball (or at will)."
> "Field goal on the ball."
> "Extra point on the ball."

"On the ball or at will" means the offensive center will snap the ball when he is ready, after the punter or holder of the ball for the field goal or extra point signals to the center he is ready to receive the center's snap.

Or the signal caller in the huddle may say:

"Kick-off return middle, ready break," or "Punt rush left, ready break." Avoid wordiness. If effective teaching-coaching has occurred, the signal caller need not describe or identify blocking or rushing assignments. Nor should the signal caller attempt to coach his teammates by giving special instructions. All of the huddle commands should be short and concise.

KICKING GAME MISTAKES AND ERRORS

It appears there are incongruencies in coaching the kicking game in particular. As indicated previously, the kicking game typically has the lowest priority in that it is practiced last and receives the least amount of attention and time. Yet at the same time the tendency is to attempt to give it the most concentrated attention or to overcoach what is being taught-coached. As an illustration, a coach may have a punter with natural leg swing but poor technique although he achieves the desired results in punting the football. Too frequently the coach will overcoach this particular punter in order to get him to fit into a particular mold or style in punting. Usually the result is that his style improves in that he looks better when punting, but his effectiveness in terms of desired results diminishes. While major mistakes should be corrected, you should permit him to utilize his natural leg swing and punt the football in the manner in which he achieves the best results, regardless of his style. The same principle is applicable to place kicking for extra points and to kicking off.

THE KICK-OFF

Kick-off Team's Goals

It is important for the kick-off team to set reasonable goals, such as the following:

> Not to allow any long returns that would enable the opposition to commence its offense in good field position.
> Allow no returns for touchdowns.
> Hold return team to inside its own 20-yard line.
> Regain possession of the football for our offensive team.

Kick-off Mistakes and Errors

Mistakes and errors in this phase of the kicking game may be the result of poor attitude, carelessness, inadequate drive, or lack of knowledge of the rules or of how to perform the skills and techniques properly.

Offsides A common mistake, easily corrected, is for one of the end men to line up offside on the kick-off or for a player to cross the 40-yard line on coverage before the kicker's boot meets the football. Frequently, it is merely a matter of being overeager and can usually be handled by having the two outside people yell across the formation cautioning the players not to be offside. This problem may also be remedied by aligning your kicking team to allow vision to the football so that the latter is the focal point and cautioning players not to cross the line until they see their kicker's foot meet the football.

Bunching Up on Coverage   Losing proper spacing, which results in opening return lanes, is a more common error on almost all kick coverage. If a member of the coverage team runs around an opponent's block and does not get back into his designated coverage pattern, several players will be in close proximity to each other and there will be gaping holes in the coverage. The remedy is to teach your players on coverage not to slow up and catch a blocker but to evade blockers quickly, or to run through the blocker who overextends on his block and stay in the designated coverage lanes.

Staying Blocked   There is no disgrace in getting knocked down for this will happen in every game. Coverage team members should expect to be blocked, but they are not expected to stay blocked. They should release from their blocker as quickly as possible, and if knocked down, they are expected to bounce up immediately and pursue on course.

Loafing on Coverage   Many players unconsciously ease up when they see the ball kicked deep or away from them. Kick-off coverage requires an all-out effort to get to the ball carrier before the blocking wall can be set up in order to pin down the offense as close to their goal line as possible. The offensive objective is to advance the football at least to their own 20-yard line.

Failure to Contain   The failure to contain generally falls into three categories: lack of self-discipline, temperament, and confusion. The player who lacks the self-discipline to contain and wants to do it his way is always a problem. To put him in a contain position is a mistake. His temperament may be such that he could be better utilized as a wedge breaker or as a head hunter pursuing directly to the ball carrier. You can design your coverage specifically with his role and function in mind. However, if you assign him contain responsibility to anchor the net in order to keep the ball inside and he fails to carry out his responsibility, the ball carrier can get outside containment and the kicking team members are now chasing not pursuing the ball carrier. Anytime a ball carrier gets outside of containment, the result is usually a long gainer or a score.

Oftentimes when a team changes its coverage, contain men, or safeties in an effort to confuse their opposition or to throw off the latter's timing and blocking pattern, one or more members of the kicking team will fail to get word of the change. This may be caused in the huddle by a poor or indifferent attitude on the part of the signal caller, crowd noise, or nonchalance on the part of the contain man or safety. Other causes may be in having too many coverages with too many varieties of assignments. In an attempt to create confusion for the opposition, you must be careful you do not create even more confusion for your own players. Constant attention to detail in practice and the coaches' re-emphases will usually solve these problems.

Failure to Play Safety   The failure to be a safety when called upon usually occurs for the same reasons as failures to contain. The remedies are also essentially the same.

Check your huddle communications. Is the huddle formed as you have coached it, without confusion in terminology or duties required by coverage?

Check the attitude or temperament of the individual.

Have you incorporated too many coverages and/or assignments?

Slowing Up in Contact Zone   Oftentimes this comes about by the lack of understanding of what is meant by "breaking down or coming under control," which is a coachable item and must be drilled. Coming to balance or being under control requires work in practice. A common mistake is to instruct a player what to do in the execution of a technique but fail to give him sufficient practice in executing that technique.

Slowing up in the contact zone may also be mental to the extent that the player plays too cautiously, overly concerned that the ball carrier may evade him. The pursuer must realize that coverage is a *team* function not an individual one.

After Ten Yards It Is a Free Ball   After the ball goes 10 yards on a kick-off, it is anyone's ball. Members of the kick-off team should scramble quickly to regain possession of the football, and members on the receiving team should only try to cover the ball, gaining possession of it. Neither team should try to advance the squib kick or the on-side kick.

If the ball does *not* go ten yards on the kick-off, members of the kicking team should not touch or down the ball but crowd around it and let it keep rolling ten yards before covering it. Members of the receiving team should down the ball immediately but should not try to advance it.

Misplaying the Reverse or Bootleg   Typically, teams return a kick-off up the middle with wedge or cross blocking, or utilize a sideline return trying to get the ball carrier behind a wall and into a return alley. In actuality, relatively few teams utilize a criss-cross return with one of the twin safeties handing off or faking a hand-off to the other. However, your coverage must make provisions for the reverse or the bootleg solo, and contain men frequently play the sideline return improperly. Contain men are responsible for searching any opposing player coming to their side of the field, but they must not play their positions so deeply and loosely that the ball carrier can break back inside of the end man. Most sideline returns are designed to block the end man out anyway, aware of the fact he is outside contain oriented. By covering too deeply and playing softly he actually aids the opposition in breaking the play back inside of his outside contain position. He must "squeeze down and in" from the outside on the ball carrier, anchoring the net so other pursuers can converge and make the tackle. Pursuing directly to the ball is a mistake; it is also a mistake if he does not close the net anchoring it from the outside in.

Too Many Coverages   Doing a few things well rather than many poorly is a sound coaching principle. Therefore, it is possible to have too many types of kick-off coverage and strategy. Moving your kick-off man from sideline to sideline, changing positions or personnel of your safeties, may appear to be relatively simple, but it may create more problems for your players than for the opposition's. The amount of details and techniques your players must master in several coverages is not overwhelming unless some of your players are also involved with other areas of special teams, plus perhaps playing defense and backing up on the offensive unit. Keeping your coverage simple and getting outstanding performance in execution is more sound than trying to teach-coach multi-coverages. The on-side or short kick-off should never be excluded, however.

The On-side Kick   The term "on-side kick" is actually a misnomer, erroneously labeled because the football must travel at least ten yards in order for the kick-off team to be awarded possession if they recover the short kick. However, the short kick is commonly referred to as the on-side kick, and it is an important phase of the kicking game. It also requires practice. Often the on-side kick technique is not practiced enough to guarantee a high percentage of success.

The decision to go for an on-side kick should be made as far in advance as possible. Lining up quickly and utilizing the on-side kick without the appearance of preparing to do something special may force a mental mistake on the receiving team in terms of readiness or substitution. Sideline conferences, given the tactical situations, often alert the opponent's defense to a sure on-side kick and allow proper substitutions to be made.

Frequently the kick is made and recovered only to be short of having moved forward ten yards. Repetitive practice of this type of kick is essential, and the use of a specialty or pre-practice period for the kicker to work on this technique daily will help.

Some teams have had excellent success using a starter or the man next to the regular kicker to handle this duty; this leaves him free to work on this special technique daily. Setting a target at eleven yards downfield will aid the kicker. During the game have a coach or manager stand on the sideline a distance of eleven yards from where the ball is lined up. The drawback is that the kicker must change sides of the formation when his team changes ends of the field, although this can be built into the team coverage rule by having him always be to the side of the kicker away from his own bench.

Regardless of whether the ball goes ten yards or not, the personnel designated as "gunners," those who are going directly to the football, must sell out and cover the kick. The prevention of the ball getting out-of-bounds is the responsibility of these gunners. They will ensure this naturally if they are giving 100 percent effort in getting to the football.

All personnel not designated as gunners are responsible for maintaining their proper lane coverage. They should not be overeager but should carry out their designated coverage responsibilities. Someone must be designated to be sure that the football does not rebound backwards toward the kicking team's goal line; this is usually the safety's responsibility.

The Free Kick after the Safety

There comes a time each season where taking an intentional safety can ensure a team victory. There are also times when a safety is given up unintentionally. In either event, the team taking the safety must be able to utilize the free kick.

Intentional Safety A plan for taking an intentional safety should be part of each team's total package. When you are being handled physically late in the game it is often better to give up two points and get the ensuing free kick than risk a blocked punt or long punt return that could result in a possible loss of the game. Three methods of taking an intentional safety are as follows:

To have the center snap the ball over the punter's head out of the end zone.
To have the punter receive the snap and step out of the end zone.
To allow the punter to wait, run around in the end zone consuming as much time as possible, and then step out-of-bounds or fall down before being tackled.

The first two are low risk tactics, and the third involves the risk of a fumble and a resulting touchdown if the punter (or quarterback) is tackled before he steps out of bounds or falls to the ground in the end zone. In all cases, however, the person handling the ball must *not* try to make a big play no matter how open it may seem.

Kicking Off after the Safety   In covering the kick-off following a safety, a team is wise to use the same coverage as on a regular kick-off. When kicking off with the regular kick-off man, everything will remain constant. However, when using your punter, he must be aware he now takes a position *one and one-half yards ahead* of the cover team.

Punt or Kick-off   The coach should select his best kicker here. Whether the safety is intentional or otherwise he must get the best possible field position from the ensuing kick. The height of the kick is a decided factor in this selection. Distance is important but only in terms of *maximum coverage* versus the abilities of the return men. Consistency is imperative in a free kick situation, as a sliced or shanked kick is likely to give your opposition immediate field position. The time remaining, the weather, and the score should also be considered in making the selection of whether to punt or kick off in each free kick situation. The coverage mistakes and errors have been discussed previously.

POINT-AFTER-TOUCHDOWN AND FIELD GOAL ATTEMPTS

One of the primary mistakes relevant to the extra point is the failure of the staff to decide during a scoring drive whether to go for two points or for one. Such indecision usually prevents a smooth transition to the next phase of the game with resulting penalties for too many or too few men on the field or taking too much time, or having to waste a time out. These may also occur as a result of indecision on whether to go for a touchdown or to attempt a field goal.

Another area of concern is the failure to have the kicking team together on the sideline in advance of the time of need. Drills against the clock on running onto the field, lining up with no huddle, and getting the play off when no time-outs remain, will also pay dividends.

Personnel Errors

The most common errors for the kicking team are failure to get the snap count in the huddle, including kicking at will, and failure to align properly. The players should align from the center out.

For the center, the failure to make a perfect snap is a common error. The center's first responsibility is a perfect snap. He must not be intimidated by sudden movement or false starts by the defensive front or linebackers.

Holder   The holder may commit the following errors:

1. Failure to align properly. The kicker will set the alignment, but the holder must also check so he is not too close to the tee to inhibit the kicker nor so far that he must overextend to place the ball on the kicking tee.
2. Not concentrating on the ball on the snap. The holder must follow the ball all the way into his hands.
3. Iron hands. The holder should be selected with care—a primary consideration being quick hands. He must take the ball at its highest point, relax his hands, catch the ball, and make the smooth accurate transfer to the tee.

Kicker   The kicker may commit the following errors:

1. Failure to align properly. The kicker must be constantly aware of where he is kicking from. The position of the football in relationship to yard line and hash mark are critical in ball placement with reference to both his formation and the goal posts.
2. Failure to take a comfortable balanced stance. He must assume a stance from which he can move quickly and smoothly into his kicking motion.
3. Failure to concentrate. The kicker must concentrate totally on the task to be attempted and the spot at which the ball will be placed. This concentration will allow him a slight correctable margin of error in case of a misplacement, as well as maximum contact of his foot with the football.
4. Stepping technique. Proper timing is essential in stepping to kick the football. Too few steps will cause a lack of smooth kicking motion and lack of power; too many steps will result in reaching for the ball and a poor kick.
5. Looking up. The kicker cannot hit squarely what he cannot see. Keeping the head down and following through is mandatory. Crowd noise and the scoreboard will indicate success or failure of the kick. Having the kicker pick up a blade of grass or the tee before looking up have been successful methods in keeping his head down.

Field Goal and Extra Point Protection

Protection for the kicker, whether area, zone, or man-on-man, will vary with the coach's philosophy and his personnel. Common mistakes and errors are as follows:

1. Failure to block gaps. Rules must be devised to block gaps first in this situation.
2. Chasing upbacks. Not blocking—the basic rule—and going out chasing the outside rusher, leaving the inside seam open.
3. Overanxious center. The center's primary responsibility is to make a perfect snap first, then to block.
4. Improper offensive stance. Too much weight back on the heels or tail allows the defender to overpower the offensive blocker.
5. Being offside, either by alignment or moving prior to the snap, is a common mistake.

Field Goals   Protection rules are usually the same for extra points and field goals. However, in the field goal attempt as in the punt and kick-off, patterned coverage is essential. Common failures in the field goal coverage are as follows:

1. Failing to sustain block. While coverage is important, protection for the field goal attempt is imperative.
2. Failing to release downfield. Center should call "cover," alerting his teammates to release downfield and not remain at the line of scrimmage after the ball has been kicked.
3. Failing to fan out to cover the field. Coach your team to fan out covering the width of the field rather than remaining bunched up in coverage.
4. Failing to maintain patterned spacing. Set the net for the defender trying to return the field goal attempt should the kick be short.
5. Failing to identify the direction of the kick. The kicker should call the direction of the kick, which will help the covering team to control the return if the kick is unsuccessful.
6. Overanxious center. Failing to make a perfect snap in preference to blocking first.
7. Chasing by upbacks. No blocking the gap and leaving too soon to contain.
8. Failing to contain. The upbacks forgetting responsibility to contain outside.
9. No safety support or failure of holder and kicker to cover to their respective sides. Usually the holder will cover to his right and the kicker to his left (opposite for a left-footed kicker).
10. Failing to cover. The linemen must block first, then get out and cover. They cannot be held up or remain at the line of scrimmage watching what occurs.

Kicking from the Hash Mark   While the protection and coverage rules are the same whether attempting the field goal from the middle or the hash marks, in the latter situation common critical mistakes are as follows:

1. Failing to call "cover," and offensive player not allowing for the wide side of the field in coverage.
2. Failure of the kicker to call the direction of the kick. This is a *must*.
3. Improper alignment of holder and kicker. The kicker must take into consideration the angle of the kick as it is more acute the closer you are to the opposition's goal line. Some highly successful teams have gone to unbalanced line protection to the wide side on field goals kicked from the hash mark.

No-chance Field Goal or Extra Point Play

It is important to have an alternative plan when the snap is mishandled for some reason. Many teams will have an automatic pass or run for such an occasion. When this fails, it is usually because of:

1. Illegal receiver downfield on the pass. The kicker must immediately call "ice," "fire," or some other designated term to alert linemen to stay with his block and not go downfield. Such a call will also notify the ends and upbacks to release to get open as receivers.
2. Failure of receivers to get sufficient depth on a pass. In the field goal situation that breaks down, the ends and upbacks must get enough depth for the first down if a pass is indicated.
3. Failure of receivers to adjust routes. Eligible receivers away from the passer should work in the direction the passer scrambles.
4. Failure of kicker or holder to block. The player not recovering the snap must block the most dangerous rusher. Too often he becomes a spectator and merely observes what is occurring.
5. Failing to cover. In the broken field goal attempt, the line must cover as on a regular pass. The passer must make a direction call in the event of an interception.

Special Plays from Extra Point and Field Goal Formations

Special plays—runs, passes, and screens—are the products of individual head coaches and their staffs. The danger is in becoming too involved in trying to fool the opposition and taking away from the basics.

There may be a time in a game or against a certain opponent when including this type of play might be a bonus in terms of scoring, taking advantage of the overzealous play of a particular defensive player, or slowing up the rush or certain stunts of the opposition. If this is the case, it might be well to add a play as a special or momentum changer.

SPREAD PUNT

The punt is an excellent weapon when used properly and when mistakes are minimized.

Formation Selection

Great care should go into the selection of the primary kicking formation. The ultimate selection should be based on

1. Maximum protection—two upbacks versus three deep backs.
2. Center's deep snap capability in terms of accuracy, speed, and distance. If your center cannot get the ball back accurately thirteen yards in .07 to .09 seconds, the kicker should not be aligned thirteen yards deep.
3. The kicker's ability to get the kick away in 1.3 to 1.5 seconds. Getting the ball away quickly is imperative. If the total time exceeds 2.1 seconds, the chances of the punt being blocked escalate greatly.

Center   Common errors and mistakes made by the center are as follows:

1. Failure to make the deep pass consistently to the punter with speed and accuracy within the prescribed time stated above. Constant practice while working on weights or with a weighted ball aids performance.
2. Releasing the ball too late; this causes the snap to be too high.
3. Releasing the ball too early; this causes the snap to be too low.
4. The target for the center is the inside thigh of the punter's kicking leg. If the pass is not on target, time is expended positioning the football.

Punter   Common mistakes and errors made by the punter are as follows:

1. Not concentrating on the snap, flight, and trajectory of the ball. He must focus on the ball all the way through from its

position on the ground as the center holds it until he "sees" his foot into the football.

2. Not being in a relaxed, balanced position. He must be able to adjust to a snap from center that is off target vertically and/or laterally.

3. Releasing the ball too quickly, which results in a poor drop; the ball is literally thrown at the foot.

4. Dropping the ball too low, which results in the line drive kick, which in turn is usually either blocked or returned for a long run.

5. Dropping the ball too far outside, which results in a sliced or shanked kick.

6. Adjusting or "molding" the ball too slowly, which in a hurried finish to the smooth kicking motion usually results in a blocked kick or a poor punt.

7. Dropping the ball too close to the body, which results in a loss of power and usually a muffed punt.

8. Overstriding. The results are an uneven drop, caught too far out on the toe, and an end-over-end or line drive kick.

9. Trying to overpower the ball. As in golf do not try to kill the ball. Strive for a smooth, rhythmical leg swing and punting motion.

10. Lack of knowledge of the situation and rules. On a bad snap on fourth down the punter must punt the ball, even if he must execute a running punt. On third down the punter may try to advance the ball, providing he has possession of it, but it is safer to fall on the ball, retain possession, and punt on fourth down.

11. In kicking from the end zone, stepping on the back line of the end zone is an automatic safety. The personal protector should be given the assignment to alert the kicker prior to the snap, "Watch the end line."

12. Failing to work with a center. The center and the punter are a team and should work together at all times.

Protectors Common errors and mistakes by protectors when in punt alignment are as follows:

1. Failing to block gaps. The blocking rules must be designed to cover basic gap situations. With two men in gap, a help call is needed. The lineman should point out whom they will block to avoid misunderstanding.

2. The upbacks releasing too soon. The upbacks must block their area first, then take the proper coverage routes.

3. Personal protector too deep. The protector must not line up too deep or step back into the punter. He should scan from the center to the kicking leg side of the punter and attack the most dangerous rusher who threatens. He must not retreat. He must be aware of an overload situation to one side or the other. He must alert the punter to end line when kicking from end zone.

4. Gunners or head hunters are those assigned to go directly to ball, and not infrequently a gunner jumps offside, forgetting to get his man blocked first.

Contain Men The failure to contain usually occurs for the following reasons:

1. A mix-up in assignment especially when you are changing up your coverage.

2. A lack of discipline in not recognizing the team role, which may be caused by being out of position or by an assignment having been changed.

3. By getting jammed inside and not getting back on his course. This player needs work on releasing through a defender.

4. Not getting off the ball. A player's technique may be poor or he may not be physical enough to release from the defender who holds him up at the line.

5. Coverage personnel may be jammed inside, may not be recovering, and may fail to run the prescribed position coverage lanes.

Punting from Hash Marks

When kicking the ball from the hash mark, it is well for the punter to kick the ball so that it lands between the near hash mark and near sideline, rather than in the wide side of the field. He must avoid the exact center of the field and wide side of the field or the ball is outside the majority of the coverage. When only part of the coverage makes the adjustment, gaping lanes are opened for the punt return and it is difficult for the offensive players to obtain proper coverage. This error occurs because of a lack of discipline and a lack of comprehension of team responsibility.

Safety If a safety fails to cover this designated area of responsibility or coverage, it is usually because he loses his perspective or misjudges his relationship to the field, and/or he loafs and uses the offensive punt coverage as a rest period.

Punter   The punter's failure to call the direction of punt right, left, or short, can cause coverage breakdown. Coverage may overrun the ball or not get desired field coverage.

Contain   The coverage must locate the football as soon as possible, each man covering in his designated lane and not following the same colored jersey. Each must then close on the ball, gathering, breaking down, and not overrunning the return man. The contain men must maintain a position to force the ball inside, keeping relative position on the ball and teammates, and not overrunning the return man or being driven outside. A container must not let a blocker get the outside position on him.

SPECIAL PUNT FORMATIONS

Tight Punt

The snap kick and general protection coverage in the tight punt are the same as for the spread punt with one notable exception: that is, all blockers hold until the ball is punted. Change-ups in head hunters and contain men may be necessary, but the coach must be wary of too many assignments being changed as this increases the opportunity of individual breakdowns.

Squib or Soft Kick

The squib or soft kick snap protection and coverage are the same as those for the spread punt except for the following:

1. The punter will not kick as hard but will simply punch the ball downfield. He should strive for height on his punt.
2. Coverage failure results when the first man down fails to keep the ball from going in the end zone.
3. The player downing the ball must not leave the ball unattended until the whistle blows the ball dead.

Special Punt Plays

You should probably have at least one running play for attempting short yardage, and possibly an option run-pass for long yardage, when you *must gamble* and *not punt*. However, there are exceptions to the rule, and you must remember the time factor and its relationship to the learning process if success is to be achieved.

RETURNS

Kick-off Returns

The kick-off return is a valuable weapon for attaining good field position, which is the returning team's primary objective. Realistically, any return beyond the 20-yard line must be considered as a plus for the receiving team; if a team does not get the ball out to the 20-yard line on the kick-off return, it is a plus and evidence of excellent coverage for the kick-off team. Unfortunately, many returning teams contribute to a kick-off team's success because they commit mistakes and errors.

Trying to teach and utilize too many different types of returns is just such a mistake. The lack of practice time to teach *and perfect* returns is always a factor.

Complicated rules cause confusion for the returning team, especially when the kick-off team crosses pursuers on their coverage routes.

It is difficult to run reverses with return men who are not quick afoot. On most teams there are usually few "blazers," individuals with outstanding speed. While your objective may be to get the ball to your speedster on the return, your opposition's objective is to keep the ball away from him. Plowhorses run best straight ahead, and trying to time out reverses with them is more advantageous for the kicking team than the receiving team.

When there is an exchange of the football on a criss-cross return or on a simulated buck lateral series with a hand-off where several players handle the football, the probability of a fumble is high.

While a coach cannot control the weather, he must consider it as a factor that does have a bearing on the type of return he employs. Footing may be a problem, too, depending on the weather and condition of the field. Across the field returns are difficult to time out in adverse weather.

Safeties   Typically, safety men make the big mistake of not communicating. The failure to call, "yours" or "mine" or "down it," the latter indicating the receiver should not attempt to run the ball out of the end zone, are the most common errors. The lack of communication may be between the players and the coaches, too, in that the returning team has too few or too many players on the field to receive the kick-off. An assistant coach on the sideline must be held accountable so this mistake does not occur; and a player on the receiving team should be designated to make certain eleven players are on the receiving team when the play commences.

Offside   Players must talk to each other about improper alignment and caution each other not to leave too soon and sustain an offside penalty.

Clipping By knowing the rule and having proper concentration and technique, a player can avoid clipping. The guideline to teach is, "If in doubt, let him go," which means do not try to block a pursuer if it is questionable whether it will be a legal block or a clip.

On-side or Short Kick Return

Having the best hands on your team line-up is important when an onside or short kick is anticipated. However, having the players with the best hands in the proper position will not be sufficient if they *fail* to do the following:

1. Recover the kick. Recovery is the single objective, not advancing the football; it requires total team discipline and an all-out effort.
2. Take good alignment. Often members of the receiving team take alignments in which their vision to the kicker and the ball is impaired or blocked by a teammate.
3. Aid the teammate who is fielding the ball. Not all of the members on the receiving team are in a position to field the ball, especially when it is kicked off to one side. If the ball bounces over the front line of players, they should block and protect, not turn back to try to recover the ball. Players in the second line will recover the ball. If the ball is kicked in front of the first line of players, those to the side the ball is kicked should attempt to recover it immediately and other players should attempt to block in front of the teammate who fields the kick.
4. Block in front of the ball so as not to clip. Most clips occur behind the play.

Kick-off Return after a Safety

Since your opposition will be putting the ball in play by a free kick from their own 20-yard line, the receiving team's objective is to *not lose field position* on the possession. Therefore, no effort should be made to get fancy. A straight ahead return will typically garner the most yardage. Many coaches substitute their punt return specialist in this situation with a three-deep secondary in order to cover the width of the field in handling the opposition's free kick after a safety.

Punt Return and Punt Block

Punt rushes and punt returns usually will vary from week to week according to the opposition's alignment and personnel strengths and weaknesses. Punt return and block schemes are designed to consider technique and timing to take advantage of any weaknesses the opponent might have.

Mistakes to Avoid　The following are punt return and punt block mistakes and errors:

1. Being offside, which may be caused by improper alignment or failure to communicate with each other. Inform your players to key the ball properly in order to avoid being offside.
2. Roughing the kicker. This usually results from failure to aim at the point where the punter's foot will *meet* the football, not where he lines up to punt.
3. Clipping downfield. This is the result of failing to read the path and action of the pursuer to be blocked.
4. Letting the ball hit the ground. All kicks should be fielded whenever possible.
5. Fielding the ball inside the 10-yard line.
6. Being hit with the bounding ball. Each team should have a designated call, such as "Peter," as an illustration, which informs teammates to get away from a bounding ball.
7. Being surprised. Always have a "spy," a player designated to check the run or pass.
8. Turning back on the football getting into the wall before the ball has been punted.

Not-sure Kick Situations

In every game there are situations where a coach and his team are uncertain whether the opposition is definitely going to kick the football despite the fact they are in a punting, field goal, or extra point kicking formation. Generally, tactical factors such as the score and time remaining to play will determine whether you rush, return, or play it safe defending against a pass or run from the kick formation.

Extra Point Try　As an illustration, if your opposition is behind by one point, the point-after-touchdown try will usually be a placement kick attempting the extra point. Typical strategy would be to rush hard to try to block the placement attempt. However, if the opposition is down by two points and lines up in a place kicking formation, it would be wiser *not* to have an all-out rush but to play a safe defense looking for the pass or run. While pressure will be minimal with contain men only, should your opposition go ahead and successfully kick the point-after-touchdown, you still have a one-point lead.

Field Goal Whether to rush, return, or play the field goal attempt safe looking for the pass or run, would depend on the same tactical factors as above, plus the ability, distance, and accuracy of the opposition's field goal kicker. Wind and weather conditions may be a factor, too.

Punt Formation A run or pass from punt formation, when you are expecting the punt, is probably the most critical error and probably the most embarrassing, too, because it permits the opposition to keep possession of the football. Therefore, you must have a safe defense, usually a read type with zone or secondary coverage, as your primary objective is to prevent the pass or run for the first down. If the football is punted, usually the return is unorganized to the extent that each member on the return team blocks the nearest pursuer and the player who fields the punt tries to get all of the return yardage he can. If man coverage is used involving linebackers and secondary defenders, a single safety can be freed up to play the deep zone and field the ball should it be kicked. Otherwise if he plays at his usual depth and has pass responsibility, it is likely the opposition will punt the ball over his head, and much yardage and field position will be lost because you have neither a rush nor a return. If a team were to go into a punt formation on other than fourth down, you would be compelled to play a safe defense expecting the pass or run. Should they continue to employ the same tactics whether on third or fourth down, then you must decide whether to play your secondary normal or to free up a single safety as indicated above to return the punt. Should you choose the latter, although you will be utilizing man coverage, which is not as safe as zone coverage, at least you will have a player in position to return the football for some yardage, and you will not be sacrificing field position every time your opposition employs this kicking game ploy.

Field Goal Rush

Each team should have some method designed to put maximum and minimum pressure on the field goal attempt, as indicated above. The basic errors to avoid are:

1. Being offside, either by alignment or quick charge, which may be avoided by looking into ball (vision) and helping each other out (communication).
2. Getting "juked"—not having someone designated as spy to key fakes and assign pass coverage responsibility.
3. Failing to return a short or errant kick. Even though this kick may be returned, many teams fail to go into a precalled return

pattern. Players feel their job is to rush hard, and if they do not block the kick, they become spectators.

SUMMARY: KICKING GAME CHECKLIST

Every coaching staff should prepare a kicking game checklist. Such a list may be designed in many different formats, but regardless of the method of presentation it should serve as a quick reference for the players of critical mistakes and errors to be avoided in the kicking game. The following is a suggested kicking game checklist:

1. *Punt block rules.*
   a. Get off with the ball; do not be offside.
   b. Look at the ball.
   c. Go to the kicking area.
   d. Do not rough the kicker.
   e. Automatic return away from block side or wide side of field.
   f. Partially blocked punt crossing line of scrimmage is as if it had not been touched.
   g. Fourth down punt not crossing line of scrimmage will be our ball, so try to advance it.
   h. Third down punt not crossing line of scrimmage is a free ball, so get possession.
   i. Field goal block and return procedures same as punt block and return procedures.
   j. Know who has spy responsibility and know which side is rushing.

A BLOCKED PUNT IS USUALLY GOOD FOR A TOUCHDOWN!

2. *Punt return.*
   a. Safety is responsible to set backs to cover field. Know where you field ball in relation to return.
   b. Do not be offside. Yell across.
   c. Do not rough the kicker.
   d. Do not let the ball hit the ground.
   e. Do not clip.
   f. Call "Peter" if not handling the ball. (Get away from the ball).
   g. Know who has spy responsibility on return and block.
   h. Generally, do not handle punts inside our 10-yard line.

i. Never go into return unless sure punting situation. Know our procedure for unsure kicking downs.

j. Know the rule of first touch. Official downs the ball.

EASY WAY TO MAKE BIG YARDS. EACH TIME THE SITUATION COMES UP, YOU MUST THINK THIS IS THE BIG PLAY!

3. *Punt protection.*
   a. Be sure you are in a legal formation!
   b. Cut down splits when kicking within 3-yard line. Punter check the dead line (back line of end zone).
   c. Personal protector, check your position in relationship to punter—eight yards in front—and remind punter of end line.
   d. Personal protector, do not give ground and take alignment on correct side. Get into return alley.
   e. Personal protector calls when all are set and alerts for overload. Know blocking rules and be ready for alert call.
   f. Early down kicks should never be blocked.
   g. Be alert for punt check-off.
   h. Line may adjust splits until personal protector gives "set" command when going from an up position.
   i. Center must wait one full second after "set" command before snap.
   j. Punter alerts team to ball direction, "right," "left," or "short."

A PUNT MUST NEVER BE BLOCKED. HAVE PRIDE IN YOUR PROTECTION.

4. *Punt coverage.*
   a. Know our coverage call.
   b. Do not hold back—RUN!
   c. Stay in lanes and fan out.
   d. Must allow a 5-yard zone between you and the receiver. After the catch the first man down should take a shot across the bow.
   e. If you have contain responsibility you must contain. Be aware of a reverse.
   f. Do not overrun the ball, balance up and take hitting position.
   g. Down the ball only if it is going into the end zone or bouncing toward your goal line.
   h. You cannot touch ball until it touches the ground or your opponent.

i. On downing the ball, do not leave it. Official stops the play.

PUNT COVERAGE IS A TRUE INDICATOR OF A TEAM'S DESIRE TO WIN. PUNT RETURNS ARE CAUSED THROUGH CARELESSNESS OR LACK OF CHARACTER.

5. *Kick-off return.*
   a. After ten yards, it is a free ball. It must be handled.
   b. Have five or four men between ten yards and fifteen yards from ball. The middle man is the group leader. Make sure you have a complete team.
   c. Be sure of a deep kick before turning your back on the ball.
   d. Know the approximate depth and location of the ball before executing a block.
   e. Safety man, use judgment on handling and returning the ball from the end zone.
   f. Safeties, know who the call man is and the direction of return.
   g. Know your on-side return and regular return.

NO PENALTIES, FOR WITH EXTRA EFFORT THIS CAN BE A GAME BREAKER.

6. *Kick-off coverage.*
   a. Kicker, count your team.
   b. Do not be offside—call across.
   c. Ball is free after ten yards or if touched by a receiving team player.
   d. You will run past most potential blockers—if you run.
   e. Keep your spacing.
   f. Evade early blockers and return to your lane.
   g. Run through the blocker immediately in front of ball carrier.
   h. Contain man, be alert for reverse and unusual returns.
   i. Know your on-side or squib kick responsibility. Know who folds as safety and contain.
   j. Go after the ball.

FORCE OUR OPPONENT TO PUT THE BALL IN PLAY INSIDE HIS 20-YARD LINE.

7. *Field goal and extra point defense.*
   a. Move into your block alignment in sure field goal range and situation.
   b. Know who has spy responsibilities. (Make sure of fake.)

    c.   Single safety back, be conscious of field position, time, and score.

    d.   Be alert for a fake field goal.

    e.   Automatic return away from the block side or to wide side of field.

    f.   Rules are the same as punt on field goal.

    g.   Know which is our rush side. Rush from one side only.

DO NOT BE OFFSIDE, BUT GET OFF WITH THE BALL—BLOCKING A FIELD GOAL OR EXTRA POINT CAN WIN!

8.   *Field goal and point-after-touchdown protection.*

    a.   Kicker will bring in the play.

    b.   Be alert for "no huddle" if time is a factor on field goal.

    c.   Field goal must be covered—know your coverage.

    d.   Be alert for a "fire" call on a bad snap.

    e.   Field goal coverage rules are the same as punt rules.

A PLACE KICK MUST NEVER BE BLOCKED.

9.   *Procedure after taking a safety.*

    a.   Kick-off coverage team puts the ball in play.

    b.   20-yard line is the restraining line.

    c.   Line up on the 15-yard line.

    d.   Have five men on each side of the kicker. The kicker is the safety.

    e.   Any intentional safety will be a bench call and taken from punt formation.

    f.   Ball will be put into play either by a punt or a place kick.

10.   *Receiving the ball after a safety.*

    a.   Kick-off return team on the field.

    b.   Move up the restraining line.

11 POST-GAME ANALYSIS: HOW TO CORRECT MISTAKES AND ERRORS

Analyzing game mistakes should be a total evaluative process. Coaching is always a race against time and the tendency is to want to move on immediately after one game to get ready for the next. However, you must do more than just a cursory analysis and an oral correction, merely commenting on the mistakes and errors in the game just completed, in order to prepare for your next opponent. Otherwise, whether you won or lost, your players and coaching staff are likely to make the same mistakes and errors again. Getting ready for your next opponent *is* analyzing and correcting previously made mistakes and errors. Post-game analysis in actuality then is the oral wrap up of one game and the beginning of preparation for the next game. Effective coaching requires indepth evaluation of all phases of each game played in preparation for the upcoming games.

ANALYZING YOUR TEAM'S MISTAKES AND ERRORS

Typically when a team loses the tendency is to comment on the obvious, such as blocked punts, intercepted passes, completions of long passes or runs for touchdowns, and fumbles. When a team wins, frequently even the obvious mistakes and errors are overlooked. In the loss, some or many of the mistakes may be corrected; in the win, few or none may be corrected. Whether a team loses or wins, the game should be evaluated

completely, and *all* mistakes and errors should be corrected. As an illustration, what about the hidden yardage plus the penalty yardage that
was lost by your offense after a good gainer; or what about the time you
stopped your opponent for no gain in a critical situation, only to have
the play nullified because of a penalty on your defensive team; or what
about your opposition's third- or fourth-down incompleted pass that
meant he would have to give up the football and field position, only to
have a pass interference away from the intended pass receivers called
on your defensive team; or what about your average of forty yards per
punt, countered by your opposition's average of twenty-two yards per return? These mistakes and errors make up the game, whether your team
lost or won; and usually the team that makes the fewest mistakes wins.

Your Coaching Situation

We recognize that in the average high school there may not be the
number of coaches, the amount of film coverage, and the extensive com-
puterized statistical information that exist at the major college or professional levels. Most high school and small college coaches have class
preparation and other job related duties that impede their ability to
spend much time in compiling game results. However, none of these
facts relieve the necessity of gathering, studying, and implementing the
needed corrective measures. Regardless of the situation, more effective
coaching demands these time-consuming tasks be done. Certain techniques can be utilized to make the task less time consuming. However,
there must be a plan for obtaining pertinent information, which is the
responsibility of the head coach. First, he must decide what information
and what type of statistical breakdown are needed and can be assimi-
lated in his particular coaching situation.

How and Why Did Your Team Win or Lose?

The starting point of your post-game evaluation should be to determine
how and *why* your team won or lost. As we pointed out in Chapter 1, it
is an established axiom in sports that in order to win, your team must
not beat or defeat itself. You and your staff should be seeking answers
to the following types of questions.

How and Why Did You Win? Was it because of your superior personnel, execution and performance, preparation and game plan, and/or
conditioning? Was it because your opposition played poorly, committed
mistakes and errors, and beat themselves? Were you lucky to win?

How and Why Did You Lose?   Did your opponent defeat you, or did you beat yourselves? Did you have opportunities to win but fail to capitalize on them? Why? Where did you break down? What were your mistakes and errors? Was their personnel superior to yours? Were your preparation and game plan sound? Were you outcoached or out-conditioned? Was your opponent "lucky" to win? Should you have won?

Merely securing answers to the above questions will be of little value unless you intend to correct the mistakes and errors prior to the next game. Methods of garnering pertinent information are listed below in order to answer the above questions and the following one: "What must we do and how will we correct our players' (and coaches') mistakes and errors in this week's practice so they do not occur again?"

METHODS OF EVALUATION FOR EFFECTIVE COACHING

There are numerous methods of compiling data for analysis, two of which are drive sheets and grading player performance on films. While the films may be prohibitive because of either finances or time in some situations, drive sheet information can be acquired during a game so that it is available immediately after the contest. From offensive and defensive drive sheets (which can aid in evaluating and grading player performance on film, too), such pertinent information as rechecking your game plan, types of penalties, third down success offensively and defensively, goal line offense and defense, and so on, can be obtained. All of these will be discussed in detail below.

Drive Sheet

The preparation of complete offensive and defensive drive sheets during each game is essential to a head coach. They should be available to him immediately following the game and are a prime source of information to initiate the analyzation and correction of game errors.

Offense   For a high school or small college that is unable to have an entire game filmed, it is imperative that an assistant coach, manager, or statistician compile a drive sheet indicating the following:

Down, distance, and field position; formation and each play run in sequence; yardage gained or lost; what stopped each play or drive and any other pertinent information. From this sheet it is possible to scout your own team obtaining the following statistical breakdown:

1.   Complete tendencies of the offense by down, distance, and field position, which is the same information that your opponents'

scouts are obtaining. Such information may be readily transferred to large formation charts by game and cumulatively for evaluation and study by your offensive coaches and quarterbacks.

2. The drive chart may also be used to determine the consistency of plays in the offensive package by formation, down, or distance.

3. It will readily reveal what stopped each drive, namely the opposition or your own team. If you stopped yourself, how and where? And was your drive stopped by a penalty, fumble, interception, breakdown, busted play, or were you forced to punt or fail to make a fourth down running or pass play for the necessary yardage?

4. It will also give the coaching staff information on how well or how poorly you maintained field position. In which parts of the field did your team operate offensively (and defensively)?

5. The effectiveness of your offensive kicking game will be revealed.

Defensive   The defensive drive chart will reveal the effectiveness of your defenses. What defenses were used, and where were they analyzed?

1. A coaching staff is able to scout themselves defensively.

2. You can determine the effectiveness of the different fronts as related to your theorized defensive game plan.

3. You can also determine the effectiveness and consistency of your defensive alignments (reads), stunts, pass rushes, and coverages.

4. Did you stop your opposition by forcing them to punt? On what downs? Did you force a fumble? Were your players able to make the big play? Number of fumbles recovered? Passes attempted, completed, intercepted?

5. What was your *must* down success? You can check your defensive key down success, third down and short and/or long yardage in the third-down zone; fourth down and short and/or long yardage in four-down territory.

6. Did you force them to critical *must* down calls (that is, the offense *must* make the necessary yardage to retain possession) and if so did you stop them?

7. Did your defensive team ensure the offense good field position? How effective was your kicking game?

While the value of the drive sheet is enormous, no matter how well prepared and organized it is, it serves no purpose if the data is not utilized. The head coach and staff must secure the information with the objective of utilizing it to improve the football team and program.

Film Evaluation

Individual budgets and coaching situations vary. Many high schools and small colleges do not film complete games or all of the games on their schedules. At the major college level of competition, football films are broken down for offense, defense, and kicking game, as well as having a sequential copy of the complete game or film. Since most high schools and small college football coaching situations are different, compiling a complete offensive and defensive drive chart is a great time saver in allowing the coach to zero in immediately on critical errors that may have occurred in the game just terminated. Almost *all* coaches utilize drive sheets as a guide when grading films since the information is sequential and speeds up the grading process considerably.

Since film grading is a necessary time-consuming process, a coaching staff should begin as soon as films are available from the processor. Recognizing the fact that many coaches may be unable to secure one-day service from their film processor, if the films arrive on Sunday then the task of grading the films should not be postponed till Monday. Few football coaches *prefer* to work on Sunday, but *most do* by necessity. If the films arrive late Sunday night or early Monday, at least a cursory look at the film, along with the drive sheet information, will aid in setting up Monday's practice schedule. If the films do not arrive until Monday afternoon or evening, the value acquired from filming your games versus their cost may be questionable.

However, film errors are readily observed: alignment, assignment, technique, and physical mismatches are all readily verified and gradable, and positive correction can be initiated. Yet if the complete game is not filmed, grading will not reflect a total performance. Since time is of the essence, do *not* get overly involved in unneeded detail and keep the grading process relatively simple. It is well to remember, too, that you and your coaches are actively evaluating your teaching and their learning.

Grading System   The following is a simple grading system used effectively by a PAC 10 football coaching staff:

(+)—The player gets the job done; for example, he blocked his man. The coach should note if the player's technique needs polish.

(−)—The player does not get the job done. The coach notes the reason such as alignment, stance, not firing out, failure to follow through or improper execution of assignment.

E—An error, such as a penalty, fumble, bomb, or any other critical error that will stop a drive, lose field position, or put points on the opponent's side of the scoreboard.

RBI—Indicates a big play that advances the runner. A key block, quarterback sack, excellent pursuit, second effort, and the like (from baseball, run batted in).

Home Run—A big play, one that turns the game around for the team. It may be a great *third* effort. Scoring a touchdown may or may not be graded an HR; the ball carrier may have had such great help (RBI) that almost any player could have scored had he carried the football.

U—No grade. Impossible to grade, because of poor film coverage or the scope of film did not include a split receiver or a secondary defender, or the photographer did not get the entire sequence.

C—For coaching. This is the important grade. Are we teaching? Have we spent enough time on this technique? Is it designed properly? In checking the practice schedule records you might discover you spent a total of ten minutes on some phase of the game, three games ago.

Players Grade Themselves   In grading film it is well to have each player grade himself. Most times the players will be more critical of themselves than their coaches. They have also been known to play the game and score according to just what they feel their coach will accept.

When you are going over the film with your squad members, praise the RBI's and home runs as defined above. If something humorous happens, enjoy it with them. Point out to your players the +, −, and *E* performance grades, too, lauding the first and correcting the latter two. Most *E* grades are especially critical and *must* be corrected. Anyone can point out mistakes and errors. The players probably can recognize most of them by themselves. However, a player will not perform more effectively unless he is taught how *not* to make errors and is given the opportunity in practice sessions to correct them.

The passing of film grades has as many pro's as con's. However it is handled, the end result of film grading should be improved individual, group, and team performance.

Analyze the Game Plan

Was your game plan sound? Did you follow it, or did you panic and start "slot machine" selecting plays? Was it sound offensively, defensively, and in all phases of the kicking game? Where were the breakdowns? Why? In each of the three phases of football, were the breakdowns the result of poor execution, technique, penalties, or possibly poor physical condition?

If the game plan needed adjusting during the game, did you adjust it on the basis of what was actually occurring or on what you thought might occur? Did you adjust it on the basis of what your opponent had done in previous games? If you altered your game plan during the game and you lost, try to determine if you made the changes too soon or too late.

Physical Condition   Were your players physically ready to play? Were you playing starters who had sustained injuries and were unable to perform at the expense of reserves who could have gone full speed? Were they able to go all out for four quarters? Were any players tired? Did you run enough or too much during the week? Answers to these and similar questions will aid your coaching staff in making plans for the upcoming game.

Were You Mentally Ready?   What was your approach to getting mentally ready? Did the staff do a good teaching job in preparing the team? Did the players get with it or merely go through the motions? Did your staff overplay or underplay the abilities of your opponent? If any answers are negative, they must be corrected during the week in getting ready for the next opponent.

Penalties   Did you stop yourselves with penalties? In what areas of the field and at what time during the game did you sustain these penalties? The loss of yardage from the penalty itself does not always tell the whole story. It is the hidden yardage, the loss of forty yards on a punt return plus the penalty, the quarterback sack on third down for minus fifteen yards only to be offside defensively, taking the minus five yards of the offside plus the continuation of possession by your opponent—these mistakes do the damage.

Penalties are mistakes that few teams can afford. It is important to recognize them as mistakes and to correct the causes so they do not recur. The following are typical causes:

1.   A *lack of knowledge* of technique on pass block usually results in a holding penalty.
2.   A *lack of poise* when held, pushed, hit, or shoved creates the "hit back" syndrome.
3.   *Overeagerness* usually incurs the offside penalty.
4.   *Lack of discipline* usually is responsible for aligning up incorrectly and being offside.
5.   *Mix up in snap count* causes offside or illegal motion.
6.   *Lack of communication* between coaches and players is the cause of too many or too few players on the field.
7.   *Confusion* causes delay of the game, mistakes in coverage, and breakdowns in assignment.
8.   *Lack of condition* usually is the cause of lack of concentration, and the results are myriad mistakes and errors.
9.   Grabbing a player by the face mask, spearing, running into the kicker, holding, pass interference, hitting the quarterback after the ball is thrown, piling on, and rule infractions and violations of a similar nature can occur because of lack of knowledge, lack

of poise, overeagerness, lack of discipline, lack of conditioning, poor concentration, and/or lack of coaching. All are correctable and must be corrected.

Bench and Sideline Control and Communication   Did the information that was sent down get communicated to the appropriate coach and players? Or had the assistant coach hung up the phone to talk to a player who needed a jersey change, turning the phone to the equipment man who was busy putting ice on a sprained ankle for the trainer who was chewing out the officials? In the meantime were substitutes standing on the phone line to the head coach's head set, who really only wanted to know where the football was spotted? Were players readily available for substitution and on quick turnovers? Each job on the sideline requires special handling. The plan must be constantly scrutinized and upgraded.

Sideline to Field Communication   Were the players getting the information exactly as it was relayed to the field or were they interpreting what they thought the coach said or meant to say? If hand signals were utilized, were any misread or misinterpreted offensively or defensively? Why were there breakdowns on the communications system? How can the situation be improved?

Half-time   Was half-time in the locker room business-like, confident and orderly, or panicky, chaotic, and confused? Was it organized for the adjustment of the plan to better prepare the team for the second half? Did the team perform better in the second half? Can your half-time organization be improved?

Scout Yourself   Knowing your own team's tendencies in all phases of the game is essential. Chart them and attain balance in your approach. Where total game films are available, this is handled rather easily by the staff. They can use the press play for accurate down and distance information only filling in the hash mark and keying off the drive sheet for pertinent information. Where complete films are not available, the drive sheets are critical and must be relied on for the majority of the information.

AFTER INCURRING A LOSS

Probably the most common failure or error after a big loss is to panic, want to change everything, tilt windmills, have witch hunts, and fail to evaluate objectively the causes for the loss. Sometimes things snowball: you make errors against a good football team, they go for the jugular immediately, and once they get momentum it is difficult to stop them from scoring. Assess the damage coolly and make the required corrections in preparation for your next game.

Another mistake is losing heart, losing faith in your plan, and failing to maintain a positive approach. Your feelings ring out loud and clear to your players. Do not go into a shell or find a whipping boy, pop off or blame officiating, weather, or the pre-game meal. Take a confident, objective approach to solving the real issues. Stress the "we" and "us" factor. If you have taken time to devise a plan, do not abandon it in desperation. Coach-teach what you know best. Some critical areas to give special attention to are discussed below.

Continue to Teach the Basics

An outstanding former Big Ten coach who was known for his winning record and producing physically tough football teams would inform his staff upon sustaining a loss, *"This week we're going back to teaching the basics.* Our players are confused. We have too much offense, too much defense, and we're not doing anything well. We don't have time to coach it all, and our players don't have enough time to learn what we are trying to teach." The offensive and defensive game plan for the upcoming opponent would be basic and fundamental, and seldom were two consecutive games lost in a single season under this veteran coach's sage leadership.

It is well to remember that it is not plays or systems that win, it is players able to execute what has been taught to them. A common coaching mistake is to try to teach too much, when the players do not have sufficient time to master what has been presented to them. Mastering numerous plays, alignments, and coverages involves both cognitive and psychomotor skills. The element of time alone may prohibit learning from occurring, despite the fact the coaching staff may feel they have covered offensive, defensive, and kicking game maneuvers and strategies in practice. Always teach the basics first, and return to teaching the basics when your players are not performing well. These are sound principles that are often violated.

Critical Areas of Play

The critical areas of play offensively and defensively are at both ends of the field. From the offensive standpoint it is imperative that you analyze how well you did with your goal line or scoring zone offense when you got to the 10-yard line, and when you had the long end of the field in front of you when you were operating in your danger zone offense coming out from your own goal line to your 10-yard line. Conversely, it is imperative that you analyze how well your defense did when they were at their goal line defending the short end of the field versus the opposition's scoring zone offense, and when they had the opposition back in their end of the field operating their danger zone offense.

Offense   How many times was your team successful in scoring when they got into the scoring zone? How did they score? Why did they not score? How can this be corrected and improved upon? You should get at least three points when you get to this area: "Put points on the board *every time* you get inside the opposition's 20-yard line."
   How many times did you get possession of the football inside your own 10-yard line? How many times were you successful in getting the football out of that area? How many times did you accomplish your objective of getting one or two first downs before punting? Breakdowns? Why? How can you improve your play offensively in this area of the field?

Defense   It is not the number of times a team gets into scoring position that is important, what counts is the number of times they score when they have the opportunity to do so, especially from within the offense's 20-yard line. Therefore, you should analyze how many times and how well your team defended its own goal line. How did your opposition get possession of the football in this area? How many plays were in each of the opposition's scoring drives? Did you stop (defense) the opposition or did they stop themselves? Breakdowns? Why? How can you improve your play defensively in this area of the field?
   Conversely, when a team has the opposition pinned down in its own danger zone frequently it has a tendency to let up. If you shut off the opposition there, inevitably your team will gain good field position immediately when your opponent is forced to punt from deep in its own territory. To let them escape by driving the football for several first downs and then punt to your team is to nullify an immediate advantage. To allow an opponent to break a big gainer from deep in its own territory gives that opponent confidence and momentum. Therefore, it is important to analyze what you have done defensively versus the opposition's danger zone offense despite the fact your team was defending the long end of the field. Analyze the breakdowns. Not infrequently they may be attributed to the defensive coordinator calling a stunting defense, which may result in man coverage, and the opposition either breaks a running play at a void in the defense or a receiver beats man coverage for the big gainer. It is probably more dangerous to gamble defensively in this end of the field than in the short end since the field must be covered in depth and width. When in your goal line defense at the short end of the field,

there is little depth to cover since the opposition needs less than 10 yards to score.

You should analyze the offensive and defensive mistakes and errors that have occurred at both ends of the field of play and correct them since these are the critical areas where a single mistake generally results in a score for your team or the opposition's.

Third Down Success

The most critical down in football is the third down. In the three-down zone of play if a team stops its opposition on the third down most of the time the offensive team will turn over possession of the football by punting it downfield on fourth down. Occasionally a team in the three-down zone will attempt to run the ball on fourth down, gambling they will make it, instead of punting the football. Without considering any tactical factors, usually that team is *not* playing percentage football. Once a team gets to its four-down zone its fourth down play is not nearly as predictable, since it will be based on what the team has done on third and short yardage or third and long yardage. Therefore, once again the critical play is the third down play. Probably most teams in a third and three situation in the four-down zone will try for the first down by running the football inside, although some coaches may go for the big play or score with an option or an option run-pass play or a play action pass, since they still have the fourth down to attempt to get the first down if their attempted pass is unsuccessful. Third and long yardage situations are more predictable, as are fourth and long yardage situations in the four-down zone. In the latter most teams must revert to the pass for the necessary yardage, or depending on their position on the field, the ability of their field goal kicker, and the score, they may attempt a field goal. Even if the attempt is successful, the defensive team has done a good job in forcing the opposition to settle for a field goal rather than a touchdown.

Analyze your third down plays offensively and defensively very carefully since these are the *must* situations in football. On offense in the three-down zone you *must* make the first down to retain possession; in the four-down zone you *must* get sufficient yardage on third down not to have to gamble or be limited only to a field goal attempt on fourth down. On defense you *must* stop the opposition so they do not retain possession, or you must force them into a gambling situation or a punt (or field goal attempt) on fourth down. For the most part your third down success or the lack of it on offense and defense will also determine whether your team is kicking off or receiving and which end of the field they will be playing on for most of the game.

Sudden Changes

How did your team and coaching staff handle sudden changes in situations, like giving up possession of the football on a quick turnover? Did you retain your poise or panic? What caused the turnovers to occur? Breakdowns? Did the opposition score quickly or did you shut them off after they gained possession of the football on the turnover?

Probably a blocked punt is the most demoralizing turnover, especially if it is advanced for a score. The records reveal that a team whose punt is blocked for a touchdown seldom wins the game. However, if the ball is not advanced for the score and the defensive team is alert, not infrequently the opposing team will go for the big gainer or try to score on its first down play usually by a pass. Should the defense intercept the ball they can nullify their opposition's blocked punt advantage immediately. It is important for your players to keep their poise and not panic when a sudden change works adversely against them.

Conversely, if your team got possession on a sudden turnover, how did your players and coaches handle it? Did they take advantage of the situation? Did your team score? On what selection of plays? Was your strategy sound? If your team failed to score, you should analyze why and correct the situation before your next game.

Two-minute Offense and Defense

In the event you utilized your two-minute offense, you should examine this phase of the game, too. Was it productive? Did you move the ball? Were your time-outs used with discretion? Was your quarterback able to save the clock, using it to his team's advantage? Were your ball carriers and receivers able to get out-of-bounds to stop the clock? If errors and mistakes were made, correct them.

An underclass quarterback of a major college football power got rattled while operating his team's two-minute offense; he attempted to stop the clock by grounding the ball on a high sideline pass well over the receiver's head. His intent was obvious and the strategy was appropriate as he wanted to set up one last play. Unfortunately it was *fourth* down, instead of third down, and possession of the football went over to the opposition. Part of the confusion obviously was caused by the pressure of the situation: little time remained to play in the game and his team's time-outs were expended. But some of the confusion might have been the result of oral instructions and animated gestures by coaching staff members on the sideline.

The opposite situation of above is how well did your team play the prevent defense? Did you bleed the clock properly? Did your players keep the opposition's ball carriers inbounds? Did your team prevent the score? Breakdowns? Why? Was your strategy sound?

PRINCIPLES AND SUGGESTIONS FOR CORRECTING MISTAKES AND ERRORS

Did you force the opposition to play your game or were you forced to play theirs? Did your offense move the ball without mistakes, keeping their defenses off balance, and not give up the ball without kicking it? Did they give your team opportunities to win? Did you exploit them?

Did your special teams ensure field position, prevent the long returns, block a punt? Breakdowns? Why? Did you adjust your rush when needed?

Additional questions could be asked in an effort to analyze and correct mistakes and errors for more effective coaching but the above will suffice. Much of the information to the questions can be gleaned from the offensive and defensive drive sheet if it is complete and has been well prepared. However, the manner of correcting mistakes and errors is important, too, and suggestions and principles are offered below.

Do Not Harp on Past Errors

While it is important to analyze, call attention to, and correct errors, it is important to move on to the upcoming game and to get off the subject of errors or mistakes that have already occurred. Otherwise the players involved and the other team members will begin to develop negative attitudes feeling everything they do is going to be wrong. There is little to be gained by constantly carping and harping about mistakes and errors.

Illustration   The captain of a professional football team got confused in his selection of goals after having won the toss of the coin and made a serious judgmental error. Prevailing wind was the determining factor, and it was evident to almost everyone, including the television audience, that whoever won the toss would elect to defend so that his team would have the wind when they get possession of the football in the first quarter. The opposing captain's choice was a simple one in that since his team did not have the wind his team should at least receive and have possession of the football. When the opposing captain indicated defend, the home captain replied to the referee that he wanted to kick off, which meant the opposing team would gain possession of the football immediately *and* have the wind to their backs. The television announcer tried to explain the foul up, the referee appeared to be confused, the captain was more confused, and the coaching staff was the most confused. However, the coach, an experienced professional, quickly called for his specialty kick-off team instead of his receiving team, and gave the outward appearance this is what he had intended to do. The error was obvious. However, to have carped on it and to have been demonstrative about such a stupid mistake would have probably upset the entire team; they might not have regained their composure. The error was not fatal and eventually the home team won with superior personnel and coaching. The error was so glaring that the newspaper accounts of the game also referred to it the following day. However, once again, the coach minimized the captain's mistake and merely stated the captain got confused. To the best of our knowledge the mistake was not referred to again in the media, although one does not know what the coach actually said to his captain about that wrong decision he made.

Never Blame a Player for Your Mistakes

There are coaches who pretend they never made a mistake because they never want to look bad. While no one wants to look bad or appear to have made a football mistake, a coach should never place the blame on a player when the coach himself is responsible for the foul-up.

Illustration Suppose the defensive coordinator calls a stunting defense and the opposition cracks or breaks the defense for a big gain or a score. There is a void or a weakness in every defense, and finding it is a guessing game between the offense and defense. Suppose all eleven of your players do what they are supposed to do, but the opposition cracks the vulnerable part of the defense. The defensive coordinator put the team in a bad alignment and he should take the heat, not the players. However, if the defensive coach calls a stunt and a defender falls down or lines up incorrectly or does not get to his area of responsibility on the pattern defense, the player's error will be obvious when you are viewing the films.

In both illustrations it is easy for a coach to place the blame on a player. Should he do so and it is not a player's mistake, the coach's behavior is unethical. Just as a coach knows when he makes a mistake, the player knows when the mistake is his or the coach's. Players will lose confidence in their coach if they are being blamed for coaching mistakes. They are very likely to lose confidence in him, too, if he calls too many "bad defenses." They and others are likely to recognize the fact that he simply does not have the necessary technical knowledge of defensive football to handle his position. Through study, hard work, and experience he can learn technical football. But if he blames a student-athlete for his mistakes, he is likely to lose more than he will ever gain.

Correcting Mistakes, Not Merely Talking about Them

There is a difference between merely talking about mistakes and correcting them. In the former, no follow-up is undertaken and the player or players are merely informed orally they made mistakes. Therefore, the players are likely to make the same mistakes again.

Illustration   In his first football game an offensive center had two bad snaps to his punter, which set up two opposition scores. The punter had one punt blocked and he punted poorly because of a tough punt rush a second time. When reviewing the films, his coach merely pointed out the center's poor passes for punts and the resulting scores. The following week the center made another poor deep punt pass and set up another score. If the coach did not give the center extra practice during the week making deep passes for punts under pressure, but instead merely talked about the mistake, that was a grave coaching error on his part. The only thing more serious would be the coach's failure even to discuss with his center the mistake and what caused it. Otherwise the player might not be aware of the fact that he did make a mistake.

Illustration   The opposition scores from five yards out on the option, with the quarterback, as he is tackled, pitching back to the tailback, who runs into the end zone untouched. As the defensive team comes off the field after the try for extra point, the defensive coach makes no effort to get the defensive team together to correct the error. In effective coaching in order to defense the option properly someone is assigned to take the quarterback and another the pitchman. In this illustration no one was on the pitchman—the assigned player failed to carry out his responsibility. If the head coach merely shakes his head, walks away to the other end of the bench, and does not correct the error at that time, it is likely the next time he sends out his defensive team, they will see the option again and make the same mistake.

Playing Performance or Potential

Are you playing your best performers or your potential performers? Ability comes in any size, although at times a coach becomes blinded by a candidate's speed and size. He may be reluctant to give the player of small stature sufficient opportunity to prove he is a footballer, while making every opportunity available for the big, well-muscled candidates. While size and speed are important in a contact sport like football, if a player cannot perform and will not hit on offense or defense, do not be blinded by his potential. Make your choices based on performance, not size and speed. A winner is as easy to identify as a loser. The latter generally does not have the "heart" for football. The great majority of a team's players are those between these two extremes, ones who must be cultivated and developed. However, the mistake is to do so at the expense of the footballer who may be on the sideline and should be in the game. Since ability comes in any size, an effective coach plays ability not just Mr. Potential, until of course Mr. Potential becomes a performer.

"What If" Syndrome

Did you spend too much time practicing on what your opposition *might* do and not enough time preparing for what it actually did? Probably very few coaches go into a contest secure in their own mind they are totally prepared for everything; they usually feel they need something else since the opposition might do such and such. There have been game plans that have been revised and/or added to on the day before a contest because of the "what if" syndrome.

It is not well to worry and confuse your players with all of the "what ifs," although most coaches do think about them. From a defensive standpoint what you must do is to defense your opposition's favorite plays and prepare to stop what they do best. Should they do something unexpected, such as run trips or twins or double-wing or go unbalanced, and they have not done so previously, adjustments must be made on the sideline quickly and relayed to the field. To spend valuable practice time during the week defensing these formations and plays while neglecting what the opposition does the most and the best based on previous game tendencies, would be an unwise use of time. In pre-season planning and practice usually these situations are covered and general rules are given for defensing the unusual quickly. Obviously special defenses need to be reviewed during the season, but this can be done on a cursory basis and entire practice sessions need not be devoted to covering unusual formations and gimmicks unless a team is known for employing them frequently in their game plan.

Continue to Teach-Coach

Losing your poise does not help in correcting at the expense of teaching-coaching. Usually a player knows when he has made a mistake. Typically a person feels embarrassed as the result of making a mistake. Little is gained, except venting your own frustration, by verbally undressing the player about his making mistakes. Even if you have no alternatives in terms of teaching and coaching, hollering at a player is not the solution to the mistakes and errors.

A coach does well to remind himself frequently that he is a teacher, and in the scholastic and collegiate ranks of coaching he cannot trade or draft student-athletes. Therefore, he must continue to teach-coach the players he has available if their performance is to improve. It should be pointed out that even in professional football the *consistent* winners are the teams where *consistent* teaching occurs. Those coaches recognize the importance of good teaching.

Were You Together as a Team?

Did you have it all together as a cohesive team? Since there is much individual and group work in practice sessions, the transition to team unity for the game is not automatic. The offensive line and the offensive backs might not be fully coordinated, or the defensive line, linebackers, and secondary might not be fully coordinated. Or the rivalry in practice that prevails between the offensive, defensive, and special teams might prevail in the game, too, so that one unit might be blaming the other for poor field position, failure to score, failure to keep the opposition from scoring, poor coverage, fumbling, blocked punts, and so on, instead of encouraging each other. When this occurs, it is a *coaching staff mistake* that must be corrected. You have let the friendly rivalry between the units of your team get out of control. Mentally the players are not ready to play as a team. The emphasis should be on *we* and *us*, not fragmented on *I*, *you*, and *they*, if team unity and cohesiveness are to be achieved.

Goal Setting

Setting seasonal goals is important and each game's mistakes can be weighed against your seasonal goals. If goals were achieved your players should be commended; if they were not, they should be reaffirmed. It might be well to establish some special goals for the upcoming game. For goals to be effective the players must be dissatisfied and motivated to improve individually and as a team. Even if goals were achieved a concerted effort must be made to motivate your players to do better. Effective coaching is establishing team consistency and avoiding the inconsistency of uneven performances.

Various charts may be worked out but one we have found effective is painted on a full sheet of plywood and is hung in the varsity locker room (see Diagram 11–1). This board is brought up-to-date after each game by the coaching staff. Usually helmet decals are awarded for the winners in each category.

DIAGRAM 11–1
Football Award Board

FOOTBALL AWARD BOARD

19__	HAWKS	VANDALS	GOPHERS	HOOSIERS	DUCKS	BEAVERS	COWBOYS	INDIANS	SUN DEVILS	HUSKIES
BEST DEFENSIVE LINEMAN	Knecht	Dolby	Knecht	Clark	Andros	Mason	Knecht	Mason	Dolby	Andros
BEST DEFENSIVE BACK	Riley Nelson	Brooks	Riley Brooks	Herndon	Brooks Nelson	Athon	Riley Herndon	Riley Athon	Brooks	Athon
BEST BLOCKING LINEMAN	Bogosian	Kolberg	Partenan	Kolberg	Anderson	Kolberg	Bogosian	Partenan	Crakes	Anderson
BEST BLOCKING BACK	Scott, G.	Smith, G.	Shanley, J.	Marvin, J.	Marx, G.	Scott, P.	Marvin, J.	Shanley, J.	Scott, G.	Smith, G.

4'

8'

Are Your Players Doing It Your Way?

Evaluate your players' game performance in terms of their getting the job done. The free spirit or free-lancer may get the job done three times out of ten because he is playing it his way on defense, as an illustration. The player in a coordinated defense must learn the team way. While you do not want to stifle his aggressiveness and desire to hit, his free-lance play does more overall harm than good. He is the sort of player every coach is seeking on a dog, blitz, or tough rush coming off the corner. Therefore, put him in a position to perform this function within the team concept.

Practice Plan

Evaluate the previous game's mistakes in terms of practice time spent in the respective problem areas. If time spent seems reasonable, check your what and how of teaching. Do not be misled by a detailed and comprehensive practice plan on paper. While such a plan is highly desirable, you must be certain you and your staff are not merely filling segments of time. If learning is not occurring, your teaching is ineffective. If the center-quarterback exchange is a problem, for example, devote more time to perfecting it and less time on some other aspect of the practice plan.

Are you teaching on the field or holding coaching clinics and seminars for your players? Give them the theory in meetings, and coach them on the field. Have the players perform.

Losing Your Game on the Practice Field or in Meetings?   Your specific situation usually dictates how much time is available for practice sessions including meetings. Despite the fact that coaching is a race against time, and probably no football coach ever feels he has sufficient time to get his team ready to play, remember that practice time is limited. Probably more games are lost on the practice field as the result of extending scrimmages, going over it one more time, than are lost in actual games. Many teams are beat up so badly or are so mentally and physically tired by the time they play the scheduled game, that they are unable to perform well. The head coach and his staff may be tired, too, as the result of extended, frequent practice sessions and meetings. They are too tired to be on top of everything during the game and they make mistakes and coaching errors, too.

Lengthening the Practice Schedule   While a coach may work out a detailed and comprehensive practice schedule, unless he is disciplined he may not adhere to it. As an illustration, he may have three minutes of agility drills scheduled where there should be no more than five repetitions in one segment in order to develop reaction and quickness. However, if the players do not react quickly and they round corners in their movements, the coach may extend the number of repetitions and the duration of the drills so that they become conditioning instead of agility drills. Also, the length of time expended on the drills and additional changes in other activities must be added on to the practice session if the situation permits. If the length of practice time is fixed, then the schedule must be adjusted or some phase of the game will receive less than its allotted share of time and attention.

Deviating from the Practice Schedule   A worse situation is to deviate radically from the designed practice schedule. As an illustration, an objective may be to have a limited, controlled goal line offense versus the scout squad running the opposition's goal line defenses for ten minutes, but it turns into a thirty-minute "meat" scrimmage because the offensive team is not running its plays properly. The mistakes multiply and the longer the players practice the more the *mistakes become perfected.* No team ever won a game, much less a championship, by practicing and perfecting mistakes. You must remember what you are teaching and the objective and purpose of your drills, including your scrimmages. Have a plan. Polish and hone what is in your plan. If you are not getting the job done, evaluate why. Come back to your plan, possibly the next day, and do it right. If your players are leg tired, act as if they are in a trance, and play poorly, the chances are they are leaving their game on the practice field or suffering from too many meetings. They can absorb only so much, and if they are not motivated to learn, their learning of new material or perfecting what they have learned will be minimal.

Press

Before you have a chance to evaluate your previous game completely, objectively, and unemotionally, do not be a "pop-off." Control what you say and where necessary educate your staff and players to do the same. Many times a loss has been compounded by a coach or players without their intending to do so.

Illustration   An excellent PAC 10 sophomore football player sounded off before a game with a traditional rival about the questionable skills of the upcoming opponent. That was all the opposition needed to get stoked up to defeat a team with probably better personnel. After getting beaten, the same sophomore player made a post-game statement boasting, "There is *NO WAY* that team can beat us with our vastly superior material three years in a row." Each year the main topic in the opponent's locker room the week before the traditional game was the pop-off statement by that player. Three years in a row it was enough to stoke up the opposing team for a win.

A coach should also be careful of passing a defeat off as luck or robbery. Players read their coach's comments and the following year when he's trying to get them "up" they may be playing a step slow waiting for the ball to bounce differently. After all, they think, the other team was lucky or our team got robbed in last year's game.

A fumble is not a break if it is a result of a good hit. A pass interception is not a break if you coached the technique and it was executed properly. There are no such things as breaks where coaching is involved and techniques are executed. Your players have to understand, too, that 9–6 is getting beat, 52–28 is getting beat, and 14–13 is getting beat. Yet, if they read in the newspapers that it was not bad, or it could have been worse, and their coach confirms this, it may well be worse the next time the teams play.

Do not harp or nitpick after a tough loss. Evaluate, be firm, and be fair. Correct the mistakes. Learn from the history but do not dwell on it. Get your players ready to play the next game.

12 ANALYZING AND CORRECTING SEASONAL ERRORS

With the post-game analysis of the final game of the season, the wheel has turned full circle and the process is ready to commence again. Each aspect of the total program must now be studied in depth, corrected and improved, or eliminated.

STATISTICAL BREAKDOWN AND ANALYSIS

A complete compilation of data and analysis of your season's entire offensive, defensive, and kicking games is the starting point. Illustrative diagrams for doing this will be included throughout this chapter. Providing the individual game sheets have been religiously maintained, determining seasonal averages for the various phases of the game is not as difficult as it would be if you had to go back through offensive analysis (see Diagrams 12–11, 12–12, 12–13, 12–14, and 12–15).

Offense

Offensively the head coach would want to determine the effectiveness of the following:

Offensive Sets   Which of your sets were effective, and which were not?

Plays   Which plays were high yield plays (three plus yards), and which had the best average; which the poorest (less than three yards) and why? Which plays should we retain, and how can we improve on them?

Your Offense versus Your Opponents' Defense   Which defensive alignments, techniques, stunts, and secondary coverages hurt us the most? Why? Was it because of superior personnel or better techniques? Break it down, analyze and evaluate each segment.

Also evaluate the following phases of your offensive game:

Two-minute offense.
Short yardage offense (third and less than two, fourth and less than
   one)
Long yardage offense
Total passing game
Audibles

Analyze everything in your offensive package. We will discuss common coaching failures relevant to offensive football shortly.

Defense

The coach should evaluate his total defense for the season and find out all that he can about his alignments, stunts, coverage, and personnel, such as:

Set Evaluation   What offensive sets gave you the most trouble, and could you adjust to them quickly?

Play Evaluation   Analyze the opposition's plays and offensive series that hurt your team the most.

Defensive Fronts   Analyze your defensive fronts. Which were strong? Which weak? Why?

Linebackers and Secondary   Analyze which were acceptable and unacceptable. Which would be retained and reused? Were breakdowns because of design, personnel, technique, or too complicated? How can we improve our linebacker and secondary play?

Stunts   Were they effective? Which ones were ineffective? Why? Personnel, design, technique or too complicated? How can we improve?

Long and Short Yardage Defensive Play Outside the Scoring Zone   Analyze and determine which were effective and ineffective based on field position and offenses. Again seek improvement of the product.

Goal Line Defenses Versus Opposition's Scoring Zone Offense   If we bent on defense out on the field, did we hold on the goal line? What hurt us? How can we improve?

Kicking Game

Evaluate each phase of the kicking game: alignment, protection, coverage, and the special skills of the centers and kickers. Know the statistics. Have understanding of why some aspects were good and others poor. Solidify the thinking on the good aspects, evaluate, adjust, and improve them; and discard the poor ones. Constantly look for better ways to attain better results.

Common coaching failures relevant to the kicking game will be discussed shortly.

COMPILING DEFENSIVE SEASONAL STATISTICS

At the close of the season the defensive coaches should evaluate totally the defensive play as to individuals, groups, and the whole team. Such aspects as game performance, practice time spent, and techniques taught should be considered and analyzed, including the statistics of the defensive front and secondary and the alignments, stunts, and coverages utilized in the games throughout the season.

Defensive Fronts

Each defensive front should be analyzed with specific detailed scrutiny given to the prevention of the opponent's third down success and all goal line defense. Each statistic obtained should be weighed against the personnel doing the job and their techniques. Can we use a better technique for our returning players to give more success?

Diagram 12–1 illustrates how the seasonal statistical breakdown for the defensive fronts would be compiled in order to be analyzed, and it reveals that of the three defenses listed the 4 Flex Strong proved to be the poorest in each of the categories. A scrutinizing analysis of the Flex defense would be in order, examining personnel, technique, what was taught, and what was learned; game strategy would also be taken into consideration.

DIAGRAM 12–1
Defense Front Seasonal Statistical Breakdown

Front	Games	Attempts	Yards Gained	Yards Lost	Total Yards	Yards Per Play	Sacks	Forced Fumbles	TDs	Prevention Third Down Success
4 Base	11	320	690	50	640	2.0	2	5	3	85%
4 Rush	11	125	375	80	295	2.36	6	8	1	78%
4 Flex Strong	11	110	590	40	550	5.0	4	2	6	10%
4 Flex Weak	11	90								

Secondary Performance

Data on the defensive secondary's seasonal performance may be compiled and evaluated as illustrated in Diagram 12–2. Considerations are personnel involved in the coverage, their assignments and techniques, and the total amount of practice time spent on each coverage. The latter may reveal a direct relationship to the results obtained. Holding one's opponent to less than 50 percent completion and 5.5 yards per completion is considered excellent. Cover II Red in Diagram 12–2 would need close scrutiny in terms of percentage of completions, touchdowns, and third down success.

Stunts

Each stunt should be evaluated for its effectiveness in terms of use, yards gained and lost, sacks, and average yards per play. These areas of performance should in turn be compared to the personnel performing the stunts. Consider the purpose and design of the stunt and how well the technique was mastered. What was each stunt's total effect in relationship to the defensive game and/or team package? Diagram 12–3 illustrates the defensive stunts seasonal statistical breakdown. The statistics in Diagram 12–3 might indicate that all three stunts were adequate but that the easy stunt was the most effective in sacks and average per play.

COMPILING KICKING GAME SEASONAL STATISTICS

Just as cumulative seasonal statistics are compiled and analyzed for all phases of defensive play, information on all aspects of the kicking game

DIAGRAM 12–2
Defensive Secondary Coverage Seasonal Performance Statistics

Coverage	Games	Attempts	Completions	Percent Complete	Yards	Average per Completion	TDs	Interceptions	Longest Completion	Knock Downs	Third Down Success
Cover I (Free Safety)	11	97	40	42.2%	360	9.0	3	9	15	7	3/20
Cover II Red	6	30	19	63.3%	95	5.0	5	0	8	0	9/9
Cover III Trey	4	24	8	33.3%	24	3.00	0	2	10	6	0/5
Cover IV Rotate Zone	11	10									

DIAGRAM 12–3
Defense Stunts Seasonal Statistical Breakdown

Name of Stunt	Games	Times Used	Yards Gained	Yards Lost	Total Yards	Sacks	Average per Play
Twist	11	65	195	40	155	8	2.38
Easy	11	74	180	70	110	10	1.48
Sam	8	38	92	15	77	3	2.42
Will	8	39	85				
Omaha	11	40					

should be compiled and analyzed, too. Usually coaches analyze their offense first, then their defense, and if time permits they look at limited phases of their kicking game. The cursory consideration that some coaches give to the kicking game is a mistake.

The Punting Game

Not only should the mechanics of the punt be studied, but also the execution by the offensive front in terms of protection and coverage. The center is studied for his contribution in terms of perfect snaps. Diagram 12–4 illustrates the compilation for analysis of punting game statistics for the season.

If punts have been blocked or returned for touchdowns, the causes must be determined and the problems corrected. In Diagram 12–4, Column 4, the Penalty Yards are those that cause a team to punt again or

DIAGRAM 12–4
Punting Game Seasonal Statistics

Name	Year	Number Games	At- tempts	Penalty Yards	Kick Aver- age	Return Aver- age	Return for TDs	Blocked		
								Center	Kicker	Front
S. Mobley	Sr.	7	35	45	40.1	2.7	0	0	0	0
D. Kloser	Jr.	4	15	0	39.9	11.8	0	2	0	0

to turn over possession in poor field position. Often the results are difficult to offset in a game.

The Quick Kick

Although few college football teams utilize the quick kick these days, it is still an excellent weapon when used successfully as an element of surprise. When it is used, it should be evaluated. Diagram 12-5 illustrates how statistics may be compiled for analysis. In the event of a blocked kick, whether a punt or quick kick, the cause should be determined and remedied.

Punt Returns and Blocks

The various returns and punt blocking schemes should be analyzed and upgraded. Correct faulty or too difficult technique requirements. It is possible that a certain coverage or blocking scheme must be eliminated. Diagram 12-6 illustrates a statistical breakdown of a team's punt returns and punt blocking schemes for the season. In analyzing the results, Punt Return I and Punt Blocking Scheme II were more productive than the others.

Kick-off Statistics

Diagram 12-7 illustrates a statistical breakdown of kick-off coverages and returns utilized during the season. A cursory analysis readily reveals that the coverage needs improvement and the second kicker needs to improve his technique as is evidenced by the number of times he shanked the ball. The latter affects the morale of the covering team members.

DIAGRAM 12-5
Ground Quick Kick Seasonal Statistics

Name	Year	Number Games	At-tempts	Kick Average	Number Blocked	Return Average	Penalty Yards	Blocked Center	Front	Kicker
D. Kloser	Jr.	2	2	50.4	0	0	0	–	–	–
D. Newman	Soph.	1	1	0	1	0	0	–	–	1

DIAGRAM 12–6
Punt Returns and Punt Blocking Scheme Seasonal Statistics

Type	Number	Yards	Average	Fumbles
Return I	3.0	450	15.0%	0
Return II	1.0	9.6	9.6%	0
Block I	18	0 blocked	0 %	1
Block II	12	6 blocked	50 %	1

Extra Point Effectiveness

The extra point is *not* automatic. The teamwork of the center, holder, and kicker is essential as is excellent protection. A poor snap or fumble requires an immediate "ice" call to turn a potential bad play into a completed pass and two points.

Diagram 12–8 illustrates extra point results for a season, with the indication being that additional practice time and drill should be given to the center, holder, and kicker for a better coordinated effort.

Field Goal Statistics

Field goal data are analyzed in Diagram 12–9 in the same way as the extra point with the additional requirement that the kick must be covered. Coverage is all important as a field goal attempt may be returned, possibly for a long run or a touchdown. You might also want to analyze whether any field goal attempts were nullified by penalties, delay of game, holding, and so on.

Extra Point and Field Goal Prevent Statistics

When preventing extra points and field goals, blocks, forced shanks, and prevention of completed "ice" calls, are all plusses, as illustrated in Diagram 12–10. In this category of play, penalties often become critical areas. Diagram 12–10 indicates excellent results in this phase of the overall kicking game, with the exception of needless penalties.

DIAGRAM 12-7
Kick-off Coverage and Return Seasonal Statistics

Names	Number Games	Total Kick-offs	Cover 1	Cover 2	Return Yards 1	Return Average 1	Return Yards 2	Return Average 2	End Zone	Inside 10	Shanked	TDs
D. Kloser	8	33	20	13	70	3.5	195	15	9	11	2	0
J. Crakes	3	6	1	5	25	25	100	20	1	1	4	0

DIAGRAM 12–8
Extra Punt Seasonal Statistics

Name	Year	Number Games	Attempts	Made	Per-cent	Shanked	Holder	Center	Front	Kicker	"Ice" Calls Made	Missed
								Blocked				
S. Mobley	Sr.	7	25	22	88	2	0	1	0	0	2	1
D. Kloser	Jr.	2	5	4	80	0	0	1	0	0	1	0
Gary Smith	Soph.	2	3	3	100	0						

DIAGRAM 12–9
Field Goal Seasonal Statistics

Name	Year	Number			Per cent	Longest	Hash Mark			Shanked	Blocked			Kicker	"Ice" Call	
		Games	Attempts	Made			L	M	R		Holder	Center	Front		Made	Missed
S. Mobley	Sr.	7	11	9	81	47	3/3	3/3	3/5	1	0	0	0	0	1	1
D. Kloser	Jr.	2	4	2	50	49	1/3	1/1	1/1	0	0	1	1	0	0	0
Greg Smith	Soph.	3	3													

DIAGRAM 12–10
Extra Point (Top) and Field Goal Prevent (Bottom)
Seasonal Statistics

Number Games	Attempts	Made	Blocked	Shanked	"Ice" Calls Made	"Ice" Calls Missed	Penalties against us that gave second chance	Percent not made
11	15	10	3	2	1	1	3	33%

Number Games	Attempts	Made	Blocked	Forced Shank	"Ice" Calls Made	"Ice" Calls Missed	Penalties against us that gave opponent second chance	Percent not made
11	18	9	4	5	0	0	5	50%

Other Kicking Game Areas to Be Analyzed

The on-side or short kick from both the offensive and defensive point of view should also be considered in the total kicking game. The use of your eleven best ball handlers in the sure on-side kick situation is done by many teams and like any other skill should be practiced weekly. The technique of kicking the on-side kick and utilizing your fastest players in its coverage are important.

The art of taking an intentional safety and kicking off after a safety also require practice weekly.

COMPILING OFFENSIVE SEASONAL STATISTICS

The offensive staff must analyze its mistakes in order to make plans for the upcoming season, and this analysis must cover all types of individual, group, and team activity. Offensive activity will be reflected in the game situation but will be a result of practice, the techniques taught and utilized, and the individual abilities of the participants. All of these factors are interrelated.

The Quarterback's Passing Game Mistakes

In analyzing the passing game of the quarterback, you must also consider receivers and front play or protection. The season should be closely observed with regards to total results. Particular emphasis should be placed on interceptions, passes that were knocked down, and sacks, as illustrated in Diagram 12–11. Knocked down passes and interceptions may

DIAGRAM 12–11
Passer's Performance Seasonal Statistics

Name	Year	Games	Attempts	Completions	Interceptions	TDs	Knock Downs	Yards Gained	Yards Lost (Sacks)	Percent Complete
K. O'Brien	Sr.	11	180	96	4	16	2	1075	0	53.3%
O. Carlson	Jr.	4	60	37	5	10	7	370	40	61.5%
B. Eacrett	Soph.	1	22							

be due to improper passing technique by the quarterback or inadequate protection.

Offensive Front Play in the Passing Game

Each type of pass protection should be analyzed in terms of protection afforded, completions, passes knocked down, percentage of completions, interceptions, and touchdown passes thrown. Diagram 12–12 illustrates the seasonal statistics of the protectors' performance and indicates excellent results in all areas with the possible exception of the completion percentage in the sixty series, and the interception and the sack results in the seventy series. These failures should be analyzed and the causes determined. Are the breakdowns attributable to the protection rules or to techniques, or do they fall in the quarterback's realm of responsibility?

Receivers

The passing game results are not complete without an analysis of receivers with regard to passes dropped, yardage gained, touchdowns, and percentage of completions as illustrated in Diagram 12–13. An analysis of these statistics indicates superior receiver results with the exception of dropped passes. These errors can usually be reduced by re-emphasizing fundamental techniques, especially concentrating the eyes on the football.

Running Game Analysis

The running game may be evaluated by many criteria, the most common being ball carrier (back), hole, blocking scheme, and play. The average per gradable unit, the number of touchdowns, and the number of turnovers are additional considerations. Diagram 12–14 illustrates a method of evaluating the running backs' performance. And Diagram 12–15 illustrates a method of analyzing both the offensive running hole and blocking scheme. You might also wish to make a comparison of your running plays for projected improvement or exclusion.

ADDITIONAL PHASES OF THE GAME TO BE ANALYZED AND EVALUATED

Additional phases and aspects of the game that should be analyzed and evaluated as to coaching effectiveness are discussed below.

DIAGRAM 12–12
Protectors' Performance Seasonal Statistics

Type	Games	Attempts	Completions	Yards Gained	Knock Downs	Interceptions	Sacks	Average Completion	TDs	Percent Complete
Fifties (Sprintout)	8	20	11	97	2	1	0	8.8	4	55%
Sixties (TB Action)	4	10	3	36	5	2	0	13	0	30%
Seventies (Dropback)	11	95	45	515	0	6	8	11.4	10	47%
Nineties (Automatics)	11	50	33	195	2	0	0	5.9	4	66%
Play Action	11	35	20	312	0	4	0	15.6	2	57%

DIAGRAM 12–13
Receivers' Performance Seasonal Statistics

Receiver	Year	Position	Games	Pass Attempts	Passes Caught	Passes Dropped	Total Yards	Average Yards	Percent Complete	TDs
J. Maloney	Jr.	X	11	59	41	5	501	12.2	69%	6
J. Kirk	Sr.	X	7	45	36	7	424	14.5	80%	4
J. Hodges	Soph.	X	11	21	16	5	319	19.9	76%	3
D. Kloser	Jr.	Z	11	50	37	6	410	11.1	74%	7
G. Jacobs	Jr.	Z	7	23	18	2	120	6.6	78%	2
C. Bisharat	Jr.	A	11	22	18	0	160	8.8	81%	1
A. Ferrie	Soph.	A	8	19	12	0	85	7.0	63%	3
M. Moretti	Sr.	B	11	17	14	0	97	6.9	88%	1
V. Bertoloni	Sr.	B	14	10						

DIAGRAM 12–14
Running Backs' Performance Seasonal Statistics

Name	Year	Number Games	Attempts	Yards Gained	Yards Lost	Average per Carry	TDs	Fumbles	Average per Game
C. Bisharat	Sr.	11	127	1295	20	10.3	16	3	115.
V. Bertolani	Jr.	11	80	500	0	6.2	5	2	45.13
A. Ferrie	Sr.	9	50	416					

DIAGRAM 12–15
Offensive Running Game by Hole and Blocking Scheme
Seasonal Statistics

Hole and Scheme	Attempts	Yards Gained	Yards Lost	Average Yards	TDs
8 Pitch	50	612	24	11.7	6
8 Toss	20	165	0	8.25	3
8 Sweep	20	45	5	2.0	0
6 Power	65	700			

Communication

Did your offensive quarterbacks and defensive signal callers understand what they had been taught, and were they able to communicate it to their teammates? By analyzing broken assignments, unnecessary time-outs, and improper alignments, you should have a strong indication of whether there was a communication/learning problem. Is your system indication easily understandable? Have you taught it well? Can you adjust it to make it do a better job? How can you better train your signal callers? Would it be better if the calls were made by the coaches and sent in or flashed to the signal callers?

Penalties

Study your penalties closely, evaluate their causes. Are offensive offsides the fault of your cadence? Do your flankers clip on crackback blockers because the players are undisciplined or have you taught the technique improperly or poorly? Do your players fold on pass blocking because they are inexperienced, use poor techniques, or are not in good condition?

Analyze Fumbles

If they were fumbles on the center-quarterback exchange analyze, what caused them? Is there an easier, more natural, better method? Is the center overstriding on the snap? Is the quarterback keeping firm upper hand pressure? Is the center firing the ball up hard? Is the quarterback pulling away too soon from his center?

Examine and determine why there were fumbles on handling punts, options, pitchouts, and hand-offs. Analyze the technique that you have taught. Is there an easier, more natural, better method?

Evaluate Your Losses

Evaluate why you lost; that is likely to reveal more than evaluating why you won. However, you should not take your wins for granted. Did you win or did the other team lose? That may appear to be a rhetorical question, but it may be that your opposition beat itself and as a result your team could not lose. Did you lose or beat yourself? Was your team defeated when it should have won? Why? Identify any mistakes and errors and correct them so you can avoid them in the future.

Study Strategy

Study your strategy in all areas of the game. Try to pinpoint possible errors and determine responsibility for them. The latter is not done in order to lay blame but in order to improve. You will probably find questionable areas where the strategy was not understood.

Illustration   During a key PAC 10 game that decided the Rose Bowl representative several years ago, an incident of above type occurred. Oregon State was leading Stanford University 11–0 with forty-nine seconds remaining in the first half. Oregon State recovered a fumble in their own territory near midfield. Oregon State's young quarterback ran onto the field and went immediately to a no huddle offense. The quarterback dropped back to pass, was tackled for a loss of yardage, and fumbled the football; Stanford recovered and scored in two plays. Although Oregon State still led, 11–7, Stanford scored again in the second half winning the game 17–11 and with it the Rose Bowl bid.

The young quarterback's reasoning for attempting to pass on first down was that he wanted to improve his team's field position immediately, setting up either a touchdown or at least a field goal. His rationale was logical, but his play selection may not have been that of the coaching staff. While the veteran head coach of the losing team was as perplexed as his assistants, later he said this to his staff: "What was our thinking in that situation? Did our quarterback know our strategy? The young man's strategy had come from us, and we failed to emphasize that *time* was a factor in this decision. Actually the boy's only mistake was in fumbling the football. And then Stanford still had to move the football more than forty yards to score."

The head coach's point was well made, and his staff learned from the experience. The quarterback was not criticized for his play calling strategy in this particular situation; he was instructed only on how to protect the football when being sacked. Later through his leadership and ability, this quarterback became a seasoned performer and directed Oregon State to several upset wins.

Study Current Trends, Get New Ideas

After the season is the time to study in depth current football trends and possibly to get some new ideas. While you may not want to change entire phases of your coaching, you may discover more effective teaching methods or coaching techniques or a play or two that will fit into your offensive package. You must be careful, however, that you do not end up with a collection of single plays taken out of context from sequential systems. Also keep in mind the skills of the individuals necessary to operate those offensive and defensive systems effectively as compared to your available personnel.

Even though you may be content not to change any phase of your coaching (which would be unusual for most football coaches), all coaches should try to attend clinics, spring practices of successful college teams, and midsummer professional football practice sessions. They should study available college and professional football films and read coaching books and articles for professional growth. While you may not be able to do many of the things you hear about and see performed, this does not mean that your opposition will be unable to do them in their coaching situations. Knowledge is power. You may not be in the same coaching situation for all of your professional career, depending on your goals and aspirations.

Film Study—Training Films

After analyzing game films at the end of the season, most coaching staffs make a hi-lite film that can be used later as a training film and for public relations. It illustrates the good points and proper execution of your team's seasonal play. You may also make a lo-lite training film of the mistakes and errors made in games throughout the season. This film is strictly for teaching purposes. Some staffs, with more sequences of plays and passes, retain these over the years. Each new season when teaching the veer option, as an illustration, the films are used as training aids.

Regardless of how the films are broken down and cut up, it is suggested you keep a copy of the entire game. On large staffs usually films are cut up and spliced together with a print being made of the segments cut from the film. Then the originals are removed from the training film mock up and spliced back in place again in their proper sequence. Obviously this requires much time and several coaches who have a knack for detail work. While the cost may be prohibitive in many high schools and small college coaching situations, if you are fortunate enough to have game films, utilize them optimally. Many coaches look at a film after a game and do not view them again until the following year before they play that particular opponent again.

Reevaluation of Personnel

The evaluation of personnel is going on continuously. At the conclusion of the season remove the names of your seniors from your personnel board and start slotting players. Rather than move players up automatically into vacated slots, reevaluate what each player does best. Where does he fit in? What does it change? Will these losses change your team concepts? Coach John McKay has been quoted as stating, "The coach must make changes to learn and master what his players do best." The ever constant evaluation and counseling of players over the entire year is probably the single most important factor in a winning program.

Making Changes   Before making any changes on the personnel board, you should list under each player's name his correct height, weight, age, class, and an accurate timing of his speed for the 40-yard dash. Such information will aid in your decision making. A common coaching mistake is for coaches to become so engrossed drawing up the X's and O's that they fail to take into consideration personal attributes, including the physical skills of the X's and O's. The personnel available for coaching and where you slot them determine your offense, defense, and, to some extent, your kicking game. If you slot all of your best players on defense, the players who remain will determine what you can and cannot do offensively. The possible exception would be found in your quarterback, and his abilities will influence many of your decisions.

Size and strength as compared to quickness in your offensive line determine the technique and style of your offensive line. It would follow that the size and speed of your backs and the strengths and weaknesses of your quarterback will determine your total offensive plan. The individual abilities of receivers, their best routes and speed, determine your passing game.

The special teams can utilize the best of both groups, combining offensively and defensively with four or five of the ornery, pesky types that you have to find a spot for.

Locate Your Best Players

While every coach would like to fill out his depth chart to four complete offensive defensive teams, seldom is this realistic. Even at the major college level of competition the drop-off in player performance after the first offensive and defensive units is usually quite evident. Many are fortunate to get a third performer such as an offensive guard, who may swing left and right as the backup for both guards, since the calibre of play is better in that situation than if you must substitute an inept performer as a backup to either the left or right guard. Do not be misled and deluded by a depth chart showing six or eight teams. While there may be many "comers," locate your best twenty-two players if you are going to platoon offense and defense. Do not try to stack a player as a backup offensive guard, as in illustration, if he is capable of being a first team linebacker. He may have to go both ways and receive practice time and drill first as a linebacker and then as a backup offensive guard. He may be an outstanding performer on offense and defense, but many coaches would prefer not to play a player both ways. All coaches want to have backup depth in case of injury, but you must make certain your best athletes are on the field performing during the game and not in a backup position waiting to play when an injury occurs at that position. The two-way player can be used in spot situation when needed, although in platoon football he would be expected to perform both ways all of the time. He simply cannot practice effectively both offense and defense. Therefore, as an illustration, if you decide you will utilize him first on defense, he must receive *all* of the defensive work; then he can receive a limited amount of offensive work so he can be utilized in spot situations. Know your personnel and what they are capable of doing.

Improve Your Players

Assigning one or more coaches to handle the total conditioning, strength, and flexibility programs is highly desirable to ensure continuity in the program and to attain the desired objectives. These programs, which were once thought of as being necessary only during football season, are a year-round necessity for football players. During the off-season and the school year, many high schools and colleges continue these programs under the direction of one or more coaches who are assigned this specific detail. In most high school and college situations it is permissible to carry on these programs as long as football equipment or gear is not utilized, offensive plays and defensive alignments are not taught and practiced, and they are open to all students on a voluntary basis. If it is permissible for the coaching staff to conduct such programs, then by all means the coaches should do so. It is the head coach's responsibility to set them up and to assign coaches to monitor them. By encouraging all students to participate in the program, the coaches have an opportunity to observe and evaluate prospective football players whom they knew nothing about. This is especially important where one cannot go out and recruit the players, or does not have a feeder system, and must rely primarily on walk-ons.

The Summer Program   If it is permissible to set up summer conditioning, flexibility, strength programs under an individual who serves in the recreation or summer school program, the head coach should make certain his returnees and prospects participate. If an athletic coach is in charge of the summer program, this is highly desirable. The rules are similar to those indicated above, and the emphasis should be on building strength, flexibility, and conditioning. If there is no formal summer program, and it is not permissible for a coach to be present to conduct such a program, the players should be sent specific information during the summer months relevant to the strength, conditioning, and flexibility exercises they should undertake voluntarily during the summer months. It is the head coach's responsibility to give specific directions and information to his players in this important aspect of getting ready to play football. A coach cannot assume prospects will work on conditioning, strength, and flexibility without his encouragement.

Players' Attitude toward Physical and Mental Conditioning   A well-conditioned mind in a well-conditioned body is an unbeatable combination. A coach must plan and work to develop both as they are assets to the player and the team. Perhaps the most important factor in developing a proper mental attitude is getting the players to accept discipline. The physical conditioning of a player depends largely on himself and his attitude toward participating in football. A coach can advocate all types of conditioning drills and set down numerous training rules and regulations, but in the final analysis it is up to each individual whether to adhere to them. If he does not, he is probably selling himself short. A player who can discipline himself to work on his conditioning, especially during the summer months, is one who can be depended upon to get the job done during the football season. A player cannot renege on his physical conditioning and on the training rules, and have a poor mental attitude, and still expect to be an outstanding performer during the game. You should try to sell this philosophy to your players in your summer letters and not wait to pre-season to get across these points. The theme and content of summer letters will be discussed shortly.

Improve Facilities   Always work to improve your facilities. A coat of paint does wonders. If you have separate team rooms, involve the art class. Fix up the place. The same can be done with a music sound system. Scrounge around, talk to people, get them involved by selling them on their doing a worthy project for the good of the program. Set your goals, develop a plan, and go get it done.

Staff and Self-evaluation   Check your own role in the program and encourage your assistants to do the same. If you have the courage to do so ask your assistants to evaluate you and your performance honestly, especially if you have had a losing season. You may be surprised to learn of your shortcomings and that you are responsible for the losses. If their remarks are this candid, they may attribute the wins to their coaching! While you may resent their evaluation and opinions, their candid analysis may be more correct than erroneous. You may discover a communication problem or a human relations one, or that you are a good planner but a poor organizer, or that you provide no follow-up, or you have other weaknesses and shortcomings you may not have been aware of. In any evaluation, always ask for suggestions for improvement. While some may not be feasible, others will be beneficial. Your assistants may ask for more work and additional responsibilities, and this gives you the opportunity to delegate to your assistants, which in turn allows you more time to do your job as head coach.

   If you have your staff evaluate you and your performance, while not all of their remarks may be complimentary and some may be unjust, you should view them as constructive criticism. It takes a big person to be criticized by subordinates and not strike back or become vindictive toward them. If you cannot stand heat, do not ask for it. However, if the program will benefit, and you are likely to benefit personally from their remarks, then it will be worth it. One of us utilized this approach as a high school coach and heard what his assistants had to say after a losing season. Misunderstandings were resolved and the result the following year was an undefeated season and the state championship, which the head coach attributed to the hard work of his staff and players.

Evaluate Your Assistants   Evaluate your staff individually. First, however, have each assistant evaluate himself and his efforts. Then you evaluate each assistant, and compare his and your evaluations discussing the differences of opinion on his strengths and weaknesses. Last, make objective, factual suggestions for each individual's improvement and ways he can make additional contributions to the success of the football program.

If you shift coaching duties, make certain your assistants understand why, and make the shifts far enough in advance that they can plan to make the transition and get prepared for their new roles. Some may not wish to continue coaching because of personal and family reasons, usually because of "too much time," and it is best that you learn of an assistant's decision not to coach at the end rather than at the beginning of a season.

If You Change, Know What You Are Doing   If you are making a change in your game, do not do so without learning in advance all that you can about the new change. Visit a coaching staff who has been successful in performing what you would like to do. Ask many why and how questions. Get as much information as possible. Be assured in your own mind that you have staff to coach the change and the personnel to perform it. Be certain that what you would like to do can be done in your situation. A common coaching mistake is to try to adopt or copy what Oklahoma, Notre Dame, Southern California, Alabama, Penn State, Michigan, Ohio State or some other football power does, without having the staff to teach it or the players with the necessary skills to perform it well.

Football Notebooks

Evaluate Your Football Notebooks Assignment   One assistant should be assigned the responsibility for issuing the football notebooks at the beginning of the season and collecting them at the end of the season. In the off-season the previous season's notebook materials are destroyed, and the notebooks are made ready to be issued again at the beginning of the new football season. Each notebook is numbered with the player's corresponding jersey number.

The assistant who has the notebook assignment also is responsible for issuing the basic football materials that *all* of the squad members generally receive. Such information as training rules and regulations, football schedule, general offensive and defensive terms, basic offensive sets and basic defensive alignments material, and all kicking game materials, are likely to be placed in the notebooks. After the notebooks are issued, it is the responsibility of the offensive and defensive coordinators, usually through the respective position coaches, to make certain the appropriate players get the necessary materials and information. In addition, the position coaches issue notebook materials and information to their respective players.

Illustration Other than the basic offensive material indicated above, none of the defensive players receive detailed materials on offensive running plays and passes. Nor do the offensive players receive the detailed defensive materials. A linebacker, as an illustration, in addition to the basic offensive material that is placed in his notebook, initially receives all of the defensive materials including stunts and coverages since the linebackers are involved in both the defensive rush and the coverages. They also receive special technique materials from the linebacker coach, which none of the other players receive. The defensive linemen receive material relevant only to their line play, not secondary coverages.

Amount and Detail of Notebook Material While some coaches issue *all* notebook materials to every squad member, many coaches feel this bulk of material will only confuse the players. Therefore, by limiting the notebook material to the extent that each player is given only the offensive, defensive, and/or kicking game materials *he needs to know* as a player, he is more likely to study and learn his assignments. Obviously if a player plays both offense and defense, he needs all of the relevant materials. If a player is switched from offense to defense or vice versa, it is the responsibility of the position coach and coordinator to see that the player is issued the appropriate materials in order to carry out his assignments. If a player drops off the squad, it is the responsibility of the coach who is in charge of notebooks to follow up immediately and pick up the player's notebook.

Preparation of Notebook Materials All of the coaches should be involved in preparing materials for the players' notebooks. The offensive and defensive coordinators usually approve the materials to be distributed to their respective players, and the position coach is responsible for the materials he prepares and distributes at the positions he coaches. In preparing materials for distribution to the players, it is well to keep in mind the following guidelines:

1. Do not get too involved in extreme detail.
2. Do not get carried away on philosophical concepts, such as attitude and effort.
3. Do not set too many rules.
4. Too many slogans tend to be ineffective.
5. Do not use too many diagrams. Be certain the diagrams that are included are understandable.
6. Go over the notebook material and teach it rather than merely giving the material to the players and instructing them to read it.

7. Include only the material in the notebooks that you intend to use.

Summer Tasks

Summer Letters to Prospects   Each position coach is responsible for writing summer letters to the players he coaches. Assigning each coach to prepare three or four basic letters makes it possible for the head football coach to prepare a simple cover letter and to enclose position coach's letter with it. In the event an assistant is unable to write the letters during the summer, as occurs frequently at the high school level of coaching, this routine task can be handled *prior* to the termination of the school year. The assistants merely designate to the head coach the sequence of their letters and make the letter and the names of the players at their position available to the head coach before they depart for the summer. The head coach will know the names of the returnees at the various positions, but if the assistants give their list of players to the head coach, the possibility of misdirecting a letter to a prospect or overlooking a player is eliminated. If the personnel situation is such that the head coach must be away most or part of the summer, and his coaching position permits it, he, too, can set up all of the summer letters in advance and have a secretary in the principal's office mail them on specified dates during the summer months. At the college level of coaching, vacations are typically staggered and several coaches are on duty during the summer months until the staff is regrouped to commence finalizing pre-season practice plans.

Maintain Contact   Despite the coaching situation, the possibility of building a winning program is greatly minimized and the head coach is working against his own best efforts, including personal and professional goals, if he loses touch with his players during the summer months. Despite the fact that none of his assistants is available during the summer months, nor that he is unavailable due to other commitments and circumstances, a head coach is merely *hoping* for success if he does not maintain some sort of contact with his players during the summer months. While your coaching situation may be such that no assistants are available and you are not paid for your summer work, through careful planning and good organization you can set up a series of letters to be sent out during the summer months so that you are always in contact with your players.

Contents and Theme   The head coach's summer letters should follow the theme of positiveness, apprising the players of the schedule, goals, anticipated success, and topics of a similar nature. The final summer letter should deal with the specifics of reporting for pre-season practice and should cover particulars relating to eligibility requirements, issuance of equipment procedures, pre-season practice schedule and routine, and, for the high school prospects, information pertaining to insurance and parent consent forms. The assistants' letters should deal with the individuals they coach and the specifics and possibly the techniques of their position. All of the letters should be informational and motivational in content.

Game Schedule Analysis   Study your upcoming season's football schedule. Are there new teams on it? If so, this may represent new concepts and different offenses and defenses. Borrow film, break it down, talk to other coaches. Learn as much as you can about what these coaches and teams like to do offensively and defensively. Give yourself a chance to win.

You may find new coaches at old schools on your schedule. Find out about them, where they came from, their backgrounds and coaching records. Try to secure game films from coaches who played against their teams the previous season. Try to determine how they may utilize their existing personnel as you know it at their new coaching assignment after you have viewed films of where they worked previously. Both these cases could present new offenses and new defensive looks. You have to examine your plan in light of such developments.

Practice Plan   Analyze your past season's practices. Are the strengths of your program reflected in time spent on them? Are weaknesses evident, the result of too little time spent on various phases? If affirmative, then analyze your teaching, techniques, drills, and personnel.

Prepare a new master plan from the opening game through the first game. Consider all aspects of the plan: experience of the squad, the amount of new material, the success and failure of last year's plan. Planning is a year-round process and function.

Faculty Relations   The off-season is the ideal time to get to know the faculty at your school or college. While they may know *of* you and *of* your program, they may not know you as a person. The same applies to your assistant coaches. And you may know little or nothing of many of the faculty and of their programs. The off-season is a time for getting to know each other, and you must take the initiative. Undoubtedly at some time during the year football players have been or are students in their classes, and you and your coaches have talked with faculty members relevant to grade checks. It is suggested that you not restrict your faculty talks to grade checks or eligibility requirements, as they resent this and feel they are being used or manipulated for grades. While you may feel that you do not have time to get involved with faculty members, it is likely you will find it time well spent. Many faculty members would like to get involved in some capacity with athletics, and they are merely waiting to be asked. Usually everyone and the program benefit from faculty involvement.

Press "Get some ink," sell your program. Educate the press as to what you are doing. Be honest and positive. Players generally read the sports section of the newspapers religiously. Let them know you expect a great deal from them and what it takes for them to win. Share your interest in your players with the public, get them motivated and involved.

You cannot do this by sitting and complaining. The press has much to cover and cannot always get in touch with you. You must take the initiative and meet them more than halfway.

Service Clubs Get involved with the local service clubs. They are always looking for a program. Why not sell yours? Let them get to know you, what you stand for and believe in.

If people like you, they are less likely to be overly critical. Give them an opportunity to get to know you and your staff, and just as in your relationships with the press and the faculty at your institution, you must take the initiative.

Equipment Check Equipment is expensive and requires care. Probably more athletic equipment is lost or stolen through carelessness than wears out. Take care of it; know what you have; inventory it. Budgets are stringent, but it is easier to convince funding sources of your football needs when they observe that your equipment is cared for and properly secured than when it is misused and mishandled.

Conclusion

Other ancillary aspects of coaching could be included for discussion, but those we have presented will illustrate what should be included in an overall plan to achieve coaching success. A coach who is innovative and creative will include additional aspects into his plan or find his own way to organize those we have offered and discussed throughout this book. It is easy to rationalize that "I can't do that in my situation." While each coach must recognize his "as is" situation, he should work for the "could be" or "should be" situation. If you have obtained at least several ideas from this book that will improve your program and keep you from making coaching mistakes and errors that lose games, then you have improved your situation.

No coach is ever going to improve his situation if he maintains all the time, "It can't be done." Good coaching situations do not occur automatically overnight. Coaches at all levels have turned around poor situations into a good football program. Sometimes it is a long, hard climb to the top. Once you have done it, however, the quest for continued coaching success is almost insatiable. The battle to get to the top and to remain there will not be easy, but that is the challenge that coaching offers. Our intent throughout this book has been to offer numerous suggestions to aid you in attaining your goal. Good luck!